COLORADO: THE PLACE OF NATURE, THE NATURE OF PLACE

T H O M A S   P .   H U B E R

COLORADO

T H E   P L A C E
O F   N A T U R E ,   T H E   N A T U R E
O F   P L A C E

U N I V E R S I T Y   P R E S S   O F   C O L O R A D O

The University Press of Colorado is a cooperative publishing enterprise supported, in part, by
Adams State College, Colorado State University, Fort Lewis College, Mesa State College,
Metropolitan State College of Denver, University of Colorado, University of Northern
Colorado, University of Southern Colorado, and Western State College of Colorado.

Library of Congress Cataloging-in-Publication Data

Huber, Thomas Patrick.
    Colorado: the place of nature, the nature of place / Thomas
P. Huber.
        p.   cm.
    Includes bibliographical references and index.
    ISBN 0-87081-289-0 — ISBN 0-87081-290-4 (pbk.)
    1. Colorado — Description and travel.   2. Natural areas —
Colorado.   3. Natural history — Colorado.   I. Title.
F776.H85 1993
917.88 — dc20   93-21472
                                                                    CIP

The paper used in this publication meets the minimum requirements of the American National
Standard for Information Sciences — Permanence of Paper for Printed Library Materials. ANSI
Z39.48–1984

∞

10 9 8 7 6 5 4 3 2 1

The book is dedicated to Patrick, Christopher, and Nicole –
I hope the natural places of Colorado and the world will survive
for their children's children – and to Carole, whose help
and companionship have made it all worthwhile.

Contents

CONTENTS

CONTENTS

Acknowledgments

Many people were invaluable to the writing of this book. In almost every chapter, knowledgeable and dedicated natural scientists — both professional and amateur — guided me along the way. I would like to take this space to gratefully acknowledge their assistance.

Thanks go to Judy Rice-Jones for her help with references and in finding obscure facts in the library. Priscilla Neus was an outstanding resource for the chapter on the Garden of the Gods in particular and for other chapters in general. The National Park Service has some great talent at the Florissant Fossil Beds in Kathy Brown; at the Colorado National Monument in Hank Schoch and Jon Paynter; and in Libbie Landreth, Fred Bunch, and Sue Fischer at the Great Sand Dunes.

Several people at the National Forest Service were extremely helpful: Charlie Richmond and Jim Hollenback at the Comanche National Grassland; and Jim Barry, Barry Johnston, Sandy Hayes, and Ben Sprouse at the Gunnison field office. Bill Hill with the U.S. Bureau of Land Management assisted me considerably with the Piceance Basin. Dennis Scheiwe with the State Parks Department and Rilla Wiggins were very helpful with Steamboat Lake State Park. Several people including Warren Snyder, Marvin Gardner, Dave Kuntz, and Jim McDanold provided information about and insight into Tamarack Ranch Wildlife Area. And finally, Lee Carr, Dale Reed, and Mike Monahan offered excellent guidance on the Mt. Evans chapter.

A very heartfelt thank you to all of the above; without you this book would still be just an unfulfilled dream. I cannot adequately express my gratitude to Carole Huber for her meticulous editing and constructive ideas, and to my children who have helped in significant yet unseen ways. All responsibility for any errors or confusion, of course, still lies with me.

COLORADO: THE PLACE OF NATURE, THE NATURE OF PLACE

1

INTRODUCTION

Colorado. The mere word conjures up many varied visions: the official "Colorful Colorado" of the state bureaucracy; the Colorado of high peaks (fifty-three, more or less) above 14,000 feet; the Colorado of the Continental Divide; the Colorado, which is the river of the same name that impacts so many other places; the Colorado of the high, dry plains where short-grass prairie and dust bowl currently have an uneasy peace. This book melds these and other images of our state into a coherent scene of the natural environment. It describes and explains the how, the why, the where, and the when of the natural development of the multitude of Colorados enclosed in the geometric borders of our state.

The twelve places chosen for inclusion in this book are intended to inform, tantalize, and sensitize. First, I want to inform you about some of the special places in the state that exhibit peculiar and at the same time representative qualities of the natural environment of Colorado. The places were chosen not for their popularity but for their character. It is my hope that as you learn about, see, and experience these places, you will learn, see, and experience much of what is both wonderful and typical in Colorado.

Second, I hope that the book tantalizes you into learning, seeing, and experiencing more of the state. Whether you concentrate on the places presented here or visit others — do learn more! Only with greater knowledge can we all properly care for this special place we call Colorado.

Third, I hope this book will sensitize you to the precariousness of the beauty and natural richness of the state. For those of you who are not from

Colorado, welcome; take with you memories, knowledge, and understanding. For those of you who live here, take the same but also take the pains to help ensure our lasting natural legacy. For all who visit the natural wonders of our state, keep in mind the comments made by Henry David Thoreau a century and a half ago: "This curious world which we inhabit is more wonderful than it is convenient; more beautiful than it is useful; it is more to be admired and enjoyed than used" (Krutch 1962, p. 5).

My ultimate goal is to create an inquisitiveness and respect for this curious collection of natural regions known as Colorado. The twelve places presented in this book are but a small, albeit select, sample of the diversity and complexity of the state. Each was chosen to demonstrate its unique qualities and characteristics that fit the general pattern of landscapes occurring in Colorado. The examples range from the grasslands and broad river valleys of the eastern plains to the brusque transition of the foothills; from the mountainous environments of the montane and the subalpine to the alpine land above the trees. Almost all climatic regions and geologic provinces have been included. Among these are some of the most pristine places in the world, and some of the places that have been most affected by humans. In essence, this is a cross-section of Colorado's natural history.

In order to provide you with a foundation for understanding the natural processes at work, the following sections give a brief overview of the entire state's geology, landforms, elevation, climates, and vegetation zones.

THE GEOLOGY

Geology is the oldest of the natural factors that make up the natural world of Colorado and is therefore a good place to start — to lay the foundation, so to speak. In a very tangible way, geology is the canvas upon which the natural portrait of Colorado is painted.

When you look at even a general road map of Colorado, you see distinctive regions set off by settlement distributions, river patterns, and road networks. If you were to look at a geologic map, you would see why these regions show up so well: the geology coerces certain patterns. Three major and two minor geologic provinces exist in the state (Figure 1.1). The major provinces include the Great Plains, the Southern Rocky Mountains, and the Colorado Plateau. These three provinces constitute about 95 percent of the state (Great Plains 40%, Southern Rocky Mountains 35%, and Colorado Plateau 20%). The two minor provinces lie in the far northwest

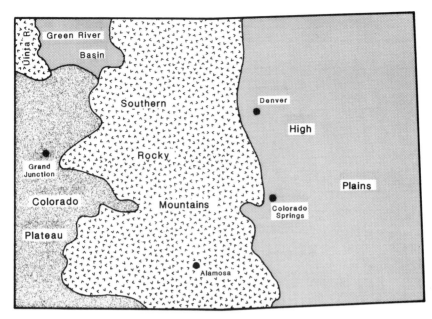

Figure 1.1. Map of Colorado showing the general location of the three major (Great Plains, Southern Rocky Mountains, and Colorado Plateau) and two minor (Green River basin and Uinta Range) geologic provinces.

corner of the state and include small sections of the Wyoming, or Green River, basin, and the far eastern edge of the Middle Rocky Mountains (Uinta Range). The elevations in the state range from a low (about 3,387') near Holly along the Arkansas River to a high in the mountain province at the top of Mount Elbert (14,433').

Four important river systems begin in Colorado, fed mostly by snow meltwater from the high elevations in the Southern Rocky Mountain province. The Colorado River, with its major tributaries the San Juan, Gunnison, White, and Yampa, drains the western slope of the Continental Divide and empties, or at least quits, at the Gulf of California. The Rio Grande begins in the San Juan Mountain range, flows through New Mexico, and borders Texas on its way to the Gulf of Mexico. The North Platte River drains the far north-central part of Colorado and meets the South Platte, which drains the Front Range and South Park, in Nebraska. The Arkansas River starts among the high peaks near Leadville and Tennessee Pass and flows east to meet the Mississippi River in the state of Arkansas.

Table 1.1. General Geologic Column for Two Colorado Regions

Geologic Period	Front Range	Central Colorado Mountains
Cretaceous	Laramie Fm	
	Fox Hills Fm	
	Pierre Shale	Pierre Shale
	Niobrara Fm	Niobrara Fm
	Benton Group	Mancos Shale
	Dakota Group	Dakota Group
Jurassic	Morrison Fm	Morrison Fm
	Ralston Creek Fm	San Rafael Group
	Entrada Sandstone	Entrada Sandstone
Triassic	Jelm Fm	Chinle Fm
		Moenkope Fm
	Lykins Fm	State Bridge Fm
Permian	Lyons Fm	S. Canyon Creek Fm
	Ingleside Fm	
	Fountain Fm	Maroon Fm
Pennsylvanian		
Mississippian	Beulah Limestone	Leadville Limestone
	Hardscrabble Limestone	
	Williams Canyon Ls	
Devonian		Chaffee Group
Ordovician	Fremont Dolomite	Fremont Dolomite
	Harding Limestone	Harding Limestone
	Manitou Fm	Manitou Fm
		Dotsero Fm
Cambrian	Peerless Fm	
	Sawatch Sandstone	Sawatch Sandstone
Precambrian	Pikes Peak Granite	Silver Plume Granite
	Idaho Springs Fm	Idaho Springs Fm

Colorado possesses a phenomenal array of examples of geologic activity. Within the state borders you can see evidence of most types of tectonic and geologic activity including fault block and folded mountain terrain, volcanic eruptions, marine submergence, erosion and deposition, geothermal springs, and more. Table 1.1 is a generalized geologic timetable useful for reference in the following sections. A more detailed discussion of each of the provinces follows.

Figure 1.2. Exposed and upturned beds of sedimentary rock visible in the foothills near Pikes Peak.

THE GREAT PLAINS

The Great Plains are essentially the depository of generations of senescent mountains. Whenever land is uplifted potential energy is produced that, when transformed to kinetic energy by water, wind, and ice, begins to wear away the rock of the uplifted mountains. This detritus is deposited down the energy gradient in convenient places such as Colorado's eastern plains. The overall surface area of the plains is flat with an imperceptible slant (about 18.5' of drop per mile traveled) toward the east. The sedimentary rocks formed by this debris are mostly sandstones, limestones, and shales, depending upon the particular environment in effect at the times of erosion and deposition. The geologic "law of superposition" dictates that the newer rock lies nearer the surface with progressively older rock lying increasingly deeper below. With the more recent uplift of the mountains, these sedimentary layers have been bent upwards on the western edge of the plains (Figure 1.2).

The sedimentary rocks of the Great Plains province hold evidence of diverse paleoenvironments that range from marine coastal lagoons to shallow seas to ancient desert sand dunes. Fossil remains found here include shark teeth in the Cretaceous period Pierre shale, and dinosaur bones held fast in the shales, sandstones, and gypsums of the Jurassic period Morrison formation. The Morrison formation is also abundant in the far northwestern corner of the state, in and around the Dinosaur National Monument. Younger sediments of the Great Plains, mostly gravels and eolian (wind) deposits of the Pleistocene epoch, veneer much of the older, partially folded rock of the plains.

The surface of the slightly tilted plane of the eastern side of Colorado is broken by four distinctive landforms. The wide and relatively fertile valleys of the South Platte and Arkansas rivers are verdant anomalies amid the stark browns, reds, and yellows of the remainder of the plains. The Palmer Divide is a folded upland that stretches eastward from the mountains between Denver and Colorado Springs, almost reaching the eastern border of the state. Toward the western side of the divide, the land is distinctive because of the forests of ponderosa pine that are a contrast to the typical short-grass prairie of this environment. Along the far southern part of the plains, extensive volcanic activity has created a dramatic landscape of mesas, buttes, and deep canyons quite out of character with the flat land of the Great Plains province. Raton Mesa and Mesa de Maya are the two most expansive examples of this volcanic activity. The Palmer Divide and the volcanic landscapes of the south exhibit characteristics of both the Great Plains and the Southern Rocky Mountain provinces.

THE SOUTHERN ROCKY MOUNTAINS

When people think of Colorado, most think of the high, majestic mountains. They envision one spectacular mountain view after another, with little variety among the sights. The mountains of Colorado, however, are a multifaceted agglomeration of high-altitude lands. They are not only spatially, genetically different depending upon where they occur, but also chronologically, some being raised while others were quiescent. Indeed, there have been a multitude of mountains through the eons. Parts of the Southern Rocky Mountain province are the result of five major mountain-building episodes and subsequent erosional cycles.

The older mountain-building episodes, called orogenies, left behind two types of evidence: remnants of rocks produced by the heat and pressure of mountain orogenies; and sedimentary rocks produced as a result of the uplift, subsequent erosion, and eventual deposition of those remnants. In the Front Range, for example, the oldest known orogeny occurred about 1.8

billion years before present (ybp) and is indicated by the Idaho Springs formation, a metamorphosed volcanic and sedimentary rock formed when the heat and pressure of the orogeny changed the structure and chemistry of the original rocks. The next episode of mountain-building in the Front Range (1.05 billion ybp) is indicated by the Pikes Peak granite, a molten rock injected into overlying formations that lifted them to create a new mountain range. A third orogeny, sometimes called the "Colorado Orogeny" (300 million ybp), produced the mountains known as the Ancestral Rockies and left behind sediments created by uplift and erosion. These sediments accumulated to form the Fountain formation, a coarse-grained conglomerate sandstone. Only a rapid uplift and high energy (i.e., high relief) event could produce such a grain-size distribution in a sedimentary rock.

The remaining two episodes of orogeny are more easily seen by the untrained observer. The Laramide Orogeny, which occurred primarily between 65 and 70 million ybp, produced our highest mountains and the tilted sedimentary rock beds that bend upwards in places such as the Garden of the Gods near Colorado Springs, Red Rocks near Denver, and the Flatirons near Boulder. We also see sedimentary evidence (much like the Fountain formation) in the Dawson arkose, a coarse-grained sandstone that caps many uplands along the mountain front. Whenever mountains are pushed up, the counteracting force of erosion immediately begins to wear them down. This process makes the Front Range mountains nearly uniform in elevation; the Laramide Orogeny mountains were worn down to this level by erosion in the ensuing millennia. During the fifth orogeny, this erosion surface was uplifted to an elevation between 2,000 and 4,000 feet above the plains to the east. This uplift occurred during the early Tertiary period (between 25 and 30 million ybp), a time that also saw extensive volcanic activity around the state. Some of these volcanoes created welded ash deposits that cap many of the mesas and buttes between Denver and Colorado Springs (Figure 1.3). Many geologists believe that this last orogeny is part of the Laramide Orogeny, which is itself part of a worldwide series of orogenies that have produced such mountains as the Andes, Alps, Atlas, and Himalayan ranges.

After absorbing all of the above information, a reasonable question might be: what can generate the incredible force necessary to lift billions of tons of rock several thousand feet in the air? While there is not, as yet, a definitive answer, recent geologic theories suggest a probable explanation. The general name for this collection of theories is plate tectonics. The concept is relatively simple: steady and continuous nuclear reactions taking

Figure 1.3. Butte between Colorado Springs and Denver capped by volcanic tuff from the Guffey volcanic field southwest of the Florissant Fossil Beds.

place at great depths within the earth produce internal convection currents of molten rock that, in turn, push less dense plates of earth material around the surface of the globe. Sometimes these plates push against each other causing tremendous stress and strain. Colorado's position in the *center* of a relatively stable plate seems to dictate that it should *not* be tectonically active. However, the state lies along a weak zone where stresses, primarily from the west, cause this weakened area to uplift, fold, fault, and erupt: ergo mountains.

Colorado has plenty of mountains, but all mountains are not created equal. We have mountains of almost every variety known to geologists. Although we do have a dominant type, the faulted anticline, the exception is almost the rule. The faulted anticline is an area of uplift where overlying sedimentary beds are arched, fractured, and shifted. In most cases these sedimentary rocks are worn away by erosion and only the core rock, usually Precambrian in age, remains (Figure 1.4). A variation on this mountain type is the fault block mountain system, such as the Sangre de Cristo Mountains, where faults occur predominantly on one side while the other side is "hinged," much like a cellar door. In predominantly folded mountains like the Elk Range, faulting plays only a minor role. Finally, there are the volcanic

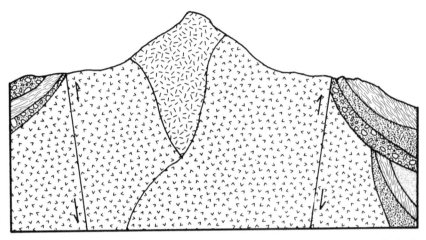

Figure 1.4. Central mountain core, an uplifted block of mostly crystalline rock flanked by upturned sedimentary layers.

mountains, such as the San Juan Range of southwestern Colorado, made up of volcanic ash, tuffs, and breccias deposited during the Tertiary volcanic period mentioned above (Figure 1.5).

Colorado has over fifty different mountain ranges, each with its own characteristics and history; later chapters will discuss many of these mountain types and the unique qualities of the localized environments that surround them.

THE COLORADO PLATEAU

The apparently flat, featureless monotony in this land of table-top mesas yields to — on closer inspection — the intricate beauty and hidden wonders of deep, steeply walled canyons (Figure 1.6). Sediments of the Paleozoic, Mesozoic, and Cenozoic eras lie nearly flat, with few exceptions. Although the layered beds of rock do not show the convulsions generated by the great orogenies of the mountain province, they nonetheless may lie at elevations well over 10,000 feet. In essence they have been uplifted en masse; only regional scale folding has created elevational differences. The particular shape of the land depends upon the hardness of the rock layers, especially the cap rock, and the weak or fractured zones that have allowed erosion by the opportunistic waters of the Colorado River and its tributaries. In a few places volcanic extrusions have added some variation to the rock types.

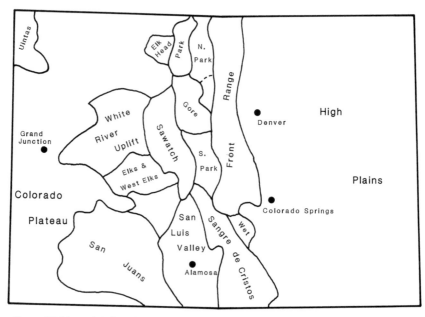

Figure 1.5. Map of Colorado showing the approximate locations of the main mountain ranges, mountain parks, and other physiologic features.

The sedimentary rocks themselves were deposited over a span of many millions of years and in many varied environments, from desert dunes to marine tidal flats to sandy beaches. Locked up in these rocks are a myriad of mineral and fossil treasures including uranium, gold, oil, and gas deposits. In fact, the Green River shales in the northern part of the plateau contain the world's largest reserve of untapped fossil fuel, impounded in rock known as "oil shale." It is not strictly oil but rather a precursor to oil called kerogen, which can become oil when released through the application of high temperature and great pressure. We may never see the full development of this resource because of economic and environmental costs associated with its extraction.

THE OTHER PROVINCES

To the casual observer the two smallest geologic provinces in Colorado are difficult to distinguish from the Colorado Plateau province. These are two sections of provinces that lie primarily in other states and are made up of sedimentary rocks lying in relatively flat strata. The Wyoming, or Green

Figure 1.6. Classic Colorado Plateau landscape of eroded rock and sparse vegetation, Colorado National Monument.

River, basin is really a structural feature that extends into Colorado from the north. The rock strata are mainly Mesozoic and Cenozoic in age and consist mostly of Green River shale (the oil shale mentioned above), dunal and stream deposits of the Brown's Park formation, and Mancos shale.

The Middle Rocky Mountain province section that lies in the far north-western part of Colorado is the final eastward extent of the Uinta Mountains of Utah. These mountains do not rise above 8,500 feet in elevation, in contrast to the very high mountains of Colorado. They are a faulted, anticlinal system undergoing severe thrust faulting. The main difference between the rocks here and those of the Colorado Plateau and Green River basin is the age of many of the sedimentary layers. Some are Mesozoic like the Morrison formation, which contains dinosaur fossils, but many are sedimentary rocks of Paleozoic age. These are real sedimentary rocks, not the metamorphosed sediments seen elsewhere in the state. They are very similar to rocks found in the Rockies of Montana and Canada.

THE LANDFORMS

The geology just discussed is the foundation upon which other natural phenomena act: the canvas that the artist uses to paint the landscape. And yet this "canvas" is used over and over again, producing a series of land-scapes that build on each other. It is a palimpsest, an old canvas with new paintings done directly over the old. The new landscape paintings are created by the forces of erosion and deposition; the basic instruments of creation are water, wind, ice, and gravity. The study of these forces and the landforms they create is called geomorphology.

Copernicus once stated that nature loves a sphere. The perfect shape for a planet, star, or other celestial body is the sphere. Any object that protrudes above the surface of the perfect sphere has the tendency to wear away; any depression below the main level of the surface has a tendency to be filled in by the material from above. When the mountains are uplifted, they are immediately and relentlessly attacked by running water, blowing wind, gouging ice, and the ever-present pull of gravity. Erosion, set into irrepressible motion by the newly produced potential energy of the moun-tain uplift, eats away at these same mountains. The debris that is dislodged and moved is eventually deposited in the low-lying areas of the earth, usually the ocean basins.

Figure 1.7. Massive erosion gullies on unconsolidated material are dramatic evidence of the power of moving water.

The most pervasive and important agent of erosion and deposition is moving water (Figure 1.7). We see the effects everywhere: in the depths of the Purgatoire River canyons, the destructive power of the 1976 Big Thompson River flood, and the lost mountains caught up in the gravels of the South Platte River valley near Sterling. The fact that much of Colorado is arid or semiarid makes water erosion even more important. Without a continuous vegetative cover to protect the soil and rock, water (when it does come) can be very effective at erosion. Much of the precipitation Colorado receives comes in the form of torrential rains from summertime thunder storms; these powerful weather systems can cause immediate and extensive erosion. It is indeed ironic that dry places can suffer most from water erosion and flooding.

The lack of moisture and vegetative cover also contributes to the potential for wind erosion. Wind is not as dominant or powerful as water, but it can create distinctive and beautiful landscapes. Many geologic formations, especially in the Colorado Plateau province, are sculpted by wind carrying sand particles much like a sand blaster on the brick of a building. Over thousands of years, this abrasion carves unique erosional ventifacts and rock formations. Wind deposition also produces distinctive landforms, seen on a large scale at the Great Sand Dunes National Monument and on a smaller scale along windbreaks and fence rows in the Great Plains province.

Gravity is the omnipresent yet insidious force that generates the need to smooth out the sphere. The power of water and wind and the pull of gravity create a delicate balance that produces the erosion and deposition cycles. But gravity, too, is an agent of erosion itself. The mass wasting in landslides, mudflows, rock falls, and snow avalanches is predominantly generated by gravity. The Southern Rocky Mountain province is especially vulnerable to mass-wasting processes because of the dramatic relief and steep slopes inherent in the high mountains.

But for sheer scenic production in the mountains of Colorado, for majestic vistas, ice is king. Over eons of time, but especially throughout the past 2 million years, glaciers have reworked the mountains of Colorado — eroding, depositing, and shaping the lay of the land. Most mountains above 10,000 feet have been affected directly by glacial ice. Mountains below this level have been altered indirectly but substantially by the side effects of glaciers, which include meltwater runoff, increased rain- and snowfall, and biotic community alterations produced by the climate changes that initially caused the glacial advance.

THE CLIMATE

Very few places in the world display in such concentration the variations of temperature, precipitation, and wind that Colorado does. Central Colorado lies at 39 degrees north latitude and is considered a mid-latitude location. Yet on the same day, different parts of Colorado can have temperatures similar to southern Florida and Iceland. We can have torrential rains or blizzards occurring on one side of a ridge when only a few miles away the land is suffering drought conditions. The variation is also quite dramatic diurnally and seasonally. In places like South Park and the San Luis Valley, the daytime and nighttime temperatures can vary by more than 50 degrees F in a 12-hour period. Colorado can have some of the best weather in the world with cool, dry, sunny days and mild nights; it can also have some of the most severe conditions imaginable — for example, we hold the 24-hour maximum snowfall record of 76 inches, which occurred near Silver Lake in the Indian Peaks region.

What causes this multifarious climatological personality of Colorado? The answer to this question is complex but can be understood by looking at the following climate factors: latitude, continental position, general circulation patterns (storm tracks), elevation, and topography.

Because of Colorado's northern hemisphere position, 37 degrees north to 41 degrees north, significant differences occur in the amount of solar radiation (sunlight) reaching the ground during the different seasons. At the summer solstice Colorado receives 2.4 times more sunlight than it gets at the winter solstice, and throughout the year our northerly position allows us to receive only about 79 percent of the sunlight that reaches the ground at the equator. This latitudinal position is the starting point for understanding our climate; all other climate factors alter the effectiveness of this solar radiation input.

Colorado lies deep in the interior of the North American continent; it is at least 600 miles from the nearest large water body (the Pacific Ocean), and the intervening space is blocked by some of the highest mountains on the continent. This separation from water results in two critical characteristics: water-bearing air masses must travel a long distance to reach Colorado, and extremes in temperature are frequent because oceans tend to modify high and low temperatures and temperature variation.

The polar jet stream is a primary control for the movement of storms across the United States. As it meanders across the continent from west to east, it essentially drags with it the major storm systems that occur in North

America. In winter the jet stream often crosses directly over Colorado, giving us high potential for large, intermittent winter storms. In summer the jet stream is usually north of Colorado, and therefore most major storms pass to the north of the state.

It is a well-known fact that temperature generally decreases as the elevation increases. This phenomenon is called the environmental lapse rate. On average, the temperature decreases 3.6 degrees F for every 1,000 feet elevation gain. On a sweltering day in Colorado Springs, a short ride up the Pikes Peak highway can take you to cool, invigorating temperatures. This temperature decrease occurs principally because air pressure decreases with altitude and the "thinning" of the atmosphere. Ironically, at the same time that air temperature decreases with altitude, the intensity of solar radiation increases. Some of the worst sunburns imaginable occur in Colorado winters when unsuspecting skiers do not use sun screening lotion. In a very real sense there is just not enough atmosphere to block the powerful ultraviolet rays of the sun.

Topography, or the lay of the land, can have a profound effect on how the other climate factors behave. Consider a valley, one side of which faces south, the other north. The south-facing slope receives more solar radiation, higher temperatures, and dryer conditions due to increased evaporation. The north-facing slope is cooler, wetter, and probably shadier because of greater vegetation growth caused by increased moisture availability. In many cases the vegetation types on the two opposing slopes will be almost totally different: dry, scrub vegetation on the south-facing slope, and possibly a lush Douglas fir forest on the north-facing slope. All of these climate factors must be kept in mind when we look at the climate patterns of Colorado.

TEMPERATURE VARIATION

As mentioned above, air temperature generally decreases with increases in altitude. Some people liken the temperature decrease for each 1,000 feet to traveling 300 miles or more north. This would make the 8,000 feet gain in altitude from Colorado Springs to the top of Pikes Peak equivalent to traveling from Colorado Springs to Great Slave Lake in the Northwest Territories of Canada. One notable exception to this rule of thumb occurs most nights, when sunlight no longer heats up mountain slopes. The air in contact with the mountainsides cools from the radiation of heat to the sky. The colder air becomes more dense and actually flows downhill. If the cold air collects in valleys or basins, it can lower the temperature drastically. In fact, the coldest recorded temperatures in Colorado occur in valleys with cold air drainage such as those near Gunnison, Alamosa, and Fraser. Another exception to the rule of thumb, slope aspect (the variation in effective temperature dependent upon which direction a slope faces), was discussed above.

PRECIPITATION VARIATION

Like other aspects of weather and climate in Colorado, precipitation is extremely capricious. We receive as little as 8 inches per year on average along the Colorado River where it enters Utah, and as much as 40 inches per year on average at the summits of some of the high peaks. The Colorado Plateau, the Middle Rocky Mountain, and the Green River basin provinces ordinarily get the least precipitation; the Great Plains province is usually slightly wetter (12 to 16 inches per year), and the Southern Rocky Mountain province even more so, although it is also the most variable of any province (15 to 49 inches per year). And we do get more than our share of extreme events — for example, the 24 inches of rain in 4 hours at Elbert in 1935, the 14 inches of rain in 4 hours near the Palmer Divide in 1965, and the 12 inches of rain in 4 hours that caused the Big Thompson River flood in 1976.

Because the Colorado mountains typically trend north-south, they tend to block storm systems and moisture-laden air coming from either the west or the east. Storms bringing moisture from the Pacific will usually drop most of their precipitation (rain or snow) in the mountains west of the Continental Divide. Storms that pull moisture from the Gulf of Mexico deposit most of their moisture on the mountains east of the Continental Divide. Some of the largest single snowfalls in the state occur along the foothills of the Front Range when moisture-carrying winds rise up the piedmont, cool to the dew point, and drop their load of snow before ever reaching the mountains. Two to 3 feet of snow in a single storm is not uncommon. However, this happens only a few times a year, and most other times little snow accumulates in the Great Plains province. The majority of precipitation in the plains and the Colorado Plateau comes from summer thunderstorms. Many of these storms are large and intense, with cumulonimbus clouds towering over 60,000 feet, heavy rains, hail, and an occasional tornado (Figure 1.8). But Colorado is not always wet and stormy; there are far more days of beautiful, clear skies and moderate temperatures than there are wet and cold or hot

Figure 1.8. Embryo of a thunderstorm building over Pikes Peak.

days. Even most winter days in the mountains are relatively mild and enjoyable.

WIND VARIATIONS

Wind is an ever-present occurrence in Colorado. Generally, the higher the elevation the windier it gets, although the flat plains can also be an area of strong and persistent wind. The dominant wind at high altitude is from the west, but depending upon weather patterns and storm systems, winds can come from any direction. Winds along the Continental Divide and the higher peaks can probably reach speeds of up to 200 miles per hour, but exact maximum speeds are unknown because there are no wind gauges at these locations.

One particularly interesting wind phenomenon is the chinook, which usually occurs in late winter or early spring when a high-pressure zone sets up over the mountains and forces air to flow eastward at high speeds. Winds reaching 137 miles per hour have been recorded at the National Center for Atmospheric Research in Boulder. These winds flow down the slopes of the east side of the Front Range and become very dry. In fact, the chinook was called the "snow eater" by Indians in the West. The strongest of the chinooks occur from Colorado Springs in the south to Fort Collins in the north and are especially intense near Boulder and the U.S. Air Force Academy.

Local climate and weather patterns around Colorado may vary greatly from the norms just discussed. It would be impractical, if not impossible, to detail every local variation of weather and climate around the state. Each subsequent chapter, however, will review the significant local weather patterns if they are considerably different from the above general characteristics and important to the understanding of the local area.

THE VEGETATION

In Colorado there are over 1,500 separate species of vascular plants, 450 species of lichen, and 250 species of mosses and liverworts. Each species has its own requirements for light, heat, water, soil, and other environmental conditions. It is a daunting task, and one well beyond the scope of this book, to explain how each species fits into the overall pattern of life in the state. Few people can ever hope to totally understand even a small portion of the complex interactions between plant and environment that take place in an area the size of Colorado. But science in general, and natural science in particular, simplify our task by categorizing plant and animal associations so that an interested person can understand at least the general patterns shown by the distribution of species. This book will go into greater detail as appropriate in each of the following chapters, but I want to introduce one way to categorize biotic phenomena.

The most general method of categorizing biotic characteristics in a place like Colorado is through the use of vertical zonation — classing types of vegetation by where they lie along the spectrum of elevation from Holly, Colorado, which is approximately 3,387 feet above sea level, to the top of Mt. Elbert at 14,433 feet. In the mid-nineteenth century, Alexander von Humboldt recognized vertical patterns of vegetation when he named the three regions in South America in or near the Andes Mountains: the *tierra caliente* (hot land), the *tierra templada* (temperate land), and the *tierra fria* (cold land) refer to the low-, medium-, and high-altitude environments of the Andes (Humboldt 1805, passim). In the late nineteenth century, C. Hart Merriam went through a similar exercise for the San Francisco Mountains of Arizona. He proposed naming the vertical zones (low to high) after the latitudinal zones (south to north) — i.e., Canadian, Hudsonian, Arctic-Alpine, etc. (Merriam 1894, passim). Merriam based his classification scheme on temperature only, which presents some problems because temperature is not the only factor involved in determining vegetation type. However, the general idea of vertical zonation is quite attractive for understanding the very real changes that occur in flora and fauna patterns as elevation changes.

Whatever the classification scheme, we are only simplifying a very complex arrangement of biotic patterns. The term that I will use to define elevation/vegetation belts is "life zones." Our basic framework consists of six life zones:

1. The Plains Life Zone (below 5,500'). This is the zone of grasslands in eastern Colorado where trees exist only along streams (riparian areas) and where shrubs are rare (Figure 1.9).

2. The Foothills Life Zone (5,500' to 8,000'). This is a transitional area between the plains and mountains. It is usually a zone of dry shrub, piñon-juniper woodland, and the occasional ponderosa pine and Douglas fir. It is the most diverse life zone because it is typically narrow and as such is invaded by species from both the plains and the mountains (Figure 1.10).

Figure 1.9. Rolling plains in eastern Colorado stretching from horizon to horizon.

Figure 1.10. Typical example of foothills vegetation showing the diversity of the foothills life zone.

3. The Montane Life Zone (8,000' to 9,500'). Here we get into the true mountains, with forests of ponderosa pine on the sunnier, dryer sites and Douglas fir in shadier, wetter places. Some ecologists divide this zone into upper and lower montane, but we will use only the overall classification of montane (Figure 1.11).

4. The Subalpine Life Zone (9,500' to 11,500'). This is quite often the most heavily timbered life zone with its large, uniform stands of Engelmann spruce and subalpine fir. Often it is a very closed, shady forest with little understory and with breaks in the forest only along streams (Figure 1.12).

5. The Alpine Life Zone (above 11,500'). Here we find the alpine tundra, the land above the trees, where only low-lying vegetation can survive the cold and drying winds that never seem to cease. In many ways the alpine resembles the tundra of the far north (Figure 1.13).

6. The Upper Sonoran Life Zone (6,000' to 7,000'). The upper Sonoran can be found in the far west and southwest of the state, where precipitation is low and semidesert conditions exist. It almost completely usurps the elevation range of the plains life zone of eastern Colorado and encroaches into what would be the foothills life zone. The term "upper Sonoran" comes from one of Merriam's zones, which refers to a cold, high, desert environment in Arizona (Figure 1.14).

These six life zones are rather simplistic, and the elevations assigned to them are merely nominal; considerable overlap can and does occur. In fact, the transition areas between zones, known as "ecotones," can be very unique environments, especially the ecotone between the subalpine and the alpine life zones.

To further complicate matters and therefore more truthfully approach reality, I will talk about individual ecosystems that occur in one or more life zones. An ecosystem is a collection of all of the organisms and physical factors of the environment that occur together in one place. The assumption, based on thousands of observations, is that this set of living and nonliving characteristics functions as a single unit with a kind of balance that provides the conditions necessary for the ecosystem to work. Many levels of ecosystem can be defined; this book will feature sixteen ecosystems that have been identified in Colorado by Cornelia F. Mutel and John C. Emerick (Mutel and Emerick 1984, passim). I will talk about each of these in detail

Figure 1.11. Parklike landscape of open ponderosa pine forests, often used to represent the montane life zone.

Figure 1.12. Subalpine life zone, characterized by dark forests of spruce and fir with sparsely vegetated alpine regions visible on the skyline.

Figure 1.13. Alpine life zone, often a landscape of stark beauty and scant vegetation.

Figure 1.14. Piñon pine and junipers, the most recognizable vegetation in the Sonoran life zone.

Table 1.2

Name	Dominant Plant Community	Life Zone(s)	Chapter(s)
Plains Grassland	Grasses	Plains	6, 7, 8
Lowland Riparian	Cottonwood/Willow	Plains	7, 8
Semidesert Shrublands	Greasewood/ Saltbush	Plains/Upper Sonoran/Montane	10, 13
Sagebrush Shrublands	Sagebrush	Plains/Upper Sonoran/Montane	3, 8, 10, 13
Mountain Shrubland	Gambel Oak/ Mountain Mahogany	Foothills/Upper Sonoran/Montane	5, 6
Piñon Pine/Juniper Woodland	Piñon Pine/ Juniper (spp.)	Foothills/Upper Sonoran	6, 7, 10, 11, 13
Ponderosa Pine Forest	Ponderosa Pine	Foothills/Montane	4, 5, 6, 10, 11
Douglas Fir Forest	Douglas Fir	Foothills/Montane	4, 5, 6, 10, 11
Mountain Grassland/ Meadows	Varied	Montane/Subalpine	3, 5, 13
Mountain Riparian	Varied	Montane/Subalpine	3, 4, 5, 9, 11
Quaking Aspen Forest	Quaking Aspen	Montane/Subalpine	4, 5, 6, 9, 10
Lodgepole Pine Forest	Lodgepole Pine	Montane/Subalpine	3, 4
Limber Pine/ Bristlecone Pine Forest	Limber/Bristlecone Pine	Montane/Subalpine	2, 5
Engelmann Spruce/ Subalpine Fir	Engelmann Spruce/ Subalpine Fir	Subalpine	2, 3, 4, 9, 12
Subalpine/Alpine Ecotone	Engelmann Spruce/ Subalpine Fir/ Limber Pine	Subalpine/Alpine	2
Alpine Tundra	Varied	Alpine	2

where appropriate in the following chapters. Table 1.2 gives a very brief outline of each of these ecosystems.

The chapters of the book are organized principally by these ecosystems. Chapters 2 through 8 move from the highest elevations in the book on Mt. Evans to the lowest elevations along the South Platte River; these seven chapters cover the range of life zones and ecosystems. Chapters 9 through

13 are devoted to other, special places that add texture to the first part of the book. Each place was chosen for some distinctive quality or set of characteristics. For example, the Great Sand Dunes add an exotic flavor to the book and the Piceance Basin speaks of oil shale and failed human hopes. Taken as a small sample of the whole of the state, these places exhibit many of the wonders of Colorado and will, hopefully, give you a yearning to see and learn more.

ADDITIONAL READINGS

Armstrong, D. M., 1972. *Distribution of Mammals in Colorado,* monograph no. 3, University of Kansas, Lawrence, Kans.

——, 1987. *Rocky Mountain Mammals,* Colorado Associated University Press, Boulder, Colo.

Bailey, A. M., and R. J. Niedrach, 1965. *Birds of Colorado,* 2 vols., Denver Museum of Natural History, Denver, Colo.

Benedict, A. D., 1991. *A Sierra Club Naturalist's Guide — The Southern Rockies,* Sierra Club Books, San Francisco, Calif.

Chronic, H., 1980. *Roadside Geology of Colorado,* Mountain Press Publishing Co., Missoula, Mont.

Chronic, J., and H. Chronic, 1972. *Prairie, Peak, and Plateau: A Guide to the Geology of Colorado,* Colorado Geologic Survey Bulletin no. 32, Colorado Geologic Survey, Denver, Colo.

Costello, D. F., 1969. *The Prairie World,* University of Minnesota Press, Minneapolis, Minn.

Elmore, F. H., 1976. *Shrubs and Trees of the Southwest Uplands,* Southwest Parks and Monuments Association, Globe, Ariz.

Griffiths, M., and L. Rubright, 1983. *Colorado,* Westview Press, Boulder, Colo.

Hammerson, G. A., 1982. *Amphibians and Reptiles in Colorado,* Colorado Division of Wildlife, Denver, Colo.

Hansen, W. R., J. Chronic, and J. Matelock, 1978. *Climatography of the Front Range Urban Corridor and Vicinity, Colorado,* USGS Professional Paper 1019, U.S. Gov. Printing Office, Washington, D.C.

Harrington, H. D., 1979. *Manual of the Plants of Colorado,* Swallow Press, Chicago, Ill.

Harris, D. V., 1980. *The Geologic Story of the National Parks and Monuments,* 3rd ed., John Wiley and Sons, New York, N.Y.

Kent, H. C., and K. W. Porter, eds., 1980. *Colorado Geology,* Rocky Mountain Association of Geologists, Denver, Colo.

Krutch, Joseph Wood, 1962. *Thoreau: Walden and Other Writings,* Bantam Books, New York, N.Y.

Little, E. L., 1980. *The Audubon Society Field Guide to North American Trees: Western Region,* Alfred A. Knopf, New York, N.Y.

Merriam, C. Hart, 1894. "Laws of Temperature Control of the Geographic Distribution of Terrestrial Animals and Plants," *National Geographic Magazine* 6, pp. 229–238.

Moenke, H., 1971. *Ecology of Colorado Mountains to Arizona Deserts,* Denver Museum of Natural History, Denver, Colo.

Mutel, Cornelia F., and John C. Emerick, 1984. *From Grassland to Glacier,* Johnson Books, Boulder, Colo.

National Geographic Society, 1987. *Field Guide to the Birds of North America,* National Geographic Society, Washington, D.C.

Nelson, R. E., 1979. *Handbook of Rocky Mountain Plants,* Skyland Publishers, Estes Park, Colo.

Peterson, R. T., 1990. *A Field Guide to Western Birds,* Houghton Mifflin Co., Boston, Mass.

Preston, R. J., Jr., 1975. *North American Trees,* Massachusetts Institute of Technology Press, Cambridge, Mass.

Richmond, G. M., 1974. *Raising the Roof of the Rockies,* Rocky Mountain Nature Association, n.p.

Sprague, M., 1976. *Colorado — A Bicentennial History,* W. W. Norton & Co., Inc., New York.

Stebbins, R. C., 1966. *A Field Guide to Western Reptiles and Amphibians,* Houghton Mifflin Co., Boston, Mass.

Taylor, R. J. and R. W. Valum, 1974. *Wildflowers 2: Sagebrush Country,* Touchstone Press, Beaverton, Oreg.

Tweto, O., 1979. *Geologic Map of Colorado,* U.S. Geological Survey, State Map G77115, U.S. Government Printing Office, Washington, D.C.

Udvardy, M.D.F., 1977. *The Audubon Society Field Guide to North American Birds: Western Region,* Alfred A. Knopf, New York, N.Y.

von Humboldt, Alexander, 1805. *Ideen zu einen Geographie der Pflanzen,* Cotta, Tübingen, Germany.

Weber, W. A., 1976. *Rocky Mountain Flora,* Colorado Associated University Press, Boulder, Colo.

Weimer, R. J., and J. D. Haun, eds., 1960. *Guide to the Geology of Colorado,* Rocky Mountain Association of Geologists, Denver, Colo.

Young, R. G., and J. W. Young, 1977. *Colorado West, Land of Geology and Wildflowers,* Wheelwright Press, Ltd., Grand Junction, Colo.

Zwinger, A. H., and B. E. Willard, 1972. *Land Above the Trees: A Guide to American Alpine Tundra,* Harper and Row, New York, N.Y.

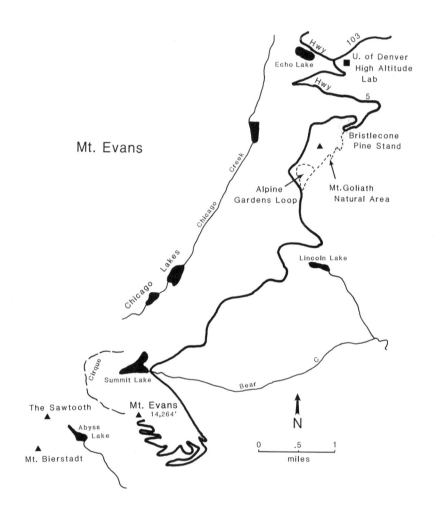

Mt. Evans

Echo Lake

Hwy 103

U. of Denver
High Altitude
Lab

Hwy 5

Bristlecone
Pine Stand

Mt. Goliath
Natural Area

Alpine
Gardens Loop

Chicago Creek

Chicago Lakes

Lincoln Lake

Cirque

Summit Lake

Bear C.

The Sawtooth

Mt. Evans
14,264'

Abyss
Lake

Mt. Bierstadt

N

0   .5   1
miles

2

MT. EVANS

Just 37 miles west of downtown Denver's skyscrapers, as the rosy finch flies, lies a high mountain, natural jewel. Mt. Evans and its surrounding wilderness area contain many examples of what people have come to think of as vintage Colorado — thousands of acres of montane and subalpine forests and meadows lying below large tracts of alpine crags and tundra. At 14,264 feet above sea level, Mt. Evans is the thirteenth tallest mountain in Colorado and lies just east of the Continental Divide. The paved road to the top of the mountain allows easy access to the world above treeline, a world that can offer a new and exhilarating perspective of Earth.

It would be a simple matter to become mesmerized by the 100-mile views from the summit of Mt. Evans (Figure 2.1), but a profusion of other important environmental features characterize the area. Amid the literally breathtaking heights lies one of the largest herds of Rocky Mountain goats in Colorado and an equally large herd of bighorn sheep. Just below treeline sits an extensive stand of bristlecone pine, one of the oldest known living organisms on Earth. Arctic-like permafrost and tundra vegetation, old forest fire zones that have yet to recover, and quintessential glacial landforms also grace the area. All of these can be seen, if not meaningfully experienced, from your car on the Mt. Evans Highway.

The road that reaches to just below the summit of Mt. Evans (14,150 feet) was completed in 1930. You can reach Echo Lake, where the road begins, from either Idaho Springs or Bergen Park via Colorado State Highway 103, which runs through beautiful forests and meadows. This paved access into wilderness is a thrill to travel and should be driven with caution — it is,

Figure 2.1. View north from the top of Mt. Evans showing the dramatic character of the high mountain landscape.

Figure 2.2. Crystalline nature of the rock, evident in outcrops all over the mountain.

however, well worth the effort and strain upon the nerves of most people. Few other areas around the world give you the opportunity to reach these high mountain elevations with such convenience.

THE GEOLOGY

Like Pikes Peak to the south and Longs Peak to the north, Mt. Evans is a Precambrian age batholith that has been repeatedly pushed to the surface. These Front Range mountains are the most dominant landforms along the linear mountain front that runs for 175 miles from the northern Colorado border to south of Pikes Peak. The rocks of this range are composed primarily of intrusive granites and diorites and metamorphic gneisses and schists. The magma that produced the rocks of Mt. Evans cooled slowly, deep within the Earth, creating rock with very large mineral crystals (Figure 2.2). Quartz, feldspars, biotite, and other mineral grains can easily be seen in the rock faces. This rock is approximately 1.3 billion years old and was formed during a mountain orogeny of that time period.

Mt. Evans, along with the other mountains of the Front Range, has been affected by orogenic forces several times since its first uplift. Just as the mountains near Pikes Peak rose 300 million years ago (mya) and again 65 mya (see Chapter 6, "Garden of the Gods"), Mt. Evans has repeatedly risen, been eroded, and risen again. The flat tops of Mt. Evans, Pikes Peak, and Longs Peak are an indication that they were all leveled by erosion in the far-distant past. Without erosion to wear away the rock after each uplift, these mountains would be very tall indeed, but erosion is an ever-present phenomenon on the Earth's surface.

THE EROSIVE FORCES

Water, wind, and ice have inextricably worn down the heights of Mt. Evans and continue to do so. Water is presently the most powerful agent of erosion, and fast-flowing streams are plentiful on the steep alpine slopes of the mountain. Each valley has its own cascades, and in the late spring the roar of flowing and falling water is heard throughout the region.

At high mountain altitudes, wind is an ever-present force. Sometimes it is a gentle breeze, but most often it is a strong and gusty gale that can occasionally reach hurricane proportions. Wind speeds of 134 miles per hour have been recorded at Echo Lake; at the top of Mt. Evans they are unrecorded but probably reach 200 miles per hour in winter. These strong winds carry small mineral particles that literally sandblast exposed rock. You can see examples of this above treeline and on the western, windward sides of rocks.

Ice accounts for a great deal of the rock weathering and landscape evolution of the entire region. Two distinctive scales of geomorphic work are performed by ice. First, massive glaciation took place here over the past 2 to 3 million years. The latest retreat of alpine glaciers from the area occurred only about 10,000 years ago — an instant in geologic time. Ice tongues up to thousands of feet thick produced a distinctive imprint on the landscape (see Chapter 9, "Silverton"). As you drive the road to the top of Mt. Evans, you will traverse a large glacial moraine just past Echo Lake. This feature, with its variable-sized boulders, is similar to glacial deposits around the world. Summit Lake is cradled in a large, natural amphitheater, a glacial cirque recently (in geologic time) abandoned by massive ice (Figure 2.3). The lake itself is a fine example of a tarn — the nearly ever-present lake associated with alpine cirques. You can see a typical glacial valley with its U-shaped form and moraine-dammed lakes if you take the short trail from the shelter cabin at Summit Lake north to an overlook onto the Chicago Lakes valley. The steep enclosure at the head of this valley is another cirque, and

Figure 2.3. Reflections in ice and water on Summit Lake seem to turn the world upside down.

the lakes that line the valley are called "paternoster" lakes because of their resemblance to rosary beads.

The second scale of activity performed by ice takes place at the level of the individual rock. Water seeps into cracks and joints of rocks and freezes. Because water expands during freezing, pressures from the expanding water and crystalline structure of ice eventually break the rock apart. Ice-shattered rock debris can be seen all over the slopes and summits of the Mt. Evans massif. Distinctive landforms called "talus" are visible throughout the alpine section of the mountain. These cones are formed from broken rock that has fallen and rolled to the areas below the standing rock walls from which they came.

THE CLIMATE

Driving from Idaho Springs to the summit of Mt. Evans takes you through a 6,725-foot elevation change and three separate life zones — the montane, the subalpine, and the alpine. Commonly, as elevation increases the temperature decreases and the precipitation increases, producing significant changes in ecosystem development. These changes are readily seen as you travel up the roadway from dense forests of the montane and the subalpine, past treeline, and into the open alpine landscape.

No permanent weather station exists on the top of Mt. Evans; however, the University of Denver's High Altitude Laboratory is located near Echo Lake. It can be assumed that weather gets progressively more severe with increasing elevation. The High Altitude Laboratory is located at 10,700 feet, in the subalpine life zone. The average yearly depth of snow here is between 400 and 500 inches; the largest accumulation of this occurs in the spring of the year. This area actually gets more snow than the top of the mountain because much of the snow that falls there is blown off of the unprotected slopes and finally comes to rest in the subalpine.

The lowest recorded temperature at the High Altitude Laboratory was -52 degrees F, and freezing temperatures may occur here during any month. Winds are often strong and constant. Summer is merely a brief interlude in a long, often severe, winter. Be assured, however, that winter can also be benign and beautiful. When the winds are relatively calm and snow is not falling heavily, many people climb to the high slopes of the mountains for skiing, snowshoeing, and other winter sports.

An aspect of the high mountains that newcomers often ignore is the intensity of the solar radiation at these altitudes. The thin atmosphere at high elevations blocks little of the sun's energy, particularly its ultraviolet rays. This means that even if the temperature is cold, you can get a severe sunburn if exposed to the sun for any length of time.

Two other weather- and/or atmosphere-related problems should always be kept in mind when traveling the alpine. The first is altitude sickness caused by lower oxygen availability at these elevations. Headaches, nausea, and dizziness are good indicators that you should retreat back down the mountain. Severe altitude sickness can be very debilitating, so heed your body's warnings. The second problem is hypothermia, the lowering of your core body temperature caused by low air temperatures and/or evaporation of water from your clothes and body. Hypothermia can occur at any time of the year, especially when the wind is blowing. Severe chills, shivering, and incoherence indicate that you have a very severe problem. The best way to combat hypothermia is to avoid it — bring appropriate, warm clothes to wear whenever you are in the high mountains.

THE ECOSYSTEMS

The typical characteristics of the montane and subalpine ecosystems are discussed in the chapters on the Florissant Fossil Beds National Monument and Crested Butte/Steamboat Lake, respectively. Therefore, these ecosystems that one encounters when traveling from Idaho Springs or Bergan Pass to Echo Lake will not be discussed here. A distinctive ecosystem not covered at length in other chapters of the book is the bristlecone pine (*Pinus aristata*) ecosystem. As one of the oldest living species on Earth, the bristlecone pine deserves special attention.

BRISTLECONE PINE ECOSYSTEM

One of the largest stands of these beautiful, gnarled trees in Colorado is located next to the road that leads to the top of Mt. Evans. As you ascend the highway from Echo Lake, a sign for the Mt. Goliath Natural Area marks the lower entrance to the nature trail that traverses the bristlecone pine stand. This trail begins at about 11,280 feet and climbs through the stand until the trees give way to the alpine landscape at 11,488 feet. The bristlecones

Figure 2.4. Twisted and eerie forms of the bristlecone pine area can be enchanting and beautiful.

are protected by state and federal law, so you cannot take any part of these trees, whether dead or alive. Please look and enjoy; do not collect.

The bristlecone pine is not a large tree but it has a very broad crown and, frequently, a twisted trunk (Figure 2.4). There are five needles per bundle, which have whitish drops of resin affixed. The trees are appropriately named because of the very sharp bristles on the cones. If you handle the cones, you will probably end up with several of these bristles imbedded in your fingers.

Living bristlecone pines that exceed 4,800 years of age have been found in the Inyo National Forest of California. Those found on Mt. Evans have not been accurately dated but are believed to be considerably younger, probably between 1,500 and 1,700 years old. These aristocratic plants grow in the most exposed and hostile regions that still allow treed vegetation. The harshness of these conditions limits many species that would otherwise invade and "succeed" the bristlecones. Evidence of the beginnings of invasion exists near the lower limit of the bristlecone pine stand, where Engelmann spruce (*Picea engelmannii*) and subalpine fir (*Abies lasiocarpa*) are starting to encroach on the pine stands. Although most bristlecones here are

Figure 2.5. "Young" bristlecone pines can be a century or more old. They must struggle long and hard to survive this harsh environment.

Figure 2.6. Krummholz, one of nature's ways to combat the elements; the low-growing form fights wind and desiccation.

past their prime, you will still find bristlecone saplings starting their slow growth toward maturity (Figure 2.5).

THE ECOTONE

I use the term "ecotone" to refer to the zone between the subalpine forest and the treeless alpine regions. In many instances in Colorado, the ecotone is identified by a modified tree structure. Timberline is the zone where upright trees cease to grow; treeline is the area where tree species are no longer found. Near timberline (at about 11,500 feet), the wind has a very drying (desiccating) effect on vegetation. This desiccation actually kills needles, twigs, and branches on the windward side of the tree. The result is "flag" trees, which have branches only on the downwind side of the trunk. In more severe circumstances the only parts of the tree that are spared from these chilling and killing winds are those covered with snow during the winter. These stunted and laterally growing trees are called "krummholz" from the German word meaning "crooked wood" (Figure 2.6). Most krummholz trees are Engelmann spruce or subalpine fir — the same stately species that grow to spirelike heights at lower elevations. Examples of these low-growing tree forms can be found at treeline near the upper levels of the bristlecone pine ecosystem. In this case the species is Engelmann spruce.

A strange and fascinating characteristic of the krummholz is that the individual trees actually migrate downwind! As the tree grows and spreads laterally, some of the branches that contact the ground will "layer" or put down new roots from the end of the branch. The older, upwind trunk of the tree may eventually die and this new root system will take over the tasks of providing sustenance for the plant. This process can repeat itself several times; as the krummholz trees move downwind they may reach ages of several hundred years and may be several yards or meters from the original trunk.

THE ALPINE TUNDRA ECOSYSTEM

Above treeline, the world appears to spread out before you. The air is crystal clear; the vantage point is high; the view is unobstructed. Most people feel awe and exhilaration when viewing the surrounding mountains and deep valleys from these elevations. Seldom can you see such an array of natural landscapes at such great distances — exceeding 100 miles on a clear day. The hues of the ever-more-distant mountains turn from dark greens to blues to purples and hold your gaze. As difficult as it is, try to pull your gaze back from the large-scale landscape to the spot where you are standing — for the tundra is much more than distant sights. It is a place where fauna and diminutive flora flourish in spite of an ominous climate, but you must view it on hands and knees instead of through binoculars. The sights, sounds, textures, and smells of the tundra are here, waiting for you to notice. With a little effort your senses will be stimulated beyond your expectations by the natural world at your feet.

The tundra is not a homogeneous collection of flora and fauna species. Considerable variation in the distribution of plants, and therefore animals, is controlled by microenvironmental conditions such as water availability, wind protection, snow depth, soil development, and rock outcrops. At least five distinctive sets of characteristics define the vegetation communities found above treeline on Mt. Evans. These include fellfields (or rock fields), meadows, wet meadows, snow accumulation and persistence zones, and rock outcrops.

Fellfields. Fellfields are areas of relatively flat ground where large numbers of shattered rocks make up the majority of the surface; significant soil accumulations may or may not exist between the rocks. Fellfields are usually on slopes exposed to wind, where snow is blown off and little moisture is available for plant growth (Figure 2.7). Weather conditions here are among the harshest: high winds, low temperatures, and no protecting snow banks. An amazing profusion of plants still survive and prosper in this seeming wasteland.

A large portion of the plants that grow here are called "cushion" plants, so named because their low-growing masses of stems, roots, leaves, and flowers resemble large pincushions. Some of the most beautiful flowers in Colorado are cushion plants that grow to heights of merely an inch or two, with flowers only fractions of an inch in diameter: the moss campion (*Silene acaulis*), the alpine phlox (*Phlox condensata*), the alpine sandwort (*Minuartia obtusiloba*), and the vibrantly blue, sweet-smelling alpine forget-me-not (*Eritrichum aretioides*). Although these plants grow in the toughest surroundings, they can be harmed by one human step; please do not tread on these tenacious yet delicate survivors.

Meadows. Meadows commonly have relatively deep soils and considerable moisture. They become verdant and lush during the short alpine growing season and can be recognized by the deep greens of vibrant vegetation growth. Most meadow plants are grasses and sedges, which provide high-nutrient forage for much of the fauna, such as Rocky Mountain elk (*Cervus elaphus*), that visit the tundra in summer. By the peak of the growing season, however, the meadows abound in a profusion of flowering plants. Of the dozens of species that grow in this environment, the most spectacular include the alpine sunflower or old-man-of-the-mountain (*Hymenoxys grandiflora*), the alpine primrose (*Primula angustifolia*), death camas (*Zigadenus elegans*), and alpine wallflower (*Erysimum nivale*).

Wet meadows. Some scientists call this environment the arctic tundra zone of Mt. Evans because it may be associated with permafrost conditions similar to those near the Arctic Circle. Wet meadows lie on flat, very wet areas (Figure 2.8) that are often devoid of snow in the winter due to high winds. Snow is a great insulator — without it, the cold winter temperatures freeze deep into the soil, and many areas remain perennially frozen below the surface. Only the top, active layer melts in the summer, giving us the telltale wet conditions. If there truly is permafrost on Mt. Evans, it is most likely sporadic and a relic from the glacial periods mentioned above.

Figure 2.7. Fellfields (rock fields) are found throughout the high mountain regions of Colorado.

Figure 2.8. Wet meadow areas on Mt. Evans, some of the most prolific and vibrant of all the ecosystems on the mountain.

Several willow species will grow in these wet conditions at or above treeline. They are very difficult to identify exactly because the identification characteristics occur during several different seasons. We do see the Arctic willow (*Salix arctica*), the snow willow (*S. nivalis*), the barrenground willow (*S. glauca*), and the planeleaf willow (*S. phylicifolia*) in or near these wet meadow areas. Forbs such as the water-loving marsh marigold (*Caltha leptosepala*) may be found in wet meadows near treeline.

Snow zones. Certain areas in the alpine are better at capturing and keeping snow than others. These snow zones retain snow longer during the spring melt and provide a ready source of moisture for plants that lie just downslope. Certain plants, like the snow buttercup (*Ranunculus adoneus*), will begin new growth and bloom while still imbedded in snow. It is quite a sight to see a large, white snow bank speckled with these small, intensely yellow flowers. Other flowers that flourish in this zone include the marsh marigold, the alpine lousewort (*Pedicularis sudetica*), and queen's crown (*Sedum rhodanthum*).

Vegetation in these snow zones will usually get a late start in the spring, but these verdant places in the alpine tundra frequently linger into autumn when most other vegetation is going dormant for the winter. The withered stems of dormant plants sit in stark contrast to the still lush areas where the snow lies late.

Rock outcrops. Talus, large rock outcrops, and imposing rock walls are prevalent in the alpine. It is difficult to imagine how any living thing could exist on these rock surfaces or in the cracks and joints amid the rocks — but life there is. Many plants survive on windblown soil that catches in the fissures of the rock and on water that seeps into these cracks. While hiking along a severe stone face, it is not uncommon to be suddenly confronted by the beautiful and striking big-rooted spring beauty (*Claytonia megarhiza*) emerging from the smallest opening in the rock.

Other plants soften the visible outlines of the rock and actually depend upon the minerals in the stone for survival. Lichens of innumerable variety and color are found on almost all rocks in the alpine. They feed on wind-blown debris, falling water, and minerals in the rock itself. A lichen is actually a symbiotic plant made up of both an alga and a fungus. Lichen survives primarily on photosynthesis performed by the alga. The fungus partner usually gets a free ride.

Alpine plant adaptations. While many of us have a difficult time convincing flowers to grow in our gardens where adequate water, fertilizer, and shelter are available, alpine plants grow and thrive under seemingly impossible conditions. Numerous adaptations enable these plants to grow and reproduce in such severe environmental circumstances. (An excellent in-depth scientific summary of these adaptations can be found in W. D. Billings's (1974) work on alpine plant adaptations and origins.) Perhaps the most important adaptation is that almost all of these plants are perennials. Only one annual, the *Koenigia islandica,* exists above treeline on Mt. Evans. It takes several years for a plant to get established here, and annuals seldom grow fast enough after sprouting to be able to survive the winter. This characteristic also allows the plant to get a head start on growth in the early spring.

Most alpine plants have very large root systems that are efficient at collecting nutrients and water. These root systems are also carbohydrate storage centers for the plants. The food stored here during the growing season allows the plant to live during the long alpine winter and is immediately available for plant growth the next spring.

The cushion plants mentioned earlier have an advantage in gathering and storing heat. Their hemispheric shape is ideal for heat retention and their low profile helps the plant avoid desiccating winds. The small stature of almost all alpine plants also helps them to avoid harsh winds and permits them to receive re-radiated heat from the nearby soil surface.

Seedling establishment in most alpine plants is slow and arduous. Much of the procreation that occurs above treeline comes in the form of vegetative reproduction. This asexual reproduction entails the growth of rhizomes, stolons, suckers, and bulbils. Asexual reproduction reduces the genetic variability of a species but allows for more dependable growth than seed dispersal. Seed reproduction does occur, but it usually takes a year or two of relatively benign environmental conditions for the seedlings to become viable plants.

There are many, many more adaptive strategies taken by alpine plants — some are drought resistant, others photosynthesize at very low temperatures and light levels, still others produce a kind of antifreeze that keeps the plant from freezing at low temperatures. Only their adaptability and tenacity for life enable flora to flourish at high elevations. When looking at the stunning colors and profusion of flowers in the mid-summer alpine, think about the struggles and triumphs over adversity each and every plant you see has gone through just to be alive. These thoughts should inspire you to take care and be gentle in this land above the trees.

THE FAUNA

The fauna of Mt. Evans are as intriguing as the flora. Here in this high-altitude world the abundance of bird life, for example, rivals that in most other parts of the state. Eagles, several species of hawk, falcons, and jays all frequent the mountain. Smaller birds are even more plentiful. The "hum" of the broad-tailed (*Selasphorus platycercus*) and ruby-throated (*Archilochus colubris*) hummingbirds can be heard throughout the summer in the subalpine. And the famous rosy finches (*Leucosticte arctoa*) of Mt. Evans are ubiquitous. There may be more rosy finches on Mt. Evans than anywhere else in the world. There are several varieties, including the gray-crowned, brown-capped, and Hepburn's finches. One large bird that stays above treeline all winter is the white-tailed ptarmigan (*Lagopus leucurus*). This bird, which has been studied extensively on Mt. Evans, survives on willow buds and twigs and a large variety of other vegetation. Ptarmigan molt three times a year, changing their distinctive plumage from the brown and black mottles of summer to the more finely mottled look of autumn to the almost pure white of the winter feathers. You might literally stumble upon one of these birds as you hike the trails of the alpine because they seldom run or fly to avoid contact but, rather, lie motionless and depend on their camouflage for protection.

THE SHEEP AND GOATS

An exciting encounter that you might have on Mt. Evans is to be driving along the highway to the summit and see bighorn sheep (*Ovis canadensis*) (Figure 2.9) and/or Rocky Mountain goats (*Oreamnos americanus*) (Figure 2.10) along the side of the road. On Mt. Evans, these majestic animals are used to people and seem to pose on rocky promontories and cliffs for photographs. If you spend any length of time here, you will probably see one or both of these animals at close range. Please do not attempt to feed or touch them — they are still wild and unpredictable.

The story behind these two species is one of coexistence and competition. The bighorn sheep are native to Colorado and exist throughout the state in small to medium herds. They often live above treeline and forage in

Figure 2.9. Bighorn sheep must struggle to survive the harsh environment and competition from interlopers like the Rocky Mountain goat.

windblown areas for food in the winter. Sheep, rather selective in using forage areas, seldom go beyond alpine meadows for food. They are susceptible to many diseases such as parasitic lungworm and pneumonia.

The Rocky Mountain goat is probably not indigenous to Colorado. Small herds have been introduced to the state since 1948; the herd on Mt. Evans was established in 1961. Goats stay in the alpine over winter and use windswept sites for foraging. They are less selective than the sheep, however, in what they eat. This, along with the goats' more aggressive behavior, gives them a competitive edge over the sheep. The Colorado Division of Wildlife has been studying the relationship between the goats and sheep on Mt. Evans for several years to identify the effects of the juxtaposition of the two species. No definite results are yet available, but it seems that the goats are better adapted to this harsh environment than even the native bighorns. For now, enjoy the thrill of seeing these two ungulates; seldom will you get the chance to encounter, firsthand, such large and stately wildlife in their natural habitat.

Figure 2.10. Rocky Mountain goats are adaptable, plentiful, and seemingly fearless on Mt. Evans.

FINAL THOUGHTS

Mt. Evans Wilderness Area. The 40,300 acres surrounding Mt. Evans was officially designated a Wilderness Area by Congress in 1980. The high peaks and glacial valleys are all available to backpackers, hikers, and cross-country skiers throughout the year. Because the "wilderness" designation means that motor vehicles are prohibited, the Mt. Evans Highway and easements along both sides of the road are not included in the Wilderness Area. Rugged alpine landscapes and scenery like those of Sawtooth, Abyss Lake, and Mt. Bierstadt are available for those willing to exert the effort.

As with most wilderness areas, the trails are often very primitive and hiking can be strenuous. Extended use of the area and long backpacking trips should not be attempted by those who are not physically ready for such endeavors. If you do go, the entire area is a welcome refuge of solitude and natural splendor within an easy drive from metropolitan Denver.

Mt. Goliath Natural Area. For those not wanting a strenuous excursion through the wilderness, but wishing to experience firsthand the subalpine and alpine environments, the Mt. Goliath Natural Area awaits. Two access points are available: one at 3.0 miles up Highway 5 and one at 4.0 miles along Highway 5. The upper access at 4.0 miles is the easier to find and use.

A .5-mile loop called the "Alpine Gardens" trail takes you around and over Mt. Goliath. Here you will see several of the vegetation types mentioned earlier in the chapter. If you wish to walk through the bristlecone pine stand, you can follow a 1.3-mile trail can be followed down the slope instead of looping back to the parking area. This is a delightful downhill hike that traverses the main bristlecone pine stand and ends in the subalpine forest of Engelmann spruce and subalpine fir. On the far upslope, near treeline, you can see some good examples of krummholz vegetation.

The human factor. It is, indeed, a paradox that the tough, tenacious vegetation above treeline is capable of surviving extreme weather conditions but is one of the most delicate floras when it comes to human disturbance. One footstep can damage or kill a cushion plant by exposing it to wind and erosion. The soil upon which most plants depend is a scarce commodity in the alpine, and it may take several centuries to replace if it becomes dislodged and erodes away. If the soil is lost, the plants are lost.

Certain plants of the alpine are more susceptible to disturbance than others. Fellfields and rock outcrop plant communities are easily disturbed and may take decades to recover. Deep-soiled meadows, on the other hand, can withstand human travel as long as the turf is not broken. Once the turf is cut, however, erosion will quickly devastate these areas and they may take up to a thousand years to heal. Winds, cold temperatures, lack of water, and intense solar radiation keep the plant communities from rapid recovery.

This means that you are welcome to enjoy and experience the alpine on Mt. Evans, but if you hike please stay on the established trails. Help preserve this legacy of grandeur and beauty for generations to come.

ADDITIONAL READINGS

Barry, R. G., 1972. *Climatic Environment of the East Slope of the Colorado Front Range,* Institute of Arctic and Alpine Research, University of Colorado, Boulder, Colo.

Billings, W. D., 1974. "Adaptations and Origins of Alpine Plants," *Arctic and Alpine Research* 6 (2), pp. 129–142.

Chronic, H., 1980. *Roadside Geology of Colorado,* Mountain Press Publishing Co., Missoula, Mont.

Geist, V., 1971. *Mountain Sheep,* The University of Chicago Press, Chicago, Ill.

Marinos, N., and H. Marinos, 1981. *Plants of the Alpine Tundra,* Rocky Mountain Nature Association, Estes Park, Colo.

Marr, J. W., 1961. *Ecosystems of the East Slope of the Front Range in Colorado,* University of Colorado Studies Series in Biology 8, Boulder, Colo.

Reed, D. F., 1982. "When Sheep and Goats Compete," *Colorado Outdoors,* Nov.–Dec., pp. 40–42.

Reiner, R. E., and L. Reiner, 1986. *The Majestic "Front Range" Region of Clear Creek County, Colorado,* The Three Rs Publishing Co., Idaho Springs, Colo.

Ringrose, L. W., and L. M. Rathbun, 1988. *Foothills to Mount Evans: West-of-Denver Trail Guide,* The Wordsmiths, Evergreen, Colo.

Veblen, T. T., and D. C. Lorenz, 1991. *The Colorado Front Range — A Century of Ecological Change,* University of Utah Press, Salt Lake City, Utah.

Zwinger, A. H., and B. E. Willard, 1972. *Land Above the Trees: A Guide to American Alpine Tundra,* Harper and Row, New York, N.Y.

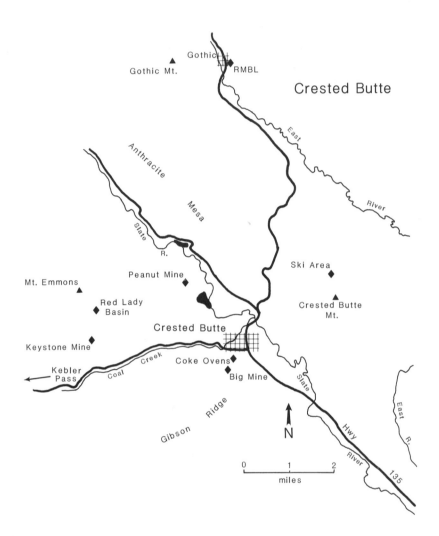

3

CRESTED BUTTE

The Crested Butte area can be considered a microcosm of the natural and human systems of the mountain world of the American West. It contains all the essential fibers that are woven into the fabric that we call the "western slope" of Colorado — wilderness, minerals, glaciers, Indians, tourism, trappers, skiing. The town of Crested Butte itself is the epitome of the once comatose nineteenth- and early twentieth-century mining town that has been revived by scenery and sport. Here the almost abandoned world of extractive exploitation of mineral wealth is the basis for a new, and so far, renewable world of cameras and skis. The visitors that use these cameras and skis are the true growth industry of the region. This relatively new enterprise is based, as its predecessors were, on the exploitation of the natural environment.

Crested Butte and its environs sit nestled in the Slate River valley at the southern limit of the Elk Mountains. The geologic history of the range is closely connected to the human history both in the distant and recent pasts. It may also dramatically affect the future destiny of this small, vibrant community. This geology is the foundation for all other aspects of the natural environment so prized by residents and visitors alike.

THE GEOLOGY

The Elk Mountains are an anomaly in Colorado geology. Most high mountains in the state consist of Precambrian intrusive and metamorphic rocks or more recent rock of volcanic origin. The Elk Mountains and the Crested Butte area consist mostly of sedimentary rocks, particularly those of the late Cretaceous and early Tertiary periods. To find other similar mountains in North America, one must travel to the Canadian Rockies. The most dramatic of the stratified mountains in the Elk Range are the Maroon Bells, 15 miles north of Crested Butte. The sedimentary rocks nearer Crested Butte are less well known than the Maroon Bells, and many have been significantly altered by folding, faulting, and igneous intrusions.

The Mancos shale and the Mesaverde formation are the most widespread sedimentary rock in the Crested Butte area. Mancos shale is very closely akin to the Pierre shale discussed in Chapter 6, "Garden of the Gods." This bed of shale with some interbedded limestone and siltstone is almost 3,600 feet thick and is highly nonresistant to erosion. Overlying the Mancos shale is the Mesaverde formation — a relatively resistant sandstone that forms cliffs in many areas because of its resistance to erosion. The upper part of the Mesaverde formation contains substantial coal-bearing layers interbedded with sand and siltstones.

THE IGNEOUS INTRUSIONS

In the mid–Tertiary period, great changes occurred that set the course for the geologic and human histories of the Crested Butte region. Massive intrusions of molten rock from deep below the surface were thrust into the overlying bedrock. This molten rock never reached the surface to produce volcanic activity but instead became intrusive stocks and laccoliths. Laccoliths of igneous rock resemble large, relatively flat-lying masses of molten rock rising from a central core. They spread out at the top like a mushroom, and replace overlying sediments already in place (Figure 3.1). The first phase of this intrusive activity occurred about 29.1 million years ago (mya) as determined by potassium-argon dating techniques.

The igneous intrusions had several important implications for the area. First, these overlying and erosion-resistant igneous rocks were much harder than the sedimentary rocks surrounding and, at times, underlying them. Sedimentary rock on top of the laccoliths eroded and left the igneous rock standing above the surrounding landscape — one of the most dramatic of these is Crested Butte Mountain itself (Figure 3.2). The softer sediments underlying the laccoliths also eroded faster than the hard, igneous rock. Unable to withstand the forces of gravity, water, and ice, these softer rocks gave way, producing a concentration of slope failures around the Crested

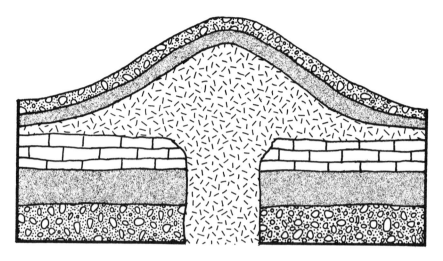

Laccolith Intrusion   A.

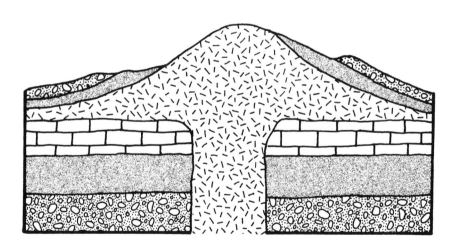

After Erosion of Sedimentary Caprock   B.

Figure 3.1. Crested Butte Mountain is an excellent example of an exposed laccolith. The above schematic diagram shows how this process occurs.

Figure 3.2. Crested Butte Mountain stands dominant over the landscape of the area.

Butte region. Fine examples of mass wasting can be seen on Gothic Mountain (Figure 3.3) and all around the flanks of Crested Butte Mountain.

A second effect of the igneous activity is the inherent hydrothermal alteration and mineralization of the zones immediately adjacent to the intrusions. The areas directly adjoining the magma intrusions were often faulted, fractured, and permeable. Fluid from deep within the Earth carried a mixture of minerals along these fissures; when the fluid evaporated, the minerals were deposited in these zones. This is a simplistic description of the complex process that produced much of the mineral wealth throughout Colorado. The great gold and silver strikes of the West are almost all the result of similar circumstances. The town of Crested Butte itself was never a hardrock mining town but rather was a service center for surrounding mining districts such as Gothic, Scofield, Washington Gulch, Kebler Pass, and the upper East River drainage.

The third major effect of the intrusions was the metamorphosis of the country rock into other rock types as a result of the very high temperatures and pressures that accompanied the original injections of magma. Contact metamorphism of this type was responsible for creating high-quality anthracite coal from the bituminous coal in the Mesaverde formation. Because of

Figure 3.3. Mass wasting is a significant geologic problem. Here you can see evidence of a large landslide on Gothic Mountain.

this transformation from good-quality bituminous coal to high-grade anthracite, the town of Crested Butte became a center of coal mining and coking for many years.

Through the vagaries of precious metal prospecting and mining, coal kept Crested Butte going. Coal began its long and vital role when mining of it began in Crested Butte in 1880. One year later the Denver and Rio Grande Railroad completed its rail route into the town. The anthracite and bituminous coals of this region were considered the equal of the best, high-grade coals of Pennsylvania; therefore, the coal was sought even though the mining and transportation conditions of the high mountains were very severe.

Local names like Anthracite Mesa and Coal Creek are indicative of the scale of coal mining in the region. Some of the largest and most productive mines were located along the north slope of Gibson Ridge, just south of the town of Crested Butte. The Jokerville Mine, about a third of a mile due west of the town, was the first mine to begin operation (in 1880). This mine was closed permanently in 1884 when gas, probably methane, in the mine exploded and killed 59 miners. Although this tragedy touched almost every citizen of Crested Butte, new and larger mines continued to be developed. In 1884 the "Big Mine" (Crested Butte Mine) was opened on Gibson Ridge

Figure 3.4. A few rusted machines, some dilapidated buildings, and rubble piles still exist at Peanut Mine.

directly south of town. The Big Mine remained open until 1952. During its 68 years in operation it produced 10,068,455 short tons of mostly coking coal for the Colorado Fuel and Iron Company steel mills in Pueblo. The Porter and the Bulkley No. 1 and No. 2 mines were also on Gibson Ridge. Other, smaller mines existed throughout the area, such as the Peanut Mine northwest of Crested Butte (Figure 3.4). At the height of the coal age, there were 150 coking ovens working around the clock in the area just south of White Rock Avenue. Hardly a trace of these large mines and coking ovens can now be found (Figure 3.5). As happens to all extractive industries sooner or later, all of the coal mines were closed. When the Denver and Rio Grande Railroad removed their tracks from the town, the era of coal was over for Crested Butte. Only the hardrock, heavy mineral mining at the Keystone Mine on Mt. Emmons west of Crested Butte kept the town feebly alive during the 1950s.

THE GLACIAL LANDSCAPE

Mountain uplifts and igneous intrusions created the bedrock and produced the elevations of the Crested Butte area, but alpine glaciation can be credited with sculpting the scenery. Most of the theory and definitions of

Figure 3.5. Remains of the "Big Mine" southwest of the town of Crested Butte are nearly invisible now.

glaciation in this book are covered in Chapter 9, "Silverton," but glaciation so altered the Crested Butte landscape it merits discussion here. The most recent major glacial advance, regionally called the Pinedale, retreated from most of Colorado about 10,000 years ago. We know this by studying places such as a bog on Mt. Emmons where radiocarbon dating has put the age of the bog at about 7,100 years old. Because the bog is in a glacial valley, it could not have existed before the glaciers retreated. Thus, 7,100 years is an absolute minimum date for the retreat of the ice; and because it may take many centuries for a bog to develop, scientists have estimated that the glacial retreat took place about 10,000 years ago. This is just one example of how dating of glacial activity is accomplished.

Everywhere you look in the Crested Butte region you can see evidence of glaciation. All of the high mountains have been scoured by ice, and many large cirques and U-shaped glacial valleys (glacial troughs) mark the landscape. Both the Slate River and Coal Creek valleys are examples of these glacial troughs. Significant evidence immediately west and south of Crested Butte suggests that several localized surges (glacial stades) and retreats of the glaciers have occurred within each of these valleys. Glaciers erode and transport millions of tons of rock and sediment from the valleys in which they move and from the valley walls above the ice. Some of this debris is deposited on the sides of the valleys — this kind of deposit is called a lateral moraine. Much of the material is carried to the snout of the glacier and is dropped as the glacier retreats — these deposits are called terminal or end moraines. The material that makes up the moraine is called "till" or "glacial drift" in older publications.

Where the Slate River and Coal Creek valleys converge just northwest of Crested Butte, there is a coalescence of lateral moraines from both drainages. If you were to look closely, you could find at least eight separate moraines at this confluence. This indicates that many small stades occurred in these two valleys. Most of this glacial oscillation took place in the Slate River drainage, which is much larger than the Coal Creek valley. This provided more ice and more rock debris to be moved by the Slate River glacier(s). Adjacent to the southern edge of the town of Crested Butte is another lateral moraine that separates the town from Gibson Ridge. This ridge and its vegetation will be discussed later in the chapter.

THE CLIMATE

The climate of the Crested Butte area, like any mountain locale, is greatly affected by topography. Crested Butte lies at 8,909 feet above sea level and is typical of Colorado mountain communities except that it has higher precipitation rates than similar elevations on the eastern slope of the Colorado Rockies. Crested Butte receives about 25 inches of precipitation and averages over 210 inches of snow annually; the high mountains surrounding the town receive significantly more. Gothic and areas north of town also receive more precipitation, as evidenced by the dense vegetation of the area. The slope angle and aspect of a mountainside influences the climate considerably. South- and southwest-facing slopes are warmer and drier, while north and northeast aspects get less sun and are therefore cooler and wetter. It is not just a coincidence that the Crested Butte ski area is on the northwest and north sides of Crested Butte Mountain.

Topography can have an even greater effect on regional climatic differences. The north-south trending valleys between Crested Butte and Gunnison (the East and Taylor rivers) allow cold, dense air in the winter to drain toward the south into the city of Gunnison. Often, Gunnison will have the coldest temperature in the state while the town of Crested Butte, which is 1,200 feet higher, has a temperature 20 to 30 degrees F warmer. Taylor Park, just northeast of Gunnison, has the second-lowest recorded temperature ever in Colorado: in 1951 it reached a very frigid -60 degrees F. Along with these much colder temperatures comes a drastic decrease in precipitation; Gunnison averages only eleven inches of precipitation annually.

As you move above treeline into the alpine region, the climate again becomes more severe. There are no weather records for these alpine slopes, but the weather will be similar to that on Mt. Evans, which is described in Chapter 2. The town of Crested Butte lies snugly between these extremes. Weather here can definitely be cold, wet, and harsh, but in general the climate is moderate by high mountain standards.

THE SKI INDUSTRY

This climate, with its combination of heavy snows, a good measure of sun, and few extreme temperatures, is perfect for the industry that has pulled Crested Butte back from the brink of economic extinction. Since its beginnings in Colorado in the 1940s, the ski industry has been the savior for many an obsolete mining town by breaking the hold of the boom and bust cycles of mining. The selection of Pando, north of Leadville, for Tenth Mountain Division training camp in 1941 was the single most serendipitous event for skiing in Colorado. Many of the men from this division returned to Colorado after World War II and were instrumental in developing the fledgling ski industry in the state. The first major ski area in Colorado began in Aspen in 1947. Since then the ski business has grown steadily larger with only a few ups and downs caused by the national economy or, more critically, low snowfall years.

Crested Butte entered the alpine ski arena in 1960 when Dick Eflin and Fred Rice opened a ski area on Crested Butte Mountain. The operation began with a handful of runs and a bare minimum of lifts. Only a few hundred skiers per hour could be handled by the small operation. The formative years of the area were fraught with problems, and in 1965–1966 it had severe financial difficulties. In 1970 Ralph Walton and Howard Callaway took over the operation, and it has been successful for years. By 1990 the ski slopes covered more than 1,200 acres, had 11 lifts, and could handle more than 13,500 skiers per hour. Development was so successful that the new town of Mt. Crested Butte was incorporated at the base of the slopes just two miles north of the original town of Crested Butte.

Skiing and the natural environment would seem to go hand-in-hand. When people around the world think of Colorado, they think of majestic mountains and skiing. Without the natural environment, the ski industry would not exist. But there are some concerns about the relationship between nature and the ski industry. Like most ski areas in Colorado, the terrain upon which the Crested Butte area is built belongs to the U.S. Forest Service (USFS). The land is permitted to the ski areas for a fee based on the revenues produced. To create the ski runs themselves, the equivalent of clear-cutting must take place on the slopes. These runs are very obvious to anyone looking at the mountains (Figure 3.6). Other concerns also exist. For example, the National Forests are designated by law to be areas of multiple use. Cattle grazing also takes place on Crested Butte Mountain, but there is little compatibility between the fences needed by ranchers and the open, unobstructed runs of a ski slope — the USFS must juggle the requirements of each of these needs. Timbering, other forms of recreation (e.g., hiking and hunting), the gathering of firewood, and other uses all make claim to the resources of the mountain. No one will be totally happy with the decisions of the USFS, but it is certain that skiing on Crested Butte Mountain will continue to be encouraged and promoted for many years to come by both private and public organizations.

THE ECOSYSTEMS

The montane life zone is not well represented here despite the fact that the town of Crested Butte is well within the altitude range for the montane. The subalpine and alpine dominate the vegetation zones in the area. Alpine life zone characteristics have been covered at length elsewhere in the book (see Chapter 2, "Mt. Evans"), but there are undoubtedly some variations in species composition and numbers. The same can be said of the Engelmann spruce/subalpine fir ecosystem of the subalpine zone. A nearly comprehensive list of plants of the region, including the spruce/fir ecosystem, can be found in the unpublished work by Paul Buck and Barbara Frase (1990), who work out of the Rocky Mountain Biological Laboratory (RMBL) at Gothic. For the serious naturalist a visit to the RMBL during the summer months is recommended. Three other ecosystems of the subalpine life zone are of special interest, however: the mountain meadow, the quaking aspen, and the lodgepole pine ecosystems.

Figure 3.6. Mt. Crested Butte Ski Area viewed from the north side of Mt. Crested Butte.

THE MOUNTAIN MEADOW ECOSYSTEM

Mountain meadows in this ecosystem can be divided into two broad categories: the dry meadow and the wet meadow. Dry meadows usually occur on moderately sloping lands that drain quickly and are thus relatively dry. These meadows occur in the mid-slopes above large, wide valley bottoms like those of the Slate and East rivers. They are dominated by grasses such as the Arizona (*Festuca arizonica*), Thurber (*F. thurberi*), and Idaho fescues (*F. idahoensis*) and mountain muhly (*Muhlenbergia montana*). Soils here are often deep yet gravelly, indicative of mass movement and/or glacial deposition.

The wet meadows of the region, however, are the more prominent and impressive (Figure 3.7). The USFS and the U.S. Bureau of Land Management own or manage much of the land in the area; in recent years they have emphasized the need to revive the vibrant wet meadows of the region. The results of these efforts are mostly positive; from Gunnison to Crested Butte along Highway 135, many of these meadows stand out as vibrant, verdant vegetation zones. Most of the natural vegetation of these meadows consists of the good forage grass known as "tufted hairgrass" (*Deschampsia caespitosa*), such flowers as the marsh marigold (*Caltha leptosepala*), and many species of sedge (*Carex* spp.). Some of the wet meadows north of Crested Butte still reflect the overgrazing that has taken place during the last several decades. These areas are usually dominated by the corn husk lily (*Veratrum tenuipetalum*), which forms a dense ground cover on the overgrazed land. The corn husk lily is very evident to anyone driving into Gothic from the south.

THE QUAKING ASPEN ECOSYSTEM

Serious discussion has taken place for many years about the role of quaking aspen (*Populus tremuloides*) as climax or as successional (seral) vegetation. There is no doubt that aspen are quite successful at invading areas that have been destroyed by fire or other disturbances. This role as a pioneer species is well known and generally understood. More recently it has come to be accepted that the aspen ecosystem can also become the climax vegetation in a region. This is particularly true in the western areas of Colorado. It does not take a keen observer to notice the large stands of very mature aspens along the valley sides in much of the Crested Butte area (Figure 3.8). These are probably climax aspen groves and may never be

Figure 3.7. East River meandering through wet meadows in the valley just south of Gothic.

Figure 3.8. A beautiful sight in this area are the many dense, old, and graceful aspen stands.

invaded by conifers, as would happen if they were seral stands. If environmental conditions change, of course, the climax character of any vegetation stand might be altered.

One explanation for this climax habit is that the aspen stands actually alter their environment to suit aspen growth over conifer invasion. Most of these aspen forests exist on deep, loamy soils that have a high potential for moisture retention. The deciduous nature of the aspen actually develops these loamy soils on previously poorer, more gravelly sites. Conifers prefer less fertile, shallower, and coarser soils and are therefore at a disadvantage once the aspen become dominant. When current, mature conifer stands are destroyed by fire and the aspen initially invade, the speed of new soil development may be the key to the fate of the aspen stand.

Many of the aspen forests in the Crested Butte area are even-aged stands. Aspen trees are relatively shade intolerant, and young trees have some difficulty surviving. In many areas, however, as the older trees die off, younger aspen sprout and thrive, keeping the conifers at bay. Aspen stands may therefore have several different-aged groupings of trees, creating a patchy visual effect. The suckering habit for aspen reproduction aids the tree in quick reinvasion of areas when sunlight becomes more available. This allows revegetation by aspen both after a disturbance like fire and after an old, single-aged stand of aspen dies.

Several different types of aspen communities develop in an area depending upon slope angles, soil moisture, and sun availability. Some aspen understories are dominated by common shadbush (*Amelanchier alnifolia*), common juniper (*Juniperus communis*), sedges (*Carex* spp.), or grasses such as Arizona fescue. These disparate understory types are evidence of the ability of aspen ecosystems to occupy a wide variety of environments. The common requirement for aspen is a site with highly moist yet well-drained soils.

THE LODGEPOLE PINE ECOSYSTEM

The lodgepole pine (*Pinus contorta*) ecosystem is similar to the aspen ecosystem in the sense that there is intense dialogue about its seral states. There is no doubt that the lodgepole pine is a pioneer species that invades areas where fire has occurred. The serotinous nature of its cones is strong evidence of this characteristic. Serotinous cones are tightly closed and sealed by resin; the seeds in these cones can remain viable for very long periods. When fire occurs it destroys the resin bond and releases the seeds from within the cone. After seed dispersal there is quick generation and growth of very dense, "dog-hair" stands of young lodgepole pine trees. Some of these forests are so dense that it is impossible for a person to walk through them without great effort. Usually there is little or no undergrowth in these forests. Lodgepole pines thrive in areas that other tree species would consider bleak; fire-scorched, coarse soils devoid of humus are the seedbed for the lodgepole pine.

Serotiny, however, is not the only seed development habit of the lodgepole pine; the trees may develop nonserotinous cones as well. In fact, the same tree may have both serotinous and nonserotinous cones. Both cone types can be the basis for lodgepole pine stands that are, in reality, climax forests. If other competitive species like subalpine fir or Engelmann spruce cannot tolerate severe environmental conditions, such as excessively cold locations with very coarse and thin soils, the lodgepole pine may remain as the long-term vegetation.

On relatively open lodgepole pine sites, the understory may include common juniper, huckleberry (*Vaccinium scoparium*), or kinnikinnick (*Arctostaphylos uva-ursi*). An example of this kind of site occurs on the glacial moraine on the south edge of Crested Butte. The olive-green hues of the lodgepole pine forest stand in contrast to the darker, richer greens of the other conifers of the subalpine. Seldom, however, do lodgepole pine stands have any extensive understory; it may be one of the most sterile ecosystems for plant and animal diversity in the Colorado mountains.

THE FUTURE

It would seem reasonable that the future of the Crested Butte region lies soundly with the economic benefits of the ever-expanding, world-class ski area. The natural beauty and majestic setting of the town and ski slopes should assure regional economic viability and environmental responsibility for decades to come. Predicting the future, however, is not a simple matter, especially when a giant, multinational corporation has the mineral rights to ore deposits of high economic value. These deposits lie under Mt. Emmons (Figure 3.9) — the mountain that makes up the skyline to the west of Crested Butte.

The mineral resource that is the focus of this discussion is a vast molybdenum ("moly") deposit under the Red Lady Basin on Mt. Emmons. Molybdenum is an element used as an alloy of steel to create a very hard

Figure 3.9. For now Mt. Emmons stands majestic and peaceful above the town.

metal used in the production of machine and cutting tools. A late–Tertiary period intrusion (17.3 to 17.7 mya) of igneous rock into the sediments of Mt. Emmons produced the molybdenum deposit by allowing injections of molybdenum carrying fluids to enter the contact zone between the igneous and country rocks. This particular contact zone is one of the richest molybdenum deposits in the world.

In 1977 the owners of the mineral rights to the ore, the AMAX Corporation, decided to "develop" the molybdenum potential of the Red Lady Basin. Modern mining technology would have allowed AMAX to literally remove most of the mountain to access the ore. Needless to say, there was tremendous opposition to the plan from residents of Crested Butte. There was also a large body of support for the scheme. After all, Crested Butte was first and foremost a mining town. Many people in the community felt that the molybdenum mine was just a logical extension of the mining history of the region. The battle raged between the two factions throughout the late 1970s and early 1980s. Suits and countersuits were filed; delay upon delay ensued.

The preliminary outcome of the controversy is that during these delays the worldwide market for molybdenum crashed. AMAX set aside, at least for now, any plans to begin production at the site. Economics, however, not the environmental impact of development, will most likely determine the final outcome of the project. Many in Crested Butte and the rest of the state hope that the demand for moly will never again be high enough to permit mining. Many others hope that someday, the era of the mining boom will return. For now the specter of vast slag heaps and toxic settling ponds is dim. When you visit the Crested Butte area, concentrate on the natural splendor, but also visualize the impact of a missing skyline to the west.

ADDITIONAL READINGS

Epis, R. C., and J. F. Callender, 1981. *Western Slope Colorado*, New Mexico Geological Society, Albuquerque, N.Mex.

Gaskill, D. L., S. M. Colman, J. E. DeLong, Jr., and C. H. Robinson, 1986. *Geologic Map of the Crested Butte Quadrangle, Gunnison County, Colorado*, U.S. Geological Survey, Map GQ-1580, Denver, Colo.

Hall, D. B., 1990. *Mountains, Minerals, Miners & Moguls*, Denis B. Hall, Crested Butte, Colo.

Komarkova, V., R. R. Alexander, and B. C. Johnston, *Forest Vegetation of the Gunnison and Parts of the Uncompahgre National Forests: A Preliminary Habitat Type Classification*, U.S. Department of Agriculture, Gen. Tech. Rpt. RM-163, Fort Collins, Colo.

Langenheim, J. H., 1962. "Vegetation and Environmental Patterns in the Crested Butte Area, Gunnison County, Colorado," *Ecological Monographs* 32, pp. 249–285.

Sibley, G., 1972. *A Crested Butte Primer*, The Crested Butte Society, Crested Butte, Colo.

Smith, D. A., 1984. *When Coal Was King*, Colorado School of Mines Press, Golden, Colo.

Soule, J. M., 1976. *Geologic Hazards in the Crested Butte–Gunnison Area, Gunnison County, Colorado*, Colorado Geological Survey, Information Series 5, Denver, Colo.

Sprague, M., 1976. *Colorado: A Bicentennial History*, W. W. Norton & Company, Inc., New York, N.Y.

Vandenbusche, D., 1980. *The Gunnison Country*, B & B Printers, Gunnison, Colo.

Wheeler, N. C., and R. P. Guries, 1982. "Biogeography of Lodgepole Pine," *Canadian Journal of Botany* 60, pp. 1805–1814.

4

STEAMBOAT LAKE

"The beautiful basin" — that is how longtime residents here describe the upper Willow Creek valley 30 miles north of Steamboat Springs. Hahns Peak dominates the skyline with its bare rock slopes and abandoned fire lookout tower. Steamboat Lake is now the centerpiece of the basin floor landscape. The open parkland, which includes the lake at the lower elevations, is surrounded and cradled by the forest that fringes the sides of the upper slopes (Figure 4.1). The beautiful basin — a name also used by the thousands of visitors who come to Steamboat and Pearl lakes each year. The landscape is like a muted spectacle: serene, vibrant, and sheltered, luring people to the slow and rhythmic lapping of waves on the shore of the lake.

THE LAKE

If you were to look at the U.S. Geological Survey topographic map that covers this area (Hahns Peak, 7.5-minute quadrangle), you would notice that Steamboat Lake is not shown. Steamboat Lake was not developed until 1967, when the dam located about 1 mile due south of Hahns Peak Village was completed. One year later the lake was filled to its current level of 8,036 feet above sea level. It is really a reservoir because up to one-third of the lake's water is being stored for use by the Colorado Ute Power Plant located on the Yampa River in Craig, Colorado. The water is reserved for cooling of the power plant during low-water conditions on the Yampa. Since 1968, when the lake was filled, there has never been a call for this water. Therefore,

71

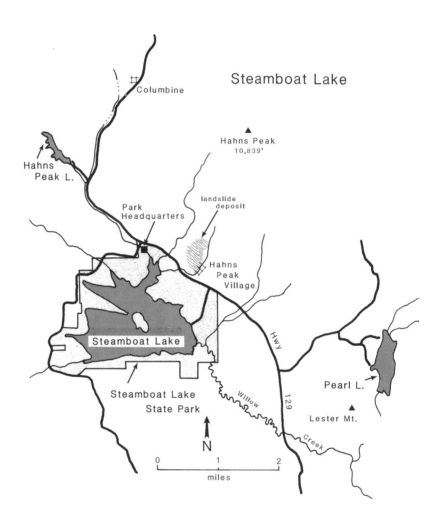

Figure 4.1. The landscape of Steamboat Lake includes mountains, forests, parks, and the lake.

the level of the lake has remained stable at 8,036 feet, and the shoreline ecosystems have been able to develop as they would around a natural lake. If this water were to be called upon for more than passing needs, the nature of the reservoir shoreline would surely change.

Unlike most water projects of the past, present, and future in Colorado, the Steamboat Lake project was not very controversial. The dam and lake were in place long before the requirements for an environmental impact statement. If the project were to be proposed today, there might well be considerable discussion of the merits of a recreational reservoir. As it is now, most people, including local residents, are tolerant of if not outright pleased by the lake's presence.

The lake was constructed by the Colorado State Parks Department to create a recreation facility, the Steamboat Lake Recreation Area. Pearl Lake (formerly Lester Creek Reservoir) State Park, about three miles east of Steamboat Lake, is also part of the recreation complex. The area inundated by the waters of Steamboat Lake was formerly an overgrazed, low-lying, grassy site in poor condition. Sparse grass covered the gentle slopes above the creek bottoms, and sedges and willows grew along the six or seven creeks that converged where the lake now lies. No timber was submerged when the waters rose to their current level.

Pearl Lake occupies a very different environment than Steamboat Lake. The land slopes steeply down to the lake and is covered by dense stands of forest. This is a much more rugged and hidden valley lying just to the east of Lester Mountain (altitude 8,827'). Pearl Lake is not a natural lake. Because it is reserved solely for recreation, there is no threat to the shoreline ecosystems from the lowering of lake levels.

Steamboat Lake covers about 1,053 acres whereas Pearl Lake has an area of 190 acres. Steamboat Lake is almost 85 feet deep near the dam but averages only 20 feet deep. Fishing is good in both lakes; Steamboat specializes in three subspecies or strains of rainbow trout (*Onchorynchus gairdneri*): the belair, Eagle Lake, and Tasmanian rainbows. Pearl Lake is especially known for its Snake River and Colorado strains of cutthroat trout (*Onchorynchus clarki*).

THE GEOLOGY

The geology of this area as described by the U.S. Geological Survey 7.5-minute quadrangle is unusually varied, with examples of igneous, metamorphic, and sedimentary rocks present. The oldest rocks in the area are the 1.7-billion-year-old metamorphic rocks, which underlie the whole region. Outcrops of these ancient rocks occur on the eastern side of the quadrangle and even more prominently just to the east, west, and south of Pearl Lake. Lester Mountain is composed of old schist, which shows up as a gray or silvery rock with significant foliations. These foliations are the layers produced in the rock from the heat and pressure that caused the metamorphism eons ago.

More recent, yet still extremely old sedimentary rocks of the Jurassic and Cretaceous periods include some of the same rock formations discussed in the chapter on the Garden of the Gods (Chapter 6). These include the Dakota and Morrison formations renowned for their fossil treasures. The most dominant sedimentary rock of the area is the Browns Park formation — a yellow to reddish fine-grained sandstone that underlies the main basin and Steamboat Lake itself. The Browns Park formation is partially responsible for the distinctly muted topography of the basin because of the ease with which it erodes. Capping many of these rocks are recent landslide deposits that line the area where the mountains meet the valleys and basin.

Hahns Peak Village is built directly upon such a deposit. Tailings from old placer mining of this loose material can be seen just to the north of the village.

The most recent rocks of the area are 12-million-year-old volcanic rocks making up parts of the mountains to the north of the lake. Small lava flows and some volcanic ash deposits cap parts of the Browns Park formation just to the north of the lake. Hahns Peak (Figure 4.2) is made of an altered and very coarse-grained rock called a porphyry, which dates from this same general time period. The Hahns Peak porphyry has been intensely weathered and broken apart. This jumble of large blocks of broken rock is easily visible on the face of the mountain. The porphyry is responsible for the lack of vegetation on Hahns Peak; these rocks move, shift, and creep downhill constantly, preventing vegetation from getting a foothold on the slopes. In fact, very little water runoff comes down the surface of this mountain because the millions of rock fractures allow the water to drain below the surface and into the groundwater system.

During the mining boom in the late nineteenth century, the area was declared the Hahns Peak Mining District. Mining exploited the faulting and fracturing caused by the volcanic and intrusive activity during the Tertiary period. Supersaturated fluids from deep within the earth carried minerals that were eventually deposited in the rock fractures when the water cooled and the minerals condensed. This was particularly the case for a circular fracture, .5-mile in diameter, that rings Hahns Peak. During the centuries of erosion following the deposition, much of the mineral wealth was washed into stream valleys and the basin bottom. These are the sources of gold and other minerals found by the placer miners who worked here late last century.

THE MISSING GLACIERS

Hahns Peak lies 2,000 feet above the basin floor, surrounded by the Elkhead Mountains to the west and the formidable Park Range to the east. Both the Elkheads and the Park Range were extensively glaciated, and numerous large glacial valleys and hundreds of smaller glacial features are remnants of that erosional period. Hahns Peak and the other mountains in the quadrangle were not touched by glaciers during the Pleistocene period. No one knows for certain why they were not affected, but there must have been a lack of heavy snows here during that time.

Figure 4.2. Bare rock slopes of Hahns Peak above the valley.

THE CLIMATE

It is ironic that there was insufficient snow during the Pleistocene period to produce glaciers here because one of the prominent characteristics of the region now is its prodigious winter snows. The staff at the state park estimates that the Steamboat Lake basin receives about 400 inches of snow per year. At Columbine, in the northwest section of the quadrangle, the average snowpack in April is 54 inches. At times there are 4 to 6 feet of snow on the level in the park. All of this snow provides an abundant moisture base for the rest of the year. This water is the lifeblood for the flora, and therefore, for the fauna of the area; it drastically affects the occurrence and character of ecosystems here.

Elevations in the quadrangle range from near 7,650 feet to 10,839 feet — from what is normally the middle montane life zone into the upper subalpine life zone. The vegetation, however, is a preponderance of subalpine species with scattered inclusions from the montane. Apparently, the large snowfalls and water availability promote vegetation types more akin to the subalpine snow forests than to montane vegetation communities.

This snow environment exists because of the location of the Hahns Peak region. Hahns Peak and the Elkhead Mountains just to the west are virtually the first high mountains encountered by storms moving into the state from the northwest. Any atmospheric moisture carried by these air masses is lifted and cooled by the upwind slopes of these highlands. When this happens the moisture condenses and precipitation results. Similarly, any storms coming into the state from the southwest dump their moisture in the San Juan Mountains of southwestern Colorado. Both regions receive heavy snows that begin in November and do not end until mid- to late May. Because most montane life zones are somewhat drier and have longer snow-free seasons, the subalpine is dominant here in spite of the elevation.

THE ECOSYSTEMS

The dominant trees of the Steamboat Lake area are the lodgepole pine (*Pinus contorta*), the Engelmann spruce (*Picea engelmannii*), and the quaking aspen (*Populus tremuloides*). There are almost no ponderosa pine (*Pinus ponderosa*) — those that do exist are old, large, and stately remnants from former times. Legend has it that in the year of the famed "Meeker massacre" (1879), the local Ute Indians burned the Farwell Mountain area just to the east and possibly the Hahns Peak area also. Their fires were said to have destroyed almost all of the then extensive ponderosa pine forests that grew in this area. These stately, montane life-zone trees have never returned and only the few scattered survivors still stand as silent sentinels here and there in the region. Apparently the climate was such that they could not compete with the lodgepole pine and aspen that became firmly established and now seem to be some of the climax species here. The only segments of the montane life zone still in existence are the patches of big sagebrush (*Artemisia tridentata*), grasslands, and some meadows that can be seen surrounding the lake like a garland.

THE MONTANE ECOSYSTEMS

The riparian ecosystem in the Steamboat Lake basin could easily be considered a wetland system. Here plant communities have developed along the shores of the new, human-created lakes where constant water levels provide a stable environment for ecosystem evolution. The lake shores are positioned so that they are transitional zones between water and land. The shores are also in temporal transition because they are slowly edging toward a time when riparian shrubs and water-loving trees will invade and become dominant. Centuries from now, if the water levels remain constant, the areas around the lakes may be a mass of willows, bog birch, alder, and Colorado blue spruce. For now herbaceous plants control this zone.

The lower elevations bordering the lake and the creek bottoms in the basin are productive, verdant, herbaceous communities (Figure 4.3). Here the increased and stable supply of water promotes the growth of moisture-loving vegetation including sedges (*Carex* spp.), bluegrass (*Poa* spp.), timothy (*Phleum* spp.), bulrushes (*Scirpus* spp.), rushes (*Juncus* spp.), and several varieties of forbs. The deep green, lush character of this land/water zone can be easily distinguished from the earth-tone, pastel colors of the areas just upslope.

These more upland areas lying between the water bodies and the mountain slopes consist of sage and grass ecosystems. The big sagebrush dominates the area with its pungent aroma and gray-blue color. There are patches of rabbitbrush (*Chrysothamnus* spp.) and bitterbrush (*Purshia tridentata*) interspersed among the sage. It is somewhat strange to have these particular species here where precipitation is high and winter snow almost always deep. We generally associate the sage ecosystem with drier, plateau regions to the west (see Chapter 10, "Piceance Creek Basin"). Apparently,

Figure 4.3. Riparian vegetation and meadows surrounding Steamboat Lake.

the Browns Park formation that underlies most of these lower levels produces a very permeable and loose-grained soil through which water drains very quickly and is therefore unavailable to the plants. Extensive sage areas in lower-lying parts of the Elk River valley are probably the source areas for these anomalous stands of sage and other brush species.

Abundant grassland areas intermingle with the sagebrush. These grasses are very similar to those farther west and to the plains far to the east. Thurber fescue (*Festuca thurberi)* and needlegrass (*Stipa* spp.) are common. The grass stands abound where the soil is more fine-grained in contrast to the coarser soils of the sage areas. Subtle differences in the soil seem to make a very significant difference in the nature of the vegetation that is able to thrive on these gentle slopes separating the waters from the mountains.

THE OTHER ECOSYSTEMS

Other ecosystems in this area are essentially subalpine by growth pattern and species type even though they may be montane by elevation range. Extensive and stable stands of aspen cover large tracts of the mountain slopes (Figure 4.4). The vibrant green of the quaking leaves on the valley sides in the spring and summer and the golden hues in the autumn attest to the widespread abundance of this species. The understory in this ecosystem is usually a dense mass of forbs, shrubs, and grasses. Sedges, peavine (*Lathyrus* spp.), yarrow (*Achillea lanulosa*), cow parsnip (*Heracleum sphondylium*), Colorado columbine (*Aquilegia caerulea*), and other moisture-loving plants spread thickly beneath the aspen crowns. This lush vegetational environment is a succulent lure for grazing and browsing animals like the mule deer (*Odocoileus hemionus*) and Rocky Mountain elk (*Cervus elaphus*) that are plentiful here in the late spring, throughout the summer, and in early fall. These animals, especially the elk, tend to migrate long distances toward the west and southwest in the winter to escape the deep snows that create the verdant forests of summer.

In contrast to the lushness of the aspen stands are the olive-green, monotonous, and almost sterile lodgepole pine forests that mark areas of former fires and ponderosa pine stands. The lodgepole forests are dark and almost lifeless places. Little sunshine can penetrate the very dense stands of trees; few plants and fewer animals inhabit the sunless ground under these trees. Their life cycle is presented in greater detail in Chapter 3, "Crested Butte."

Figure 4.4. Large stands of aspen occur throughout the area.

Engelmann spruce make up the majority of the forest areas of the higher mountains. Figure 4.5 shows the girdle of Engelmann spruce forest around the waist of Hahns Peak. This forest primeval is really a snow forest: snow provides the water that is essential for Engelmann spruce to grow, and the tree is "designed" to deal with great quantities of snowfall. The tall, spirelike shape of the tree crown facilitates the shedding of snow from the boughs so that the weight of the heavy snow will not damage or break the branches. The understory is not as lush as in the aspen forest, but there is a good distribution of plants such as common juniper (*Juniperus communis*), currants (*Ribes* spp.), and huckleberries (*Vaccinium scoparium*) on the forest floor. Although the subalpine fir (*Abies lasiocarpa*) is a constant companion to the Engelmann spruce elsewhere in Colorado, here it is almost nonexistent.

The mixture of all these ecosystems is a visual treat as they mingle and create a quiltlike pattern on the landscape (Figure 4.6). Seldom will you see the close locational setting of such diverse vegetation in a single view. This is one reason that the Steamboat Lake area is so special. The intricate mix of the ecosystems and the serenity of the placid lake together make a bucolic setting uncommon in Colorado.

FINAL THOUGHTS

This place, tucked away in the far north of the state, is a relatively unknown and enigmatic landscape. Little scientific research, save on the geology and mining potential, has been done here as evidenced by the paucity of references in the "Additional Readings" section at the end of the chapter. It is relatively unknown because it is far from the crowded Front Range corridor and at the end of a two-lane road that only recently was paved. It is unknown because it is merely beautiful and serene, not spectacular and majestic. In Colorado we tend to become immune to mere beauty because of the profusion of the extraordinary.

This place is also enigmatic because of its juxtaposition of a myriad of ecosystems and the lack of a "normal" montane life zone species — the ponderosa pine. It is a snow landscape now, but lacked enough snow in the recent geologic past to be among the glacial terrains of the other high mountains in Colorado. And it is enigmatic for another reason: of all the places discussed in this book, this almost pastoral setting is among those most altered by human hands.

Figure 4.5. Engelmann spruce forests girdle Hahns Peak.

Figure 4.6. The intermix of ecosystems is striking as you look toward Sand Mountain.

A summary of the changes induced by humans is a litany of exploitation. There were the ravages of large, uncontrolled fires that seem to have eliminated an entire montane species. These fires altered for generations past and future the look and feel of the basin. There were the additional ravages of uncontrolled mining — placer tailings and old ditches used to supply water for high-pressure destruction of the land surface in the desperate search for gold. Unbridled timber cutting and cattle grazing affected the vegetational environment subtly but permanently. More recently we have dammed several streams to create a "recreational resource." The drowning of land that was overgrazed and considered nonproductive was accepted without much comment.

One could argue that we got away with all of these transformations and created a wondrous landscape enjoyed by thousands of Coloradans and out-of-state visitors. This argument is probably essentially valid in this instance, but we should not take the view that we will always win when we rearrange nature on such a scale. Maybe the reverse is true, and Steamboat Lake, the beautiful basin, is truly the exception not the norm. We did get away with it here; we cannot expect to be so lucky in most instances. Keep Steamboat Lake and the Hahns Peak region as an example of the good we as a species can do; keep in mind that we could easily have destroyed the area for the children of the future.

ADDITIONAL READINGS

Barnwell, W. W., 1955. "The Geology of the South Hahns Peak District, Routt County, Colorado." In *Guidebook to the Geology of Northwest Colorado,* Intermountain Association of Petroleum Geologists, Salt Lake City, Utah.

Benedict, A. D., 1991. *A Sierra Club Naturalist's Guide: The Southern Rockies,* Sierra Club Books, San Francisco, Calif.

Gale, H. S., 1906. *The Hahns Peak Gold Field, Colorado,* U.S. Geological Survey, Bulletin 285-A, Washington, D.C., p. 28–34.

George, R. D., and R. D. Crawford, 1909. *The Hahns Peak Region, Routt County, Colorado,* Colorado Geological Survey, 1st Report, Denver, Colo.

Hoffman, G. R., and R. R. Alexander, 1980. *Forest Vegetation of the Routt National Forest in Northwestern Colorado: A Habitat Type Classification,* U.S. Department of Agriculture, Research Paper RM-221, Fort Collins, Colo.

Hunter, J. M., 1955. "Geology of the North Hahns Peak Area, Routt County, Colorado." In *Guidebook to the Geology of Northwest Colorado,* Intermountain Association of Petroleum Geologists, Salt Lake City, Utah.

Segerstrom, K., and E. J. Young, 1972. *General Geology of the Hahns Peak and Farwell Mountain Quadrangle, Routt County, Colorado,* U.S. Geological Survey, Bulletin 1349, Washington, D.C.

Wiggins, A., n.d. *Hahn's Peak and the Beautiful Basin,* self-published, Hahns Peak Village, Colo.

$\int$

FLORISSANT FOSSIL BEDS NATIONAL MONUMENT

The majestic mountains and spectacular vistas of Colorado often overshadow less well-known but equally intriguing landscapes. The Florissant Fossil Beds National Monument is one of these obscure treasures. An excursion here offers present beauty and reveals past marvels. As you approach the monument from the north out of the little town of Florissant, you crest the hill in your car and silently wonder, what is the big deal about this place? To you and most other casual visitors the fossil beds are, at first sight, a beautiful but unpretentious place. Your view east toward Pikes Peak is spectacular, but most of the surrounding landscape consists of only low-relief mountains and serene green forests and meadows.

The monument does have, however, two impressive characteristics that help create a most unique spot, not only in Colorado, but anywhere. First, the Florissant Fossil Beds National Monument is the quintessential example of a montane life zone. It lies at an elevation between 8,200 feet (where Grape Creek leaves the northern end of the monument) and 8,963 feet (on the eastern edge at the southernmost Twin Rock). This is the heart of the elevation range for the montane. The second and most unique characteristic is that the monument is the site of one of the world's great geologic deposits containing plant and insect fossils. Only two other places on earth, the Solenhofen limestone quarry in Germany and the Baltic amber of northern Europe, can rival the monument for its richness and diversity of fossils. This

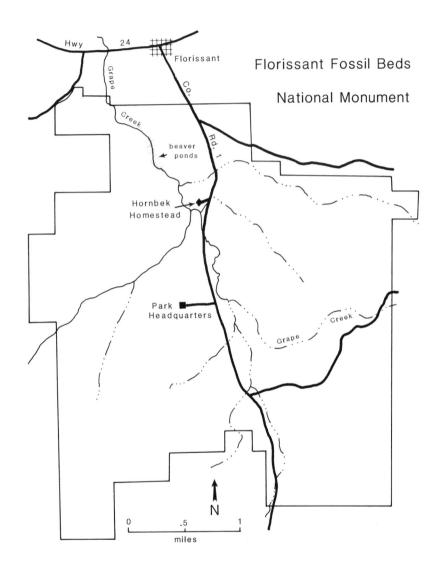

book will first discuss the present-day environment by examining the montane and the ecosystems that compose it; this discussion will be followed by an overview of the fascinating and singular past that produced such a superabundance of fossil remains.

THE MONTANE

For those serious students of ecology, habitat analysis, and botany, the monument is a wonderful laboratory in biogeography (the study of the distribution of flora and fauna). The patterns of biological distribution in the monument are striking, and the factors involved in producing this vegetational motif are dramatically displayed. For those less serious about botany, yet nonetheless devoted to the study of landscape, open space, and congenial environments, the fossil beds are an inviting outdoor laboratory for your own personal use.

One of the more significant things that we can learn from any nature excursion is that, given enough time, the plants that grow will reflect the environment; they sometimes alter the environment, but they are always in tune with the environment. Because the environment is made up of almost countless perturbations dependent on climate, soil, aspect, elevation, etc., there are also countless perturbations of plant growth and distribution. We classify plants and ecosystems, but these are crude attempts to explain the infinite complexity and wonder of life. Keep this in mind as we talk about the ecosystems of the fossil beds.

The monument is the quintessential example of the montane life zone because it has the unique characteristics of more general montane zones around the state and because it contains six of the seven ecosystems that occur in the montane life zone of Colorado (Figure 5.1). These six are the ponderosa pine, the Douglas fir, the mountain grasslands/meadows, the mountain riparian, the aspen, and the limber/bristlecone pine ecosystems. The lodgepole pine ecosystem is lacking because of the absence of fire on the monument site over the last century or so. The lodgepole pine ecosystem most often occurs after a fire because most lodgepole pine cones release their seeds only after reaching high temperatures generated by fire. All of the six remaining ecosystems can be found in this relatively small (5,992.5-acre) area.

Figure 5.1. Collection of ecosystems in the monument; the conspicuous valley in the center is the central lake area.

FOSSIL BEDS CLIMATE

The monument climate is somewhat atypical because it is slightly dryer than most montane sites. The monument gets between 12 and 16 inches of precipitation during an average year. Pikes Peak to the east acts as a barrier to the moist winds from the Gulf of Mexico that bring most of the precipitation to the eastern slopes of Colorado. Because the monument is too far from the Continental Divide to get much moisture from the occasional Pacific storms that move through the state, it is dryer than is typical for this elevation. Most of the precipitation that it does get comes during the summer when intermittent thunderstorms roll across the hills, bringing intense, but usually short-lived, downpours. The monument gets about 70 inches of snow per year, most of it coming in February, March, and April. It can get very cold here in the winter (down to -35 degrees F), but usually winter days are relatively mild with daytime temperatures in the 20s and 30s and nighttime temperatures around 0 degrees F. Summer temperatures seldom reach 85 degrees, with typical temperatures reaching 75 degrees. Temperatures at night can drop below freezing during any month, a characteristic that makes the area a poor agricultural setting.

THE ECOSYSTEMS

Ponderosa pine forest. Probably the most recognized ecosystem of the montane life zone is the ponderosa pine forest. The ponderosa pine (*Pinus ponderosa*) is a beautiful, stately coniferous tree with a broad and rounded crown (Figure 5.2). It has lovely, robust cones and a thick bark that is reddish-yellow, very rough, and smells like vanilla. The needles are the longest of any tree in Colorado (4 to 7 inches) and come in bundles of two or three. Needle length is affected by tree spacing and moisture; well-spaced trees at sites with higher moisture levels produce longer needles.

Ponderosa pine resists drought well because it grows best in well-drained, coarse soils where its main taproot can grow down to almost 35 feet to reach water. Its lateral roots, especially in more open stands, can spread more than 100 feet to collect precipitation from the surface of a large area. On the monument these trees grow best on the upland areas of coarse-grained Pikes Peak granite because this granite produces a very loose soil. The trees like sunny, warm, south-facing slopes but interfinger with other ecosystems depending upon localized environmental characteristics.

Figure 5.2. This ponderosa pine stand is typical of the ecosystem with its parklike character.

A totally natural stand of ponderosa pine usually forms very parklike conditions, with widely spaced trees generally interspersed with grasses. Most stands on the fossil beds are more densely populated because there have been few fires here over the last century. In addition, the area has averaged more moisture since the early part of this century than at other times; this has enabled denser stands to survive. Two particular pest problems arise when tree stands are so closely spaced. The first is the mountain pine beetle. These small, black beetles carry a fungus that attacks trees by clogging the cells that transport nutrients. A blue stain on a tree's wood is an indicator that it is infested with the beetle. Trees in a dense stand are less robust than in open stands and therefore cannot resist pests as vigorously. Only a few scattered trees in the monument are affected by the pine beetle. The second problem is a parasitic plant, the dwarf mistletoe, which grows from the ponderosa pine branches and disrupts normal tree development, producing swelled nodes and "witch's brooms" (massively entwined twig clusters). The mistletoe does not kill the tree directly but weakens it, making the tree more susceptible to other types of infestations. There is one area of significant mistletoe infestation at the monument. It is located on the south side of the hills just south and west of the visitor's center.

The understory of the ponderosa pine forest is variable on the monument as in other places, but certain plants are conspicuous. These are mostly grasses and include Junegrass (*Koeleria macrantha*), Arizona fescue (*Festuca arizonica*), mountain muhly (*Muhlenbergia montana*), and blue grama (*Bouteloua gracilis*). In slightly wetter areas there can be some kinnikinnik or bearberry (*Arctostaphylos uva-ursi*) and common juniper (*Juniperus communis*) among other grasses such as oat-grass (*Danthonia parryi*) and purple reed-grass (*Calamagrostis purpurascens*).

The animals of this ecosystem are diverse, and many of them are transient. The following discussion will highlight some interesting examples. Many people are fascinated by the large mammals of the area. There are a few black bears (*Ursus americanus*), an occasional mountain lion (*Felis concolor*), many coyotes (*Canis latrans*) and porcupines (*Erethizon dorsatum*), some resident mule deer (*Odocoileus hemionus*), and a large, migrant herd of elk (*Cervus elaphus*). This elk herd is particularly interesting because it was reintroduced into the region in the 1920s by a local millionaire, Spencer Penrose. The few animals that were brought in from Wyoming have now become a substantial herd(s) of about 800 to 1,200. There is a continuing research project taking place to study the elk's need and use of habitat, its migration and calving patterns, and its response to human encroachment. If you get to the monument early in the morning, you might be lucky enough to see the elk moving out from the tree stands into the meadows near the Visitor's Center to feed. They *seem* tame and do not easily shy away from view. But remember that they are wild animals and deserve to be left in peace to graze and then fade back into the trees.

There are at least 95 species of birds that inhabit or visit the fossil beds. Some common ones that use the ponderosa pine forest extensively are the red-tailed hawk (*Buteo jamaicensis*), Steller's jay (*Cyanocitta stelleri*), broad-tailed hummingbird (*Selasphorus platycercus*), mountain chickadee (*Parus gambeli*), western bluebird (*Sialia mexicana*), mountain bluebird (*S. currucoides*), pine siskin (*Carduelis pinus*), and the golden eagle (*Aquila chrysaetos*). Seeing this last species soar on thermal currents during the summer is one of the true pleasures of visiting the monument.

Douglas fir forest. Although ponderosa pine forests make up 80 to 90 percent of the forested area on the monument, the Douglas fir (*Pseudotsuga menziesii*) is also an important part of the vegetation here (Figure 5.3). There are few pure stands of Douglas fir; it is almost always mixed with ponderosa pine on the wetter, cooler sides of the hills. The spatial relationship between

Figure 5.3. The Douglas fir ecosystem is much more closed and moist than the ponderosa pine ecosystem.

the two species provides a good lesson in the concept of microenviron-
ments. Slight changes in moisture or soil type can cause notable changes in
vegetation patterns. When you walk through the forest here, notice the small
variations in temperature, ground moisture, aspect, and rock/soil makeup.
Look at how the vegetation adapts to these changes. An acute observer can
see these characteristics even if she or he is not a trained scientist.

Douglas fir is neither a true fir nor a hemlock. In fact, its scientific genus
name means "false hemlock." The tree itself is quite impressive. It is the same
tree found in the milder and wetter forests of the Pacific Northwest, where
it grows to gigantic proportions (250 feet tall, 8 feet in diameter); here in
Colorado the Douglas fir barely makes it to 100 feet tall and 2 feet in
diameter. Growth here is limited by colder temperatures, shorter growing
seasons, and more arid conditions. Nonetheless, it is a beautiful tree with
deep-green foliage and a tapered crown. Although it is not a true fir, the old
adage about "friendly firs" is an apt description of the soft, flat needles that
grow only about an inch in length. The best identification feature of the tree
is the three-lobed bract that extends from between and out beyond the cone
scales. These bracts are often called "little mouse feet" or "snake tongues"
— both appropriately descriptive.

Douglas firs are much more vibrant and resistant than the ponderosa
pine, but there has been some loss of Douglas firs caused by a spruce bud
worm infestation throughout Colorado. The best example of this problem
is seen as one travels on U.S. Highway 24 between the towns of Divide and
Florissant. You will see defoliated Douglas fir on the south side (north-facing)
of the canyon walls along Twin Creek.

Because the Douglas fir is usually mixed with the ponderosa pine, the
understory is not significantly different from that in more pure stands of
ponderosa pine. There will be more common juniper, wax currant (*Ribes
cereum*), and kinnikinnick along with the purple reed-grass, oat-grass, Junegrass, and Arizona fescue. If you are lucky you might meet the gregarious
Clark's nutcracker (*Nucifraga columbiana*) as it begs food from those who
pass. The fauna does not differ appreciably from that found in the ponderosa
pine forest because many of the animals migrate between the different
ecosystems.

Mountain grasslands and meadows. A striking characteristic of the fossil
beds landscape is the open and expansive nature of the center of the
monument. The wide, central valley that trends north-south is conspicuous
for its lack of trees. The grasslands and meadows that make up the land

cover here are indicative of two factors: the relative dryness of the site, with only intermittent moist areas; and the fine-grained nature of the rocks and soils. These rocks and soils are derived from old volcanic rocks that mark an ancient lake bed. A few of the open areas do not arise from these two factors but instead are remnants of a farm culture that existed here from the 1880s to the 1930s. A fine example of late nineteenth-century farmsteads is preserved in the Hornbek property at the north-central end of the monument. Typical cool-weather crops like hay and oats were raised, and the area became a center of seed potato production in the 1920s and 1930s. The Colorado potato beetle brought an abrupt halt to potato production during the depth of the Depression. The farms were abandoned and the grasslands and meadows that were so hard won are now being reinvaded by forest, primarily by ponderosa pine. You can see evidence of this when you see young pine saplings growing in otherwise open grasslands and meadows.

From a distance the grasslands and meadows look uniform, but closer inspection shows that they are really a quite diverse collection of plant types. Unlike most forest ecosystems, there are few dominant species; most areas of grassland or meadow have several main plant types. In the dryer grassland sites, you will find at least five main grasses with many additional, less prominent species. The five main species include mountain muhly, wild rye (*Elymus longifolius*), Junegrass, Arizona fescue, and several species of brome (*Bromopsis* spp.). In moister conditions you will find the almost ubiquitous, introduced species of Kentucky bluegrass (*Poa* spp.) along with western wheatgrass (*Agropyron smithii*) and quack grass (*A. repens*). You will also find at least two species of sage (*Artemisia* spp.), which inhabits both the grasslands and meadows. Shrubs frequently found on wetter sites include rabbit brush (*Chrysothamnus* spp.), gumweed (*Grindelia subalpina*), snakeweed (*Gutierrezia sarothrae*), horsebrush (*Tetradymia canescens*), and the Colorado rubber plant (*Picradenia richardsonii*).

The word florissant means "flowering" or "blooming" in French. These open areas bring the word to life. During the entire growing season you will find wonderful fields carpeted with wildflowers. The beauty and diversity of the flowers here have been well known for decades. Take time to learn about and enjoy the many flowering species.

Mountain riparian. The riparian ecosystem ranges from tree-lined narrow valleys to open wet meadows to marshy areas and mudflats to open water. The one common thread that connects these sites is the ready availability of water. Increased water allows for increased biomass production and a

Figure 5.4. Hornbek homestead sits amid hundreds of acres of wet meadow and riparian ecosystems caused by Grape Creek and its tributaries.

home or way station for many wildlife species in search of food and shelter. The main sites of riparian ecosystem are along Cave Creek, the main western tributary to Grape Creek, and along Grape Creek itself, especially around the Hornbek homestead (Figure 5.4). These areas lie in stark contrast to the relatively sterile ponderosa pine forest and the dry meadows that surround the riparian tracts.

In the riparian ecosystem we have an almost completely new set of vegetation. In the narrow valleys we find the Colorado state tree, the Colorado blue spruce (*Picea pungens*), as well as the river birch (*Betula fontinalis*), and the thinleaf or narrowleaf alder (*Alnus tenuifolia*). Choke-cherries (*Prunus virginiana*), willows (*Salix* spp.), and the red-osier dogwood (*Swida sericea*) are shrubs commonly found here. Willows are very prevalent in open valleys, with the lower growing shrubby cinquefoil (*Pentaphylloides floribunda*) growing around the edges of the willow masses. Cinquefoil can also be found in less dense stands on most hillsides throughout the monument. In more marshy areas you find abundant sedges (*Carex* spp.) and rushes like the *Juncus arcticus*.

A historical artifact is the presence of several old stock ponds on the monument that are often filled with runoff water and contain vegetation

Figure 5.5. Viable beaver ponds along the northern reaches of Grape Creek.

rare in the normally dry montane zone. Pondweeds and water crowfoot (*Batrachium trichophyllum*) entice several species of ducks and geese to reside in or migrate through the monument.

Because the riparian ecosystem contains, by far, the most species of deciduous vegetation at the fossil beds, this ecosystem produces the most spectacular foliage color in the autumn. The fall colors will not rival New England for sheer magnitude, but they put on an impressive display on a smaller scale. In fact, the autumn is one of the best times to visit the monument because of its cool, clear days, colorful landscapes, and the smaller number of visitors.

The beaver (*Castor canadensis*) is often credited with an ability to alter the natural world second only to that possessed by human beings. In North America the beaver is the classic example of a mammal associated with riparian habitats, and the riparian areas of the monument are no different. As of this writing there are two active lodges on the fossil beds — both of them on the far northern reach of Grape Creek. One lodge is probably the original adult beaver lodge and the second was most likely produced by the kits that were run off by the adult pair when a new set of kits was born. Although you may never actually see the beavers themselves, you can see signs of their presence all along the stream banks. Downed trees and shrubs and newly chewed bark are evident everywhere (Figure 5.5).

Aspen. The last two ecosystems to be discussed here make up only a small fraction of the vegetation at the fossil beds. They do present singular and interesting places, however. Small groves of aspen (*Populus tremuloides*) occupy a few of the wetter areas in the ponderosa pine forest and are usually mixed with Douglas fir and common juniper shrubs (Figure 5.6). Small aspen groves can also be found in the bottoms of many normally dry drainages. The understory is typical of cooler, moister places and includes the beautiful state flower, the Colorado blue columbine (*Aquilegia caerulea*). This is a deciduous ecosystem that gives a fine show of yellows and oranges in the fall. This display is much more dramatic and extensive in areas outside the monument where large tracts of aspen grow. Aspen can reproduce through seed dispersal and germination or through a process called "suckering." The latter method uses lateral suckers or sprouts to form new trees that are clones of the original. During the fall color change, you can tell what trees constitute which clones by looking at their various shades of yellow. A single clone of trees will all have similar coloration.

Limber/bristlecone pine. The remaining ecosystem is defined by two species of pine: the limber pine (*Pinus flexilis*) and the fox-tail or bristlecone pine (*P. aristata*). Both grow in relatively harsh, windblown, and rocky environments. The limber pine survives the Spartan treatment it receives from the elements by literally going with the wind. Its limbs are so flexible that you can easily tie them in knots. You will recognize the limber pine by its whitish-gray bark and its five needles in each bundle.

The bristlecone pine is the aristocrat of trees — even its Latin name means old or aristocratic pine. Bristlecone pines are some of the oldest living organisms on earth. In California they have been found to be up to 4,800 years old. The trees found here on the monument are not this ancient, but are at least 345 years old. It is sometimes difficult to distinguish the bristlecone pine from the limber pine because both have five needles per bundle. The bristlecone pine can be recognized by the resin droplets on the needles and the very unfriendly bristles on the cones — thus the name. Two sites on the fossil beds contain bristlecones: one near the west end of Fossil Stump Hill and the other just east of Grape Creek in this same area.

Figure 5.6. Aspen groves in the monument are not large or widespread, but the small stands add diversity to the flora of the area.

Concluding thoughts. The species that occur on the monument — those that have been discussed here and others that have not — will not necessarily lend themselves to quick or easy identification by the casual observer. This is due in part to hybridization, in which two separate species produce a hybrid variety, and in part to closely related species that look very much alike. Moreover, not all species flower or even grow every year. Depending on current and past weather conditions, plants may or may not grow in any given year. Nature is not static, and changes, temporary or not, are almost always the norm. Expect the unexpected; revel in the serendipitous.

The Southern Rocky Mountains in general and the Florissant Fossil Beds National Monument in particular are at the crossroads of plant migration. To the east we have the Great Plains, to the west the Colorado Plateau and Great Basin, to the north the cold, dry prairies, to the south the desert. For millions of years, particularly since the Pleistocene epoch, plants have been migrating into and out of the Rocky Mountains from all of these areas. At times the mountains are a refuge for plant species driven out of dryer or icier places. We still see some of these refugees at the monument. When looking at the flora and fauna here, keep in mind that they are not static displays in a natural history museum's diorama, but rather dynamic and adapting living systems.

THE FOSSILS

The fossil rocks of the area were well known to the local miners and ranchers at least back to the mid-nineteenth century. But credit for such discoveries invariably goes to the person who puts the "find" down on paper with pen and ink. That privilege belongs to A. C. Peale, a geologist with the 1874 Hayden Survey. Peale first described specimens of the fossils in the report issuing from the entire survey. Even before this time, however, scientific interest was piqued by a young scientist from the east, Theodore L. Mead. Mead collected many insect fossils that eventually fell into the hands of Samuel H. Scudder, who came to the fossil beds in 1877 to conduct his own collecting effort. Scudder's collection is one of the best paleoentomological (fossil insect) collections in the world and is housed at Harvard University's Museum of Comparative Zoology. To this day there are continuing studies on the paleoentomology, paleobotany (fossil plants), and geology of the beds, with new information always emerging.

Each piece of new data on the paleoenvironment of the fossils introduces new complexity to the story of the beds. Each new scientific discovery produces even more unanswered questions. That is the way of science. But we do have many answers that can give us insight into what happened to create the fortuitous convergence of geology, local topography, biology, and hydrology that has become the Florissant Fossil Beds National Monument. It is a fascinating and compelling tale of this place on Earth long ago.

THE GEOLOGIC SEQUENCE

Our story starts 36 million years ago (mya) during the early Oligocene epoch — a very long time by human standards but a mere moment in the geologic history of the Earth. (Some speculation now exists, based on fossil evidence, that it is the late Eocene epoch.) The place that we now know of as the fossil beds was rolling hill country lying at about 3,000 feet above sea level. The climate was warm and fairly moist. In fact, the weather was very much akin to what is now found along the central and northern coasts of California, such that redwood trees were able to grow here. An active volcanic field existed about 15 miles west of what is now the fossil beds. The main valley that we see today was essentially the main valley that existed then, except that the stream now flows north rather than south. The creek was dry for several months per year but flowed bank-full or even flooded during the rainy season. This period was one of great geologic activity, especially volcanic action, around the world.

Fifty miles west of the fossil beds was another volcanic field in what is now called the Sawatch Mountain Range. Between 36 mya and 35.5 mya this field was the site of a violent eruption that spewed forth a tremendous volume of ash, pumice, and cinders. This material spread east for up to 100 miles and produced a thick blanket of deposition that eventually became rock. The generic name for this kind of volcanic rock is "tuff," and the specific formation created all along the Front Range and into what is now the plains is called the Wall Mountain tuff. Wall Mountain tuff underlies much of the rock in the main valley of the monument (Figure 5.7). No fossils are found in this formation, but it does give us a reference point for assessing the timing of the events that finally led to fossil development.

The beginning of the fossil history here was abrupt and cataclysmic. Most of us have seen pictures of the Mount St. Helens eruption, with masses of volcanic debris being hurled out of the mountain. We have also seen the devastation of the area after the eruption was over. The event at the fossil

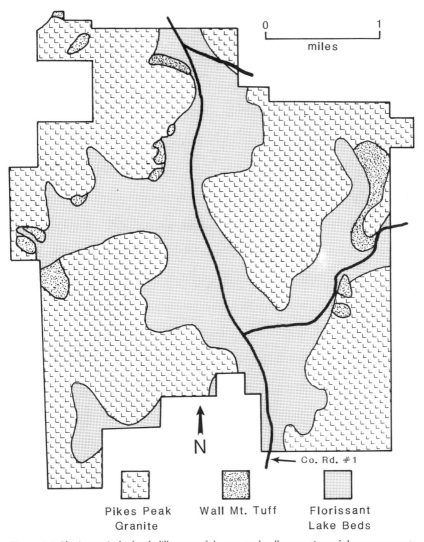

Figure 5.7. Florissant Lake beds fill most of the central valley section of the monument. Pikes Peak granite makes up most of the remainder of the exposed rock, with some minor exposures of Wall Mountain tuff.

Figure 5.8. Excavated fossilized redwood stumps provide a stunning reminder of the power in geologic events of eons past.

beds was very similar to the Mount St. Helens episode. It occurred at the monument 35.5 mya in the nearer volcanic area called the Thirty-nine Mile Field. The eruption here, like that at Mount St. Helens, produced torrential rains that turned the ash and pumice to a wet, oozing mud that flowed with great speed into the surrounding valleys. This "lahar" dammed the stream at the south end of the monument and buried the lower trunks of the redwoods, killing and entombing them in the volcanic equivalent of cement. The dam immediately caused the valley to start filling with water, and ancient Lake Florissant was formed. The forest litter and other trees were buried along with the redwoods, but more delicate leaves and insects were too fragile to survive this traumatic episode. The fossil stumps that you can now see near the Visitor's Center (Figure 5.8) show the physical impact of the lahar. Electron micrographs of the fossilized stumps show crushed inner rings that resulted from the fast-moving mud slamming violently into the trunks. Amazingly, you can still see the cell structure of the redwoods after more than 35,500,000 years! This lahar material overlies the Wall Mountain tuff and is referred to by geologists as the lower tuff of the Florissant formation.

The fossils at Florissant are world renowned because of the intricate and delicate preservation of minute detail in the plant parts and insects preserved in the rock. No lahar or lava flow could ever preserve these delicate organisms. This task was accomplished by a long series of less violent eruptions that produced ash falls throughout the region. As this ash was washed into Lake Florissant, mostly from the north, it settled gently down on the seasonal and cyclical leaf falls and insect remains. Scientists are relatively certain that it was material washed into the lake, rather than ash merely drifting down, because of the grain-size distribution of the deposit that holds most of the fossils. The shales that were formed are coarser grained near the inflow to the lake and get progressively finer grained as one moves toward the center of the lake. This is exactly how water-borne material acts. The upper or northern end of the lake also contains the bulk of the sediments, with the layers getting gradually thinner as one moves south in the old lake bed. Lake Florissant was filled with this ash over a span of about 10,000 years. These deposits are now called the lake shales and hold the vast majority of the fossil specimens.

Another major eruption of the Thirty-nine Mile volcanic field about 34 mya capped the lake shales with another layer of lahar material. This upper tuff member of the Florissant formation formed a protective cocoon for the delicate fossil remains held fast within the lake shales. Without this hard layer of volcanic material, the subsequent erosion that has taken place over the past several million years would have destroyed the fossil record. The multitude of events that occurred at this spot took place in such a sequence and at such an intensity that the fossils were preserved for our study, enjoyment, and wonder.

The final chapter of this geologic story is probably still being written. Beginning around 12 mya in the Miocene epoch, the region that extends from what is now western Kansas to the Colorado Plateau was slowly uplifted. The maximum rate of movement most likely occurred about 5 mya, but there are indications that the uplift is still active at a very minor rate. This latest movement accounts for the present elevation of the fossil beds, about 8,400 feet above sea level. This is over 5,000 feet higher than when most of the volcanic activity that created Lake Florissant took place. The movement is also responsible for some tilting and minor folding of the rock that resulted in reversing the flow of Grape Creek from its original southerly direction to its current northerly flow.

THE PALEONTOLOGY

The dictionary defines paleontology as the science of life as it existed in earlier geologic time and as represented by fossil remains. An appropriate motto for paleontologists might be, "the key to knowing the present and future is knowing the past." By looking at life in all of the forms that existed before, we can better understand many of the complex interactions of our current world. From the interaction of organisms, to paleoclimatic phenomena, to ecological relationships, we can see the consequences and implications of current environmental events. This is why paleontology is a very important science and why the Florissant Fossil Beds National Monument is such an important natural laboratory.

Although the delicate plant and insect fossil remains are impressive and very important, one of the fossil finds at the monument is particularly relevant to paleoclimatological and paleoecological studies. The giant stumps that are the center of so much attention here are the remains of huge redwood trees that lived in the valley prior to the formation of Lake Florissant. There is great scientific controversy over the naming of genus and species of currently living redwoods. It is generally accepted that we now have two main species of redwoods: the coastal redwoods (*Sequoia sempervirens*) of northern California and the giant sequoia (*Sequoiadendron gigantea*) of the Sierra Nevada.

The controversy over the ancient versions of redwoods is even more intense than that over our present species; several ancient species have been identified and named. But it has finally, at least for now, been settled that the trees at the monument are virtually the same as the contemporary coastal redwoods. The scientific name given to the monument's stumps is *Sequoia affinis*. The petrified stumps and the fossilized needles and shoots are almost identical to those of the living species. This is a subtle but profound conclusion because it implies that the climate here 35.5 mya was the same as the climate on the central and northern coasts of California in the late twentieth century A.D.

The stumps are not the only evidence for recreating the local climate of the early Oligocene, just the most visible. Other evidence lies in the vast numbers of fossil species of both flora and fauna found in the lake shales. In 1953 Harry D. MacGinitie published an account of his study of the fossils. He had been working here since 1937 and described fossil species that still exist, almost unchanged, today. His *Pinus florissantii* is nearly identical to our ponderosa pine; other similar pairs include his *Populus crassa* and our narrowleaf cottonwood, his *Salix taxifolioides* and our sandbar willow. There are oak, rose, maple, and hops genera in the fossil record here, but most telling are some of the subtropical species like magnolias that confirm the subtropical nature of the fossil beds climate in the early Oligocene epoch. It is reasoned that the more drought-tolerant plants like the *Pinus florissantii* grew on the dryer uplands, while the magnolias and other moisture-loving species grew along the creek, and subsequently, the lake shore.

The last, and in many ways the most intriguing, remains are the insect fossils that abound in the lake shales. Paleoentomologists worldwide consider the Florissant Fossil Beds among the top insect fossil sites in the world — and well they should: over 1,100 different species of fossil insects have been collected and identified by paleoentomologists. The list reads like a *Who's Who* for insects, including but not limited to:

bumblebees	whiteflies
wasps	spittlebugs
caterpillars	cicadas
beetles	cockroaches
squash bugs	earwigs
chinch bugs	caddisflies
stink bugs	lacewings
assassin bugs	termites
hoverflies	ants
syrphid flies	butterflies
crane flies	mosquitoes
robber flies	midges
snake flies	. . . and many more!

To determine and name individual species, great detail must be visible, and these fossils do not disappoint the viewer. Insect wing venation, appendages, and even the hair on insects' legs have been preserved in stone.

The actual fossilization process is fascinating because the plants and animals themselves are not actually preserved. What generally takes place is that the organic material is first trapped in sediments. If circumstance allows the organic matter to survive (e.g., under anaerobic or oxygen-free conditions), the plant or animal is available for fossilization. As water or other fluids react with the plant or animal tissue, significant amounts of the organism dissolve or become gases that are released. If the circumstances are proper, some of the carbon from the plant or animal remains and is concentrated to a thin film. This residue of carbon is what we now see in the fossils at the monument. The fossil remains are really a carbon copy of the plant or animal that has the same appearance as the real, living organism.

FINAL THOUGHTS

By an Act of Congress on August 20, 1969, this area became the Florissant Fossil Beds National Monument. In the months and years prior to that day, the fossil beds were quickly becoming a proposed site for residential development and continued to be a place for private collectors to dig and remove large numbers of fossils. If the monument had not been established when it was, the unique character of the place would have been irreversibly altered. This is, perhaps, an opportune moment to thank those unnamed few who fought so hard to preserve this natural wonder for us and future generations who will come to admire nature's work.

ADDITIONAL READINGS

Edwards, M. E., and W. A. Weber, 1990. *Plants of the Florissant Fossil Beds National Monument,* Bulletin no. 2, Pikes Peak Research Station, Florissant, Colo.

Epis, R. C., and C. E. Chapin, 1968. "Geologic History of the Thirty-nine Mile Volcanic Field, Central Colorado," *Colorado School of Mines Quarterly* 63 (3), pp. 51–85.

Epis, R. C., G. R. Scott, R. B. Taylor, and C. E. Chapin, 1980, "Summary of Cenozoic Geomorphic, Volcanic and Tectonic Features of Central Colorado and Adjoining Areas." In *Colorado Geology,* ed. Harry C. Kent and Karen W. Porter, Rocky Mountain Association of Geologists, Denver, Colo.

Gamer, E. E., 1965. "The Fossil Beds of Florissant," *National Parks Magazine* 39 (214), pp. 16–19.

Kimmett, L., 1986. *Florissant, Colorado,* revised edition, Master Printers, Cañon City, Colo.

MacGinitie, H. D., 1953. *Fossil Plants of the Florissant Beds, Colorado,* Publication no. 599, Carnegie Institute, Washington, D.C.

Malocsay, Z., 1983. *Hiker's Guide – Pikes Peak and South Park Region,* Century One Press, Colorado Springs, Colo.

Mutel, C. F., and J. C. Emerick, 1984. *From Grassland to Glacier,* Johnson Books, Boulder, Colo.

National Park Service, n.d. *Birds of the Florissant Fossil Beds National Monument,* Brochure, National Park Service, Florissant, Colo.

National Park Service, n.d. *Wildflowers of the Florissant Fossil Beds National Monument,* Brochure, National Park Service, Florissant, Colo.

Ramaley, F., 1906. "Plants of the Florissant Region in Colorado," *University of Colorado Studies* 3 (3), pp. 177–185.

Skinner, B. J., ed., 1981. *Paleontology and Paleoenvironments: Readings from* American Scientist, William Kaufmann, Los Angeles, Calif.

Tidwell, W. D., 1975. *Common Fossil Plants of Western North America,* Brigham Young University, Provo, Utah.

Zwinger, A., and B. Sparks, 1991. *Aspen — Blazon of the High Country,* Peregrine Smith Books, Salt Lake City, Utah.

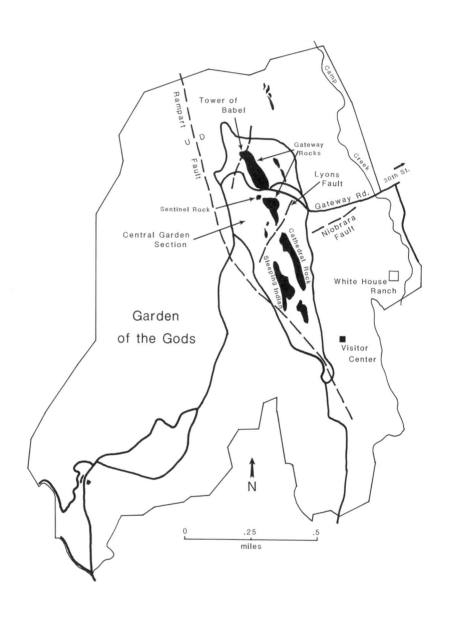

6

GARDEN OF THE GODS

The Garden of the Gods is a garden of nature. In spite of the walkways, the picnic grounds, the paved and curving roads, this is first and last a garden of and by nature. The parklike panorama, so often attributed to landscape architects, and the rock walls and ramparts were here long before humans ever set foot on this ground. In 1859 a fit of inspiration led Rufus Cable to dub the place "garden of the gods." The name was made official by Charles Elliott Perkins in 1909 when he deeded the "Garden of the Gods" to the City of Colorado Springs as a park to be open and free to the public forever. Parcels of land have been added to the original land, but it remains as a tribute to Charles Elliott Perkins and his family.

The place endures as much more than a family memorial, a recreation spot for tourists, or a photogenic landmark. Among all of the special places in this book, it portrays the geologic, biotic, and human stories of Colorado most dramatically. What is especially striking is the multitude of transitions that occur in this localized site. There are the transitions of vegetation environments that include three life zones, several ecosystems, and views to several other life zones in the vicinity (Figure 6.1); the transitions of landforms that juxtapose the plains, the foothills, and the mountains; the transitions of present-day urban and natural landscapes; and the Native American cultural transitions from the Ute Indian mountain life to the Arapaho and Cheyenne Indian plains existence.

Figure 6.1. Snowcapped Pikes Peak just visible through the gap between the Gateway rocks.

THE ENVIRONMENTAL SETTING

Any understanding of the present environment of the garden must begin with an understanding of the climate. This place we call the Garden of the Gods stands at an average elevation of nearly 6,500 feet. There is a very rapid elevation increase from about 6,350 feet on the far southeastern side of the park to almost 7,000 feet in the far northwestern corner. This is typical of foothills locations. Along with these elevation increases come climatic and environmental change. The average temperature in the garden during summer days is about 85 degrees F. However, when you are standing on a southeast-facing slope above the main section of the park during a summer day, the temperature may seem to reach into the 100-degree F range. Bright and intense sunshine and the ovenlike character of the rocks combine to make the effective temperature of this place very warm indeed. In winter the climate is usually mild, with average daytime temperatures of about 42 degrees F and below-freezing temperatures at night, but it can become cold and dreary when the north wind blows or a cyclonic storm passes through.

The garden is in a semiarid environment, which means that the total precipitation it receives is relatively small (about 16 inches per year). This average figure hides the fact that when precipitation comes, it usually comes in large quantities. Although it does not snow here often, when it does it is not uncommon for the garden to get up to 24 inches in a single storm. The rapid change in elevation mentioned above helps to cause the upslope wind conditions responsible for these big snows. The rapid rise over the land and the saturated conditions of the air moving in from the east or southeast cause the quick cooling of air and large, localized snowfalls.

Summertime precipitation, which accounts for most of the yearly total, can also be very heavy and comes primarily from thunderstorms. Most summer afternoons here have cumulus cloud buildups, caused in part by the intense heating of the Earth's surface. A few times each summer, rainfall rates from these storms can reach 2 to 4 inches per hour. Luckily these storms usually last but a few minutes; however, if they stall over the garden, they may last for hours. Flooding and erosion occur rapidly here, as in other foothills locations along the Front Range of Colorado (Figure 6.2). In general the climate of the area can be characterized as mild and serene, punctuated by severe storms and extremes in temperature. These patterns give the garden much of its personality and account for the vegetation distributions and many of the current geologic processes of the park.

THE BIOTIC ENVIRONMENT

As noted above, the Garden of the Gods spans two or three life zones, and three others can be seen from just about anywhere in the park. On the eastern edge along 30th Street, you see evidence of the plains life zone; the valley just to the west of the road exhibits the plains character. Most of the garden is in the foothills life zone with its transitory vegetation patterns, intermixture of environments, and varied collection of fauna. The montane life zone is near, if not in, the northwest corner of the park. The presence of all of these environments in such a confined area means that you can not only see many ecosystems and animal species coexisting, but also get a real feel for the variety, complexity, and rapid change possible along the mountain front. Although this book will discuss each ecosystem in turn, it is important to remember that they are not isolated, distinct units. Think of each as having a dominant vegetation type rather than exclusive flora and/or fauna species.

Figure 6.2. Large erosion gullies in Cathedral Canyon, one of the worst environmental problems in the Garden of the Gods.

THE ECOSYSTEMS

The ecosystems in the garden range from the plains grassland to the ponderosa pine and Douglas fir forests. Each is defined and regulated by a combination of climate, soil, and even geology. Subtle and gradual environmental changes make for subtle and gradual vegetation changes. There are few distinct boundaries between the various ecosystems. Keep in mind that transitions and change among the vegetation patterns are as important here as any uniform vegetation distributions.

The plains grassland. The grasslands here have little of the grandeur of the sweeping vistas only a few miles to the east. Hills and mesas limit this ecosystem to the narrow north-south valley running parallel to 30th Street. Although there are virtually no "plains" in this plains grassland, the environmental conditions for grasses to grow are very similar to those in the Comanche National Grassland (see Chapter 7), for example. This area has highly erratic but intense precipitation; it also has very high-nutrient and fine-textured soils developed from the Pierre shale underlying the valley. The grasses grow here because the limits of their competitive edge with other plants are just to the east and west, where environmental conditions change to favor other ecosystems.

The specific grass species here are very similar to those in the southeastern section of Colorado. Blue grama (*Bouteloua gracilis*), buffalo grass (*Buchloe dactyloides*), western wheatgrass (*Agropyron smithii*), crested wheatgrass (*A. cristatum*), and little bluestem (*Schizachyrium scoparium*) are all common. There are other less common species also, such as red three-awn (*Aristida longiseta*), and the bane of cattle ranchers of the eastern plains, cheat grass (*Bromus tectorum*). Spread throughout the grass ecosystem are several commonly occurring nongrass plants. They include at least three species of low-growing cacti: hen-and-chickens (*Echinocereus viridiflorus*), prickly-pear (*Opuntia compressa*), and the pincushion or ball cactus (*Coryphantha vivipara*). A common plant throughout the park and in the grassland ecosystem is the yucca or Spanish bayonet (*Yucca glauca*). This plant and an associated insect display an unparalleled case of symbiosis whereby both the plant and the animal benefit from interaction. The plant's flower attracts the female pronuba moth (*Pronuba yuccasella*), which punctures the ovary of the flower and lays its eggs. The moth has already collected pollen from other yucca plants and forces some of these pollen grains deep into the stigmatic surface. This assures plant pollination as well as a ready food supply for the moth larvae once the eggs have hatched. The plant gains pollination and the moth larvae gain food and protection.

Lowland riparian. On the western side of this valley lies the second ecosystem of the park. Here the lowland riparian ecosystem is quite evident; all one needs to do is look for the large deciduous trees that form a line along the stream bed of Camp Creek. There is little surface water in this channel, but there is considerable subsurface moisture for the water-loving vegetation in this ecosystem. Other examples of the lowland riparian ecosystem can be found in the garden, but this is the most well-developed example. This riparian ecosystem stands in general contrast to other ecosystems in the park and on the plains to the east of Colorado Springs: proof that small changes in environment in a general area of ecological stress can make significant changes in flora and fauna. Large, deciduous trees are not common in Colorado; the consistent and adequate supply of water is the primary reason that these large plants can survive and flourish in this otherwise dry environment.

Both the narrowleaf cottonwood (*Populus angustifolia*) and the plains cottonwood (*P. sargentii*) are common here, evidence for the transition between plains and mountains that takes place in the park. The plains cottonwood is predominant in the riparian areas of the eastern plains whereas the narrowleaf cottonwood is a foothills and montane species. Other riparian, woody species can be found here in lesser quantities. These include the box elder (*Acer negundo*), green ash (*Fraxinus pennsylvanica*), and wild rose (*Rosa woodsii*). One plant species that you might want to avoid while hiking around the park is poison ivy (*Toxicodendron rydbergii*); these three-leaved plants with dark green, shiny surfaces can cause considerable discomfort. We usually think of this plant as growing in damp, deciduous forests of the East, but the moisture here in the valley is enough to allow it to survive, if not to flourish. Another cautionary note is needed for a species of animal that comes to feed here on smaller animals living in the riparian. The prairie rattlesnake, a subspecies of the western rattlesnake (*Crotalus viridis*), frequents this area and is often seen sunning on the hillsides just to the west of the valley. These are small snakes, but they will make you sorry you disturbed them nonetheless.

Gambel oak/mountain mahogany. The Gambel oak/mountain mahogany ecosystem is a transition ecosystem between the grassland and the treed ecosystems of the garden. There is slightly more moisture available here than is needed for the growth of grasses, but less than that necessary for tree growth. This ecosystem extends over large sections of the park, especially the northern end. The mountain mahogany (*Cercocarpus montanus*) also occurs in the montane life zone of the Florissant Fossil Beds National Monument, but here it coexists with the Gambel oak (*Quercus gambelii*). Both species are sun-loving and grow on coarse-grained soils in mixed stands or separately. These plants will readily invade ponderosa pine or piñon/juniper areas if these areas are disturbed, but the pioneering efforts of the Gambel oak/mountain mahogany will not prevail as the trees will re-invade when environmental conditions allow.

Gambel oak grows to a height of 8 to 12 feet and has a leaf shape typical of oaks. Acorns of this species are relatively small but do attract animals, especially mule deer (*Odocoileus hemionus*), that forage these nuts. In autumn the Gambel oak gives a wonderful display of color as the leaves turn to reds, yellows, and oranges. Almost all of the stands of "scrub oak" in Colorado are made up of this single species.

The mountain mahogany is a smaller shrub that grows to only 4 or 5 feet. The oval leaves are serrated and much smaller than the Gambel oak leaves. The seeds have a very distinctive look; they are long, spiral, and hairy. When the seed matures and falls, the hairs act as a parachute to ensure that the sharply pointed tip hits the ground first. As the seed dries out, the curved tail straightens and drills the seed into the soil surface. This self-planting seed is a testament to the variety and wonder in nature.

Several species of grass will usually be a part of the understory beneath the shrubs, but the most common associated plants are other shrubs that coexist here. These include berry-producing species like the golden currant (*Ribes aureum*), wax currant (*R. cereum*), and the common gooseberry (*R. inerme*), a thorny shrub. These bushes attract many of the bird species that live in or migrate through the park. Two species of brushy vegetation that indicate sandy, dry environmental conditions are the odorous, golden-flowered rabbitbrush (*Chrysothamnus nauseosus*) and the four-wing saltbush (*Atriplex canescens*).

In many respects this scrubland is very similar to that seen in the drier, western section of the plateau region of Colorado. The main difference is moisture: this area has more; the plateau has less. Generally, the shrub species to the west are more drought-tolerant than those here on the eastern side of the mountains.

Figure 6.3. Seemingly landscaped vegetation of the central garden section in early morning.

Piñon pine/juniper woodland. This ecosystem, along with the dramatic rock formations, is responsible for the parklike atmosphere of the Garden of the Gods (Figure 6.3). The almost manicured arrangement of the vegetation here is caused by competition for nutrients and moisture. The trees will only survive where there is enough of each of these resources. This causes the naturally occurring separation of the small stands or individual trees. This wide distribution pattern allocates the food and water that maintains the viability of this vegetation community.

The piñon/juniper woodland (P-J woodland, as it is often called) is a very common ecosystem in the foothills environment of southeastern Colorado as well as in the plateau section of the state. The garden, however, is almost at the northern limit of the P-J woodland on the Eastern Slope. A mile or two north of here the P-J woodland ends, and only a small, relic stand exists farther north. This anomaly lies on a limestone formation north of Fort Collins. Eventually, the quarrying of this limestone will most likely eliminate this outlier.

Both of these trees and the shrubs mentioned earlier are xerophytes, which means that they are drought tolerant. These trees have deep taproots that enable them to survive on stored winter precipitation — even through long and relatively severe drought conditions. The junipers are more hardy and, therefore, will spread to harsher environs than the piñon pines (*Pinus edulis*). In fact, at times the junipers will act as nursery trees for the piñon pines. The pines will sprout and grow only because of the shade and protection of the juniper trees. Once the taproot of the piñon pine gets established, the tree can survive on its own.

The piñon pine is named for the pine nut that is cherished by humans and animals alike. These trees are slow-growing, and even a small plant may be several hundred years old. The piñon pine is recognized by its short, squat stature (not more than 25 feet tall) and two-needled bundles. They may be found in almost pure stands or intermixed with the junipers.

The junipers of the park include three species. The low-growing shrub known as the prostrate or common juniper (*Juniperus communis*) exists here but is not plentiful. The two more common types are the tree species, the one-seed juniper (*J. monosperma*) and the Rocky Mountain juniper (*J. scopulorum*). The one-seed juniper is a scraggly, multitrunked tree that is gnarled and picturesque (Figure 6.4). The Rocky Mountain juniper, also called the Rocky Mountain red cedar, is symmetrical, dark-green, and shapely (Figure 6.5). Several Rocky Mountain junipers were planted in the central section of the garden during the 1930s, so not all of the specimens you see are naturally occurring. These plantings were to replace lost trees, and therefore the pattern is still quite a natural one. The P-J woodland is found from the central garden section to the western edge of the park and beyond.

Ponderosa pine forest. Ponderosa pine *forest* is almost a misnomer for what exists in the garden. There are no extensive forests of ponderosa pine (*Pinus ponderosa*), but there are significant stands in the moister and higher sections of the park. These trees like sunny, well-drained sites and can be found on south-facing uplands with concentrated moisture. These pines are conspicuous because they are much larger than the piñons. The ponderosa pines are a direct reflection of the transitory aspects of the garden; montane and plains life zones come together here in what appears to be a disorderly distribution of vegetation. You need only look at the environmental factors such as wind, water, and sun to see the logic of vegetation growth here.

Douglas fir forest. The Douglas fir forest is even less of a forest than the ponderosa pine forest. Douglas fir (*Pseudotsuga menziesii*) can be found on north-facing slopes where there is little evaporation — but they can be even more selective than that: often you will find Douglas fir growing along fault

Figure 6.4. A gnarled and picturesque one-seed juniper.

Figure 6.5. The more stately and erect Rocky Mountain juniper.

zones in the park. These zones are areas where the rocks have broken and moved, creating shattered rock sections along the faults. The shattered rock is called "breccia," and its loose structure and jointing patterns allow water to collect. This increase in water availability allows the Douglas firs to grow. A good area to see this phenomenon is just to the northwest of Cathedral Rock, where three or four Douglas fir grow in a seemingly odd spot. Only the underlying fault and its attendant water supply permits these trees to flourish.

Another tree planted in the garden during the 1930s is the white fir (*Abies concolor*). This tree probably would not exist here except for these plantings. The garden is north of the normal environmental limit of the white fir, although some do exist in the deeply shaded canyon of Glen Eyrie just to the north of the park.

THE ANIMALS

The Garden of the Gods is home to some intriguing and elusive mammals, an interesting collection of birds, and a variety of insects, including one unique species that has an organization unexcelled in the insect world. In addition to the mule deer mentioned earlier, there is the seldom seen but always present mountain lion (*Felis concolor*). This usually nocturnal predator has, in the past, been presumably isolated in rugged and inaccessible parts of the mountains. In recent years the lion's shyness and fear of humans have seemed to diminish, at least in this part of the state. The growing deer population and the human invasion into the foothills and mountain areas has helped to increase the number of sightings and contacts with this large cat. You will probably not see a cougar, but be aware that they are ever present along the mountain front of the East Slope.

Another relatively rare large mammal found here is the bighorn sheep (*Ovis canadensis*). These majestic ungulates love the open shrub and P-J woodland communities located just above the park. In the past the sheep would wander down as far as the Hidden Inn by North Gateway Rock, but increased human traffic has driven the sheep up the mountain and to the north of the garden into the Glen Eyrie property. This herd is well established and relatively robust; however, urban pressures and habitat encroachment by humans cause some concern for the sheep's future viability.

The assortment of birds in the garden includes grosbeaks, pigeons, swallows, flickers, and many small songbirds. The garden is also home to three species of jay as well as the raucous and distinctive black-billed magpie (*Pica pica*). The Steller's jay (*Cyanocitta stelleri*), the piñon jay (*Gymnorhinus cyanocephalus*), and the scrub jay (*Aphelocoma coerulescens*) all reside in these mixed ecosystems. There is also an active golden eagle (*Aquila chrysaetos*) nest just north of the park on the Glen Eyrie property. These majestic raptors can be seen soaring above the garden on summer afternoon thermals in search of a meal. But the star performer of the bird class in the garden is the white-throated swift (*Aeronautes saxatalis*). The park is one of the largest swift roosting sites along the Front Range, with over 1,500 swifts roosting in the rock formations each night during fall and spring migrations. These airborne acrobats give a stirring performance with their rapid turns, dives, and other antics in pursuit of insect meals. They even manage to mate while airborne, pulling out of their precipitous fall just above the ground. As graceful as these birds are in flight, they are awkward when trying to land. Their small feet, adapted for streamlined flight, make it difficult to settle back to earth. Often you will see a swift fall out of its roost while landing; they just keep attempting to land until they succeed.

The most unusual animal in the park might be the honey ant (*Myrmecocystus mexicanus*), first discovered here in the garden. This nocturnal insect gathers honeylike nectar from surrounding vegetation and stores the viscous liquid in living mason jars. Certain members of the colony use their abdomens for storage of the honey, which consists mainly of glucose and fructose. The abdomens of these "repletes" swell to several times their normal size. Honey is regurgitated to other members of the colony when needed. The rounded ant-hill nests of these industrious insects are often found on dry, exposed ridge tops around the park.

THE GEOLOGIC STORY

The distinctiveness of the Garden of the Gods goes far beyond the juxtaposition of ecosystems in a small area. The garden is a place where the geology of the Southern Rocky Mountains comes alive and is graphically illustrated in the colors, shapes, positions, and textures of the rocks. On a short walk you can travel through millions of years of Earth history and view the evidence of several mountain-building episodes that occurred on a grand scale; those who are prepared can see the world of changes that happened here over a span of about 300 million years. Few places on Earth of a similar size can rival this natural classroom for its portrayal of the dynamism of this seemingly static and solid ground.

THE PRE-GARDEN GEOLOGIC HISTORY

The geologic story of the garden begins about 300 million years ago (mya) during the Pennsylvanian period (Figure 6.6), but the Earth's geologic history begins several billion years before that. Recall from Chapter 1 that Colorado has had up to five major mountain-building episodes. Two of these occurred before the formation of the rocks in the Garden of the Gods. Prior to the Pennsylvanian period there were sea invasions and erosion and deposition: these were the eras of the beginnings of life, of remarkable changes in the gaseous nature of the atmosphere, and of the intense deformation of the Earth's crust that alchemized sandstone into gneiss and limestone into marble. The only extant evidence in the garden of these earlier times is ancient rock fragments eroded from higher up in the mountains, transported here by water and gravity, and deposited in or on the rocks now present in the park. This older history is a shadow in the garden's past. The real story of the Garden of the Gods began when forces in and of the Earth began building a large, "ancestral" mountain system in the region.

THE ANCESTRAL ROCKIES

The mountain uplift that began around 300 mya occurred in an environment very different from that we experience today. There were lowlands with lagoons, swamps, beaches, and deltas of rivers all bordering a shallow sea. Although many different rock types were being produced, the main characteristic of the landscape was of a low, flat region. The uplift itself, called the Colorado Orogeny, was rapid by geologic standards, and most geologists believe that the mountains built by this orogeny were very high. Some geologists hypothesize that these Rockies grew to twice the height of the current Pikes Peak (14,110 feet), thus rivalling the present-day Himalayan Mountains for sheer elevation. We know or can speculate about so much of this because of what was produced by this rapid and intense movement.

The geologic concept of uniformitarianism states that the processes and physical laws we have today are the same as those that have always acted on the Earth. One of these laws states that a very rapid change in elevation brings with it a very high potential for movement of material downhill. This means that water, the main fluid in question, will be able to

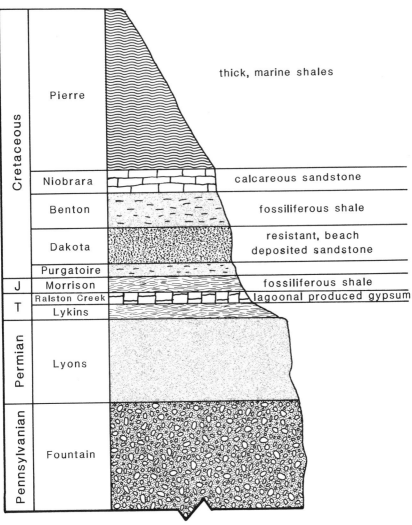

Figure 6.6. The geologic column of the rocks in the Garden of the Gods extends from the Pennsylvanian period to the late Cretaceous period — about 250 million years of geologic history.

develop torrents as it moves downslope, especially if the rains come quickly as they do in large thunderstorms. These torrents contain tremendous energy capable of moving rock fragments ranging in size from minute clay grains to boulders the size of bowling balls. When the slope angle changes rapidly at the foot of the mountains from severely angled to almost flat, all of this mixture of debris and water is deposited quickly.

The conglomerated deposit formed by this process in the Garden of the Gods has become known as the Fountain formation, named for the creek dissecting it just south of the park. The Fountain formation is a sedimentary rock called a conglomerate, meaning just that: it is made up of all sizes and shapes of sedimentary material. Of course, the many, many millennia that it took to build the Fountain formation were not just one long torrential rain and flood. There is evidence of many environmental conditions in the Fountain. The alluvial fans made up of Fountain conglomerate are intermingled with depositions laid down more gently and sorted by slower-moving waters to include clay strata that indicate nearly standing water. But the conglomerate remains the most substantial part of the Fountain formation, causing some authors, like Paul Nesbit, to refer to the rock as a "petrified flash flood."

The deep red color of the rock arises from chemical alteration of minerals like magnetite, biotite, and pyrite. Some feel that a volcanic source of iron oxides is also responsible for the color. For the nongeologist, what it boils down to is that the rock rusted!

The Fountain formation is 4,500 feet thick near the present mountain front, is the oldest rock in the park, and covers the western three-quarters of the garden. Many of the park's most well-known natural rock sculptures are made of the Fountain formation. These include Balanced Rock, Sentinel Rock, the Three Graces, Cathedral Spires, and Steamboat Rock. The angles of these rocks are a product of later movement.

THE BETWEEN MOUNTAIN INTERLUDE

Between the Colorado Orogeny and the next major uplift, the Laramide Orogeny, the area that we now know as the Garden of the Gods was shaped by many different environments. However, the overall relief was much lower than that of a mountain system. In fact, in the few million years subsequent to the Fountain formation, the area was invaded by a shallow sea known by geologists as the Absoroka Sea. This trangressing (advancing) and regressing (contracting) sea left deposits here and elsewhere, but none of these are found in the park today. The Permian period ushered in new environments and new deposition in the form of the Lyons formation.

The Lyons formation. The celebrated Lyons formation makes up the most dramatic features of the park. The Gateway Rocks, the Tower of Babel, Cathedral Rock, and Sleeping Indian Rock are all formed of Lyons and were all deposited in an almost flat and horizontal position. The Lyons is not one ubiquitous formation but includes three major members: the lower member (now the most western), the upper member (now the most eastern), and the middle member (now mostly a valley between the western and eastern sections).

There is considerable debate among geologists on the depositional environment of the lower member of the Lyons. It was probably a combination of environments including low-angle river delta muds, beach deposits, and some wind-produced dunes. Keep in mind that the deposit of any single rock formation may take millions of years. During that time changes occur; even a water level change of just a foot or two along a shore can change the way sediments are deposited. The middle member of the Lyons is even more of a mixed deposit. There is evidence of lagoon-formed shales and torrentially deposited conglomerates. This member is less resistant to erosion than the upper and lower members since it is now a topographic valley between the two more resistant rocks. The upper Lyons member is much more typical of sandstone developed from sand dunes (see Chapter 11, "Great Sand Dunes National Monument"). High angle cross-bedding and the minute markings on the individual sand grains of the rock indicate sand blown and deposited by the wind.

Apart from the size and shape of these rocks, a most intriguing aspect is the color change from the red lower member to the whitish gray upper member. The entire formation was probably oxidized (rusted) to the deep reds of the lower member. Subsequently, something happened to the red of the upper member. Three possible, and probably concurrent, processes explain this color change. First, superheated water may have percolated upwards through the upper member and bleached the oxides out. Second, the overlying strata (the Lykins and Ralston Creek formations) contained large amounts of sulfur. Hydrogen sulfide was created here and seeped down into the Lyons. This weak acid may have chemically removed the color. Third, some oil-like substance may have been produced in the shales of the middle member of the Lyons and migrated upwards through the upper member, removing the color and leaving the grayish tint in the sandstone. Of course, this is all somewhat speculative, but speculation is often necessary when discussing something that may have occurred almost 200 mya.

The Lykins formation. The Triassic period saw the development of the Lykins formation, which lies just above the Lyons in the geologic column (Figure 6.6). The Lykins was created during the transitions of advancing seas and low elevations. Shales, limestones, and gypsums are all a part of this rock formation. Each of these is produced by unique circumstances, but they all indicate a wet and quiescent region.

A most dramatic characteristic of the Lykins is the presence of large fossil remains of blue-green algae mats known as stromatolites. These are visible in the larger rocks of the formation as conchoidal inlays in the surrounding stone. Layered algae mats can be seen today in places like the tidal flats in the warm seas surrounding the Bahamas. The Sundance Sea was advancing into the area toward the end of the Lykins deposition.

The other formations. Six other geologic formations occur in the park (Figure 6.6). You can find the almost pure gypsum of the Ralston Creek formation with its sand lens inclusions; the Morrison formation so famous for its dinosaur fossils (found in other parts of the state); the monolithic, erosion-resistant Dakota sandstone standing as a gray sentinel in the sky; the weak, eroded, and fossil-rich Benton group; the low hills of the Niobrara with its cephalopod and mollusk fossils; and the youngest and weakest rock in the park, the Pierre shale. These rocks are found in descending age from west to east. The Pierre shale forms the foundation of the stream valley along 30th Street.

THE LARAMIDE OROGENY

From the Pennsylvanian to the late Cretaceous periods, this entire area was a slowly undulating and relatively low-lying region. The sediments described above were deposited close to the horizontal and more or less remained that way. According to the geologic law of superposition, the newer beds of sedimentary rock lie on top of the older strata much like new coats of paint must be put over older coats. Figure 6.7a shows a simplified version of this in the garden. At this point the stage is set for the next dramatic movements of the Earth. About 65 mya the forces in the Earth's crust began a series of events that we now call the Laramide Orogeny.

No one knows precisely what caused such tremendous pressures to be exerted on this part of the North American continent. The cause lies within the complex relationships and movements of former and current lithospheric plates around the globe, but the actual mechanisms have yet to be solved

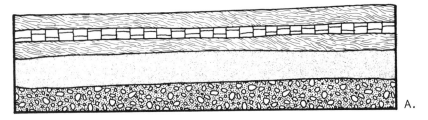

Sedimentary Layers Prior to Uplift

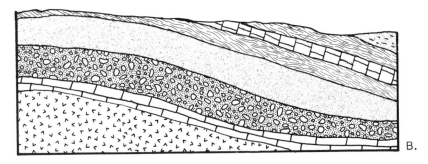

Start of Sedimentary Arching

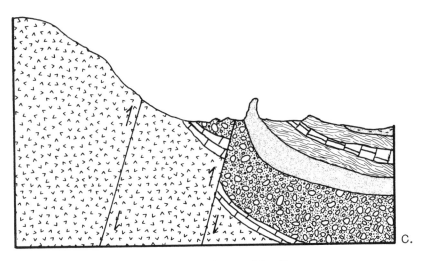

Rampart Fault after Laramide Orogeny

Figure 6.7. The sequence of events from A to B to C shows the geological creation of the Garden of the Gods.

by geophysicists. Nonetheless, the orogeny did occur with the relatively swift uplift of the deeply buried Pikes Peak granite and the arching of the overlying sedimentary rocks (Figure 6.7b). Under great heat and pressure, rocks act like malleable plastic, at least to a certain point. These "plasti-cized" sedimentary strata were bent and arched into an anticline over the Pikes Peak granite. At some point the rocks gave way to fracturing and movement along what we now call the Rampart fault (Figure 6.7c). This fault allowed the rocks on the west side of the park to remain at an angle of 45 degrees or less and ride up the growing mountain range. The rocks to the east of the Rampart fault continued to bend until some were actually more than 90 degrees from their original, horizontal position (the Gateway rocks, for example). These vertical rocks are what we now marvel at throughout the central portion of the garden. The erosion-resistant ones stand like giant guardians and the less resistant are dramatic in their absence.

As described in Chapter 1, when Earth materials are lifted above the surrounding area, there is an increase in potential energy that provides the mechanism for increased erosion. Most of the anticline overburden on the mountain side of the Rampart fault has been eroded away. Some of this material can now be found in another rock formation seen in Colorado Springs although not in the park: the Dawson formation. The mountains to the west of here have little, if any, sedimentary rock remaining over the granite core.

The other orogenies. The Laramide Orogeny lasted for several million years and then became quiescent, but the erosion of the uplifted mass continued. Uplift began again in the late Eocene epoch and continued through the Oligocene and into the early Miocene epochs. The mountains were again pushed up several thousand feet. This orogeny coincided with a period of extensive volcanic activity throughout the state (see Chapter 5, "Florissant Fossil Beds National Monument," and Chapter 9, "Silverton"). After another inactive period of about 20 million years another relatively small uplift occurred during the Pliocene epoch. This was the final period of orogeny to date. If this series of uplifts had occurred hundreds of millions of years ago, they probably would have been seen as a single orogeny. But because the evidence is still so fresh from these much more recent uplifts, we are able to distinguish between the three separate orogenies.

Figure 6.8. Niobrara formation outcrops appear as low ridges cut by Gateway Road.

THE FAULTS

Faults are like special windows into the internal dynamism of the Earth. They show the movement and the vitality of the seemingly solid and immutable crust. The garden allows us to see and touch various types of faults and to partially understand what it means to break and move millions of tons of solid rock.

The Rampart fault is the main zone in the park where the crust of the Earth moved. It is not a single break like that in a cracked dinner plate; it is a wide zone of broken and pulverized rock called breccia. In places it may be as wide as several hundred feet. It begins 35 miles to the north of the park and ends where it is cut off by the Ute Pass fault to the south. Within the garden, however, there are several less major faults and several hundred smaller faults, some as little as only a few feet long. Four of these faults deserve special discussion. For lack of better terms, these faults will be labeled for the places where they are most evident.

The Niobrara fault. Coming into the park from 30th Street along Gateway Road, you will notice that the ridge on the north side of the road does not align with the ridge on the south side of the road. The ridge is the Niobrara formation, and the reason for this offset is that there is a fault zone running just under the road at this point. The fault probably caused a weak point in the ridge that was taken advantage of by the road engineers when they laid out the road into the park (Figure 6.8).

The Lyons fault. A relatively large fault occurs just south of South Gateway Rock. You will notice that the lower Lyons member of South Gateway Rock, composed of red sandstone, aligns almost perfectly with the upper Lyons member of Cathedral Rock, composed of white sandstone. The fault has caused the south side to move toward the west a few hundred feet. No one knows positively whether this motion occurred after the uplift (a lateral fault) or before the uplift (a normal fault); probably before the uplift. The breccia along this fault allows water to collect here and is the site of the Douglas fir discussed earlier in the chapter.

The Sentinel Rock faults. Sentinel Rock is an excellent example of the smaller faults throughout the park. If you look closely at the rock itself, you will see dozens of small fractures and faults. These minor faults may be only a few inches in length and can be identified by looking at the sediments that make up the rock. See how some of the internal layers of the sedimentary strata have been misaligned within the rock. Each of these areas is the site of one of these small faults.

The Tower of Babel fault. The most visible and striking fault in the park is the Tower of Babel fault (Figure 6.9). Here you can see evidence of how the Lyons formation slid up and over the Fountain formation (Figure 6.10). You see the actual fault plane and some of the altered clay minerals that reveal the stress lines between the two formations. Seldom can you observe and touch a geologic event that occurred millions of years ago. The simple act of covering the fault with your hand can be a meaningful experience. You are experiencing the very real movement of the Earth's surface and the unimaginable power that is needed to bend and move solid rock. This may not be the most spectacular site in the park, but it may be the most stimulating.

PRESENT GEOLOGIC ACTIVITY

Geologic activity is not just something that happened in far distant eons; different facets of geologic activity occur slowly but inextricably throughout

Figure 6.9. The Tower of Babel fault can be seen in the lower central part of this photograph. The Lyons formation is the large, vertical rock; the Fountain formation is the lower rock in the shadows.

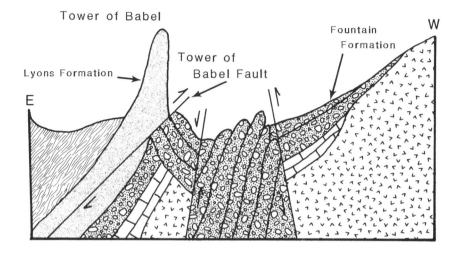

Figure 6.10. Profile of the geology of the Tower of Babel fault from the north looking south.

time. Erosion and deposition can be seen in most environments; for example, severe erosion is occurring in the valley between Cathedral Rock and Sleeping Indian Rock. Gullies several feet deep are evidence of human use combined with the effects of fierce thunderstorm activity. The park staff have slowed erosion rates in much of the garden through intensive ground work, but it is never possible to totally stop the relentless attack by the elements; gravity, water, wind, and humans merge to generate considerable erosive power. Without humans the erosion would still proceed; with humans it accelerates.

Other signs of current erosive activity are the honeycomb rocks like those above the Hidden Inn. The pockmarked surface of the Lyons sandstone is caused by minor weaknesses in the rock that have been attacked by water. Once the weak area has been altered by weathering, chemical and physical processes continue to enlarge the holes. These pitted surfaces are recent, at least in geologic terms, and did not occur prior to uplift.

Humans are contributing to the erosion and altering of the park in another significant way. The minor act of driving through the park adds sulfur and nitrogen oxides to the air that can become weak acids when moisture is present. These acids tend to attack the more fragile bonds between the rock particles. Calcium carbonate is especially susceptible to acid destruction. The processes are slow and the effects are minute, but over the long term they will alter the rock faces of the garden. Studies indicate that rock climbing frequently affects rock formations as well. The constant abrasion of the climbers' shoes and the chalk used for better grips will eventually have an impact. No easy answers exist to developing the proper balance between human desires for park use and the preservation of the natural features for which the park was ultimately created; however, we are in great danger of loving the Garden of the Gods to death.

FINAL THOUGHTS

The Garden of the Gods is a place where humans and nature have come together for hundreds, if not thousands, of years. Native Americans traveled through and camped in the area we now call the Garden of the Gods. The Utes from the mountains and the Arapaho and Cheyenne tribes from the plains all moved through here. We know little of what they thought of the place, but they certainly treated it with respect and may even have been awed by the powers of nature evident here. We latter-day visitors owe the park nothing less than the respect given to it for so long. We also owe it our best efforts at preservation.

The Garden of the Gods is a meeting place not only of the plains and the mountains, but also of common and unique features of the natural world of Colorado. We could also say that it is a meeting place of the physical and the metaphysical. Many organized and personal religions come here to celebrate. On Easter the park becomes a Christian enclave through the sunrise service. But the garden is home to other, more private forms of worship that transcend religious denominations. People come to wed, to pray, to meditate, to learn. The Garden of the Gods should remain a physical and natural place that inspires the metaphysical. If you come here, treat the park as you would a place of worship: respect the fragile nature of even the rocks and the soil, and leave the park at least as good as you found it.

ADDITIONAL READINGS

Chronic, H., 1980. *Roadside Geology of Colorado,* Mountain Press Publishing, Missoula, Mont.

Chronic, J., and H. Chronic, 1972. *Prairie, Peak and Plateau: A Guide to the Geology of Colorado,* Colorado Geological Survey Bulletin 32, Denver, Colo.

Cole, A. C., 1935. "Living Honey Jars," *Natural History* 36, pp. 117–123.

Conway, J. R., 1981. "Honey Ants: Sweet Swell of Success," *Science Digest,* August, pp. 56–59.

——, 1986. "The Biology of Honey Ants," *The American Biology Teacher* 48 (6), pp. 335–343.

Elmore, F. H., 1976. *Shrubs and Trees of the Southwest Uplands,* Southwest Parks and Monuments Association, Globe, Ariz.

Gehling, R., and M. A. Gehling, 1991. *Man in the Garden of the Gods,* Mountain Automation Corporation, Woodland Park, Colo.

Hubbard, R. L., and D. J. Wyatt, 1976. *Geology of the Pikes Peak Region, Colorado,* Century One Press, Colorado Springs, Colo.

Hutchinson, R. M., 1985. *Natural and Unnatural Stresses Upon the Ecosystem of the 1364 Acres of the Garden of the Gods Park, Colorado Springs, Colorado,* Colorado Springs Park and Recreation Department, Colo.

Johnston, M., and R. G. Beidleman, 1967. "Roosting Behavior of White-Throated Swifts," *Journal of the Colorado-Wyoming Academy of Science* 5 (8), p. 76.

Nesbit, P. W., 1968. *Garden of God's,* Paul A. Nesbit, Colorado Springs, Colo., pp. 48.

Noblett, J. B., 1984. *Introduction to the Geology of the Colorado Springs Region,* Colorado College Geology Department, Colorado Springs, Colo.

Scott, G. R., and R. A. Wobus, 1973. *Reconnaissance Geologic Map of Colorado Springs and Vicinity,* U.S. Geological Survey Misc. Field Studies Map MF-482, Washington, D.C.

Weimer, R. J., and J. D. Haun, eds., 1960. *Guide to the Geology of Colorado,* Rocky Mountain Association of Geologists, Denver, Colo., New York, N.Y.

Whitfield, C. J., 1933. "The Vegetation of the Pikes Peak Region," *Ecological Monographs* 3 (1), pp. 83–84.

7

COMANCHE NATIONAL
GRASSLAND

In 1820 Major Stephen H. Long labeled the region of the high plains from the 100th meridian to the foothills of the Rockies the "Great American Desert." His assessment had a tremendous impact on the way these lands were viewed by the people of the United States. His assessment was also inaccurate. To understand this part of the central United States, one must understand the natural and interdependent relationships of climate, vegetation, topography, and soil. This chapter will delve into these natural phenomena and look at a unique, yet quite typical, example of the high plains environment: the Comanche National Grassland.

The Comanche National Grassland is an area of southeastern Colorado managed solely by the U.S. Forest Service since 1954. It currently consists of two management units: the Timpas Unit (about 162,000 acres) and the Carrizo Unit (about 258,000 acres). A third area is slated to be added in the near future. This is a huge region of land dedicated to sound management for sustained grazing use and for recreational, cultural, and special management purposes. This dry litany of statistics and officialese obscures the true nature of this beautiful, stark, and fragile landscape; only an explanation of the character and history of this land and its natural attributes can do it justice.

The Comanche National Grassland was born from the aftermath of the great Dust Bowl of the 1930s. Drought, wind, and poor soil management combined to destroy land productivity during the period from 1931 to the

Comanche National Grassland

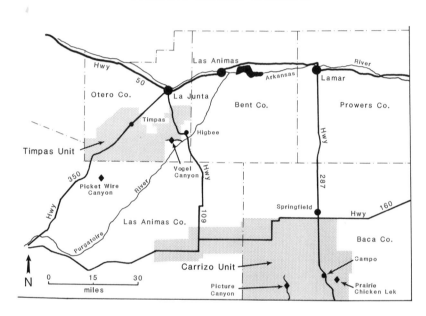

end of that decade. Dust from this region fell on places like Washington, D.C., and was carried as far as northern Africa. Fences were covered with windblown dirt, and crops and hope literally dried up and blew away. Black Sunday, April 14, 1931, was the harbinger of the almost total devastation that was to follow in areas of the Midwest and especially in the southeastern corner of Colorado. That day began the era of dust storms that grew rapidly and filled the sky with black, roiling dirt a thousand feet thick. After these storms passed no place, including people's lungs, was free of the grit. To understand the Dust Bowl is to understand the prairie; to understand the prairie is to understand the reasons for the dust bowl.

THE FACTORS OF NATURE ON THE PRAIRIE

It would not be an exaggeration to say that in the soil is written the story of the prairie. Soil and its development are reflections, on a grand scale, of the environmental factors that have occurred and are occurring in a given area. Whereas some environmental indicators, such as a certain vegetation species, change rapidly with changes in climate, the soil changes only slowly and shows a kind of cumulative environmental history of the land over hundreds to thousands of years. The material from which soil develops and the topography of a given parcel of land have some influence on how a soil develops. But soil is primarily the product of the climate of a region, the vegetative history of the land, and the long periods of time necessary for soil-forming processes to work. If climate and vegetation change over time, the soil will change in response.

Over a shorter time span, the soil here in the grassland can tell the story of human habitation and land use. As a sage, longtime resident of the region said, "Without the soil there is no life." He went on with the poignant observation that the soil here, in the country of the Comanche National Grassland, "was never supposed to be near a plow." The ranching and farming history of the grassland and the Dust Bowl era are emphatic evidence of the veracity of these two statements (Figure 7.1). To understand this tragic history, you must first understand the history of the prairie soils and the climate and vegetation of the ecosystems of the high plains.

Figure 7.1. Stark and isolated loading pen, a reminder of the ranching history of the area.

THE CLIMATE

The climate of the high plains in general and the Comanche National Grassland in particular can be summarized in one word — *extremes*. Seldom do we get the norm or average of anything here. For example, the average amount of precipitation per year in the Timpas Unit is 10.5 inches of water. But it can receive as much as 26 inches per year or as little as 1 or 2 inches per year. There is either drought or waterlogged conditions three-quarters of the time. Only 3 in 10 years receive enough moisture to grow normal crops like wheat, and the dry years seem to come in clusters as evidenced by the Dust Bowl of the 1930s and drought periods before and after this era.

Temperatures here are also extreme — ranging from 120 degrees F in summer to -20 F in winter. The warm temperatures of summer along with the 3,000 hours of wind a year combine to produce extreme evaporation and plant transpiration rates. If there were enough water available, the high temperatures and wind would combine to evaporate or transpire 72 inches of water each year; this *potential* evapotranspiration from the grassland is seven times what the area usually gets in precipitation. Because of this fact there are no perennial streams here, save those that originate in the mountains to the west/southwest and merely flow through this country. It is no wonder, then, that the natural vegetation that grows here must be tough and adaptable.

THE VEGETATION

Although there are conspicuous stands of piñon-juniper woodland among the arroyos and canyons of the grassland, this place is first and foremost a plains grassland ecosystem. Most people view grasslands as uniform, desolate places with only minor variations in plant variety; there seems to be an endless sameness that borders on monotony. This fallacy is soon disproved if you take the time to study and learn to see the subtle, yet unmistakable, variation in the ecosystem. Despite the variety there are some commonalities that allow the grasses to thrive in this hostile environment.

Almost all species of grasses and forbs in the Comanche National Grassland are perennials. A perennial life cycle allows plants in high-stress situations to grow and reproduce quickly when conditions are favorable, without the need to germinate seed or produce large amounts of biomass each year before reproduction occurs. In a very real sense, this gives the plants a head start in their competition with would-be invaders. Many prairie grasses can also produce seed very quickly when conditions are optimal. Buffalo grass (*Buchloe dactyloides*), for example, can go to seed in only 30 days. If buffalo grass were an annual, it would take most of the growing season to produce viable seed.

Another adaptation of most high plains grasses is the small size of the above-ground portion of the plant. The high plains is often referred to as the short-grass prairie as opposed to the tall-grass prairie of places east of the 100th meridian. Seldom do the grasses here exceed two feet in height. This limits the nutrients and water required for plant parts that are exposed to harsh circumstances. A corollary to this adaptation is that most of the biomass of the plants is in the root system. The blue grama (*Bouteloua gracilis*) plant is typical of this adaptation. The very large root system supports a relatively small leaf and stem mass above ground level. This high root-to-total-biomass ratio helps the plant in several ways. First, it allows the plant to capture relatively large amounts of moisture and nutrients. The root system occupies a large volume of soil, from which moisture and nutrients can be tapped. Second, this large root system must only support a small above-ground mass, thus making it easier for the stems and leaves to remain viable. Third, many of the grass species of the high plains can go dormant for long periods, up to two or three years, during which the above-ground portion of the plant appears to die, while the root system continues to live and waits for better environmental conditions before commencing new growth.

Fire is the fourth reason why a small above-ground mass makes it easier for high plains grasses to survive. Fire is an important — some would say required — part of grassland ecology. Natural or human-caused fires have swept across the plains over the past several millennia, destroying any woody plant invaders but burning only the leaves and stems of the grasses. Once the competitors are eliminated, the still viable root systems of the grasses can again produce new growth. Many of the world's great grasslands, including those of the Great Plains, are thought to be at least partially pyrogenetic — meaning caused by fire. Without intermittent fire the grasses would soon be invaded by woody shrubs and drought-tolerant trees. Fire allows the grasses to remain dominant. A consequence of these large root systems in grasses is the widely spaced and incomplete ground cover on the grasslands (Figure 7.2); water and nutrients needed for more numerous plants are already being subjugated by the roots of the existing vegetation. Since the beginning of widespread cultivation, fire has not been important for maintaining the grasses. Nonetheless, the grasses remain as a legacy to the pyrogenetic influence.

There are two broad types of grass communities in the grassland: short-grass and mid-grass. Short-grass grows in areas with fine-textured soil. Buffalo grass and blue grama grass are the primary species in this environment. In looser, sandier soils the mid-grasses thrive. Here the dominant grasses are sand drop seed (*Sporobolus cryptandrus*), side-oats grama (*Bouteloua curtipendula*), little bluestem (*Schizachyrium scoparium*), and western wheatgrass (*Agropyron smithii*). These two community types are not totally exclusive of each other; you will find mixes of these grass species as well as some other, less common, grasses and forbs.

Two native nongrass plant species sometimes found in the grasslands are the yucca (*Yucca glauca*) (Figure 7.3) and the cholla or candelabra cactus (*Opuntia imbricata*) (Figure 7.4). These plants are common only where the grasses have been seriously disturbed or where there has been extensive overgrazing. As you drive or hike through the Comanche National Grassland, notice the patterns of dominant cholla and yucca interspersed with areas where vibrant grasses predominate. These patterns give an intriguing glimpse of the history of land use here.

Figure 7.2. Open soil between plants is a good indicator of competition for moisture by vegetation.

Figure 7.3. Although the yucca plant is a native of the region, large patches of the plant mark areas of overgrazing.

The soil. The soil and its development are manifestations of the natural relationships introduced at the beginning of this chapter. Soil reacts to and develops in accordance with the environmental conditions in existence at any given moment. However, the soil changes very slowly; thus only long-range modifications in the climate will alter the way the soil changes and develops. The question that should be asked is, how does the soil character react to given environmental conditions or circumstances?

The ancestral origin for all mineral matter in the soil is the bedrock or other parent material from which the soil evolves. The minerals that exist in the soil are derived from rock through a collection of physical and chemical processes called weathering. Over the years, decades, and centuries this weathering breaks the rock down into smaller and smaller particles and even changes the chemical makeup of the fragments. Weathering is a direct result of the heat and water available, and they are directly dependent on climate. As heat and/or moisture increase, weathering increases, breaking down the parent material into smaller and more chemically active particles. In some cases the parent material begins in a broken-down state, carried from other areas by the wind. This eolian material (see Chapter 11) soon becomes

Figure 7.4. The cholla cactus, like the yucca, can be found on land that is overused and abused.

incorporated into the soil upon which it lands or, if it comes in vast quantities, soon becomes the totality of the soil.

It might seem that the parent material should determine what kind of soil is built; however, as time passes the parent material becomes less and less responsible for soil characteristics, and climate and vegetation become the primary determinants of soil character. Climate is the principal soil-forming agent because it furnishes the energy (heat) and the main chemical (water) for weathering processes to work. The more heat and water available, the more developed and weathered the soil becomes. An extreme example of this occurs in the Amazon River basin of South America where there are very high temperatures and large quantities of water available; the soil there is literally weathered to death. No nutrients remain in the soil, and only the rapid recycling of plant matter provides the soil with any fertility at all.

In the Comanche National Grassland, we have quite a different story. There is heat aplenty in the summer but little available in the winter. Therefore, chemical and physical breakdown of the soil occurs only for short periods of time each year. Even more restrictive than the lack of heat is the lack of moisture. Most of the annual precipitation that the grassland receives comes from severe thunderstorms during the summer months. This rainfall often comes in torrents that seldom soak into the ground, but rather run off and disappear in the bottoms of arroyos and canyons. Without adequate water, soil changes very slowly. The paradox of this situation is that the soils here are very fertile and productive *if* irrigated. The inherent lack of moisture here allows the microscopic nutrients to be held in the soil rather than leached out as in the Amazon.

The dominant grassy vegetation is an additional factor in the soil's high fertility. With the large biomass of grass roots, the prairie has a ready source of organic matter for decomposition after the plant dies. When this organic matter decomposes, it releases significant quantities of nutrients that are then available for use by new growth. The intrinsic fertility of the land is maintained by this recycling of plants. Vegetation also plays a role in the chemical weathering of mineral matter in the soil. Organic acids formed by the plants aid in mineral decomposition and help release more nutrients for vegetation use.

The texture or grain-size distribution of the soil here is characterized by high sand, silt, and clay quantities. The combination of climate, vegetation type, wind, and soil texture makes this region environmentally precarious and vulnerable. If a drought occurs at the same time as the natural vegetation is plowed under and the wind blows strongly, we get the black skies, soil drifts, and devastation of a dust bowl. This set of circumstances came together with a vengeance in the 1930s to produce the decisive events that culminated in the establishment of the Comanche National Grassland.

THE HISTORY OF HUMAN OCCUPATION

Semiarid grasslands around the world have always experienced droughts and wind. Dust storms are recurring events that come with the territory, but the dust storms and environmental destruction of the high plains in the 1930s were extraordinary in their severity and duration. Humans and their actions were directly responsible for the magnitude of devastation.

PREHISTORY THROUGH THE EIGHTEENTH CENTURY

During the many centuries they occupied this region, Native American nomads had only minor impact on the natural balance of climate, soil, and grass. Hunting and gathering, with some farming, were the dominant activities of the Indians who lived and passed through this area. Even when the Indians obtained horses during the sixteenth century, they hunted buffalo and other large game but did not seriously damage the character of the environment. The Indians' main impact was in their use of fire. They used fire to drive game for easy hunting, and accidental fires may have spread across the dry grasslands. These fires did not change the environment, though: the grasses kept their vegetative dominance.

The Native Americans did leave behind some significant and splendid cultural remnants. Many pictographs and petroglyphs can be found in the canyons and deep arroyos of both the Timpas and Carrizo units. These pieces of ancient rock art have been vandalized in recent decades but still elicit feelings for our connection to these ancestral peoples. The U.S. Forest Service is implementing programs to save and possibly restore some of these cultural treasures.

There were some encroachments by Europeans into the area starting in the sixteenth century, mostly in the form of Spanish exploration and occupation. The impacts of these incursions were not greatly felt in the region that is now southeastern Colorado. The one real impact was the introduction of the horse to the local native population. These nomads' lives were changed rapidly and irreversibly by their newfound mobility.

THE NINETEENTH CENTURY

The nineteenth century ushered in the beginning of real change for this region. The area north of the Arkansas River was incorporated into the United States through the Louisiana Purchase of 1803. Explorer Zebulon Pike traversed the region in 1806, and the vestiges of the historic Santa Fe Trail, first traveled in 1819, can still be seen in the northeastern corner of the Timpas Unit. Texas (of which southeastern Colorado was a part) was annexed by the United States in 1845. Hunters, trappers, pioneers, and adventurers found refuge in Bent's Fort located northeast of what is now La Junta. This outpost was built in 1833 and served for many years as a supply depot and army post along the routes from the East to the Southwest. Remnants of wagon ruts from the old Santa Fe Trail can still be seen on the grassland southwest of La Junta. The Forest Service is planning an interpretation site for visitors to see these reminders of past travels.

These incursions by Europeans were only precursors to the real deluge of immigration to come. In 1862 the Homestead Act was passed and the age of cattle began. Large herds of Texas longhorns moved slowly northward into this seemingly endless grassland. By 1876 cattle and the cowboy were king. The real harbinger of things to come, however, arrived in 1880 with the introduction of barbed wire and the accompanying farmer who could now cut off the open grazing of cattle on his or her property.

Because of the stored moisture in the soil and the fact that these years were relatively wet, crops were grown with success and more and more farmers arrived. Almost all cultivation that occurred in what is now the Comanche National Grassland took place in the Carrizo Unit. Average precipitation here is almost 15 inches per year — substantially more than in the Timpas Unit. By the late 1880s there were more than 6,000 people in Baca County (compared to less than 5,500 living there today). The 1890s, however, brought drought conditions and massive farm failures. In 1898 Baca County had only 700 people, and ranching was once again dominant over farming.

THE TWENTIETH CENTURY

The cycle of dry and wet periods continued, and the early twentieth century brought more rain and considerably more homesteaders back to the region. The period from 1903 to 1926 had the highest number of homesteads ever in this part of Colorado. Economics and weather combined to promote more and more "sod busting." High prices during World War I and adequate rains made for profitable agriculture. These good times were but a respite in the natural cycle. The soil's nutrients were being depleted, and the rains began to wane.

The market crash of 1929 brought plunging prices for farm commodities; farmers again started to go bankrupt. The dismal economy was only a prelude to more profound and long-term problems. In 1931 the rains ceased. This was the beginning of a long and desperate battle between the natural cycle of drought and the errant plowing of land not suitable for prolonged cultivation. Land and lives were critically altered. For many the realization that crops and prairie were incompatible was inescapable.

In 1933 the Soil Erosion Service of the U.S. Department of Agriculture began its program to reclaim the land and reduce the dependence of the area on farm income. The Federal Land Purchase Act of 1935 began the long and expensive acquisition of land from bankrupt or near-bankrupt farmers. The Roosevelt administration started relief efforts by the Work Projects Administration (WPA) and the Civilian Conservation Corps (CCC). Not only did these programs develop soil erosion mitigation projects, but they also provided needed jobs for the populace. Water development, erosion control, bridge construction, and fencing projects were undertaken to rescue the lives and the land. World War II ended these employment programs but did not end the federal government's involvement in restoring the depleted land.

The U.S. Forest Service began administering the recovery of the area in 1954, and the Comanche National Grassland was created in 1960. The combined efforts of the U.S. Forest Service and the Soil Conservation Service have brought the grasslands back to life. There are now controls on grazing (by permit only) and a complete ban on cultivation on the federally owned land. The patchwork quilt of private/public land evident on the Comanche National Grassland resource map (available in bookstores and at USFS offices) is also visible on the ground. But even the private land here is under more nurturing management. There seems to be an attitude of long-term commitment to conservation and wiser use of the land. At least in this corner of the high plains, overgrazing has been curtailed and cultivation has been dramatically reduced. Resource management and sustained use are now the norm rather than the exception.

MORE THAN JUST GRASS

When you visit the Comanche National Grassland, you will soon realize that, even though the grasslands are the central focus of the area, there is much more than just grass to see. This country is a complex blend of rolling plains and deeply incised canyons and arroyos; it is also home to substantial populations of unique fauna, and a place for hiking, camping, and birding.

THE CANYONS

When you first see the Purgatoire River canyon, it comes as a real shock that such a deep and spectacular landform could exist in this land of seemingly endless plains. This and other canyons are cut into the horizontally layered sedimentary rocks visible in the canyon walls. The rocks, mostly limestones, shales, and some sandstones, were laid down during the Jurassic and Cretaceous periods some 100 to 200 million years ago and have been exposed here through the slow and relentless erosion of running water. The Purgatoire Canyon is not within the current boundaries of the Comanche National Grassland but rather runs between the Timpas and Carrizo units of the grassland like a crack in a tabletop. The river begins in the high elevations of the Sangre de Cristo Mountains and flows from the southwest to the northeast. You can gain access to this canyon at dozens of places: for example, along Highway 109 in Higbee, southwest of Higbee at Cable Crossing, or south of La Junta along Rourke Road and via Minnie Canyon Road to Rock Crossing. The U.S. Forest Service resource map will be very useful for finding these access points and other areas of interest.

Three smaller canyons deserve special mention. The first and smallest is Vogel Canyon in the Timpas Unit, located 13 miles south of La Junta. The Forest Service is developing recreation facilities including parking and picnic areas here. The canyon is a wonderful place to hike and see the rock art of the early Indian occupants (Figure 7.5). This lovely place also shelters ruins of settler cabins and lush, albeit small, marsh areas that provide food and cover for fauna of the region.

The second canyon is in the Carrizo Unit and is larger and more impressive than Vogel Canyon. Picture Canyon is located about 10 miles west-southwest of Campo. While Vogel Canyon is a feeder to the Purgatoire River, Picture Canyon drains away from the Purgatoire and into the Cimarron River of the panhandle of Oklahoma. Picture Canyon and its fine examples of rock art were rediscovered in the early 1900s. The Forest

Figure 7.5. Vogel Canyon, an unexpected, dramatic, and pleasant break in the seemingly desolate prairie landscape.

Service has a protection plan in progress to help preserve and maintain the art and the natural resources here. They are developing a 22-mile trail system for hiking and camping in the canyon.

The third canyon, Picket Wire Canyon (a part of the Purgatoire River canyon), has just been added to the grassland. This large (17,600-acre) part of the U.S. Army Piñon Canyon maneuver area has now been taken under U.S. Forest Service control. Picket Wire Canyon is located southwest of and adjacent to the Timpas Unit and will be included on the next Comanche National Grassland resource map. Picket Wire Canyon may be the most exciting natural history location in all of the grassland. Current faunal residents include white-tailed deer (*Odocoileus virginianus*), mule deer (*O. hemionus*), wild turkey (*Meleagris gallopavo*), bighorn sheep (*Ovis canadensis*), and the elusive and diminutive swift fox (*Vulpes velox*). But the most fascinating aspect of Picket Wire Canyon may be the fossilized dinosaur tracks found here in the lithified sediments. This is the longest trail of fossilized dinosaur tracks known in the world. Here you will find hundreds of tracks from bipedal, herbivorous, three-toed orthopods and quadrupedal, five-toed sauropods. These giants wandered along the freshwater lake that existed here in the Upper Jurassic. By the orientation of the trails, you can even envision the ancient shoreline of almost 135 million years ago. Obviously, special precautions and management practices will be needed before visits become too numerous.

The canyons and bluffs of these areas are mostly covered by one-seed juniper (*Juniperus monosperma*) with some piñon pine (*Pinus edulis*) and occasional plains cottonwoods (*Populus sargentii*). The understory consists of grasses, yucca, and, in some cases, cholla. The dark green of the piñon-juniper woodland outlines the tops of the canyon walls and breaks up the sameness of the grasslands when viewed from afar.

THE FAUNA

It must have been one of nature's most awesome sights to see thousands upon thousands of bison (buffalo) moving as one across the virgin prairies of North America. Although this place in southeastern Colorado no longer has buffalo, there is a small section of virgin prairie remaining about three miles south of Campo where Highway 287 jogs to the southeast. A marker may soon be erected here by the Forest Service to indicate this prairie remnant. This piece of land has been selected as a Research-Natural area for the preservation and study of the relic shortgrass prairie.

The buffalo may be gone, but there are many other interesting animal species here. Pronghorn (*Antilocapra americana*), not a true antelope, are making a comeback after being greatly reduced by hunting and habitat loss. You can now spot small herds in most areas of the grassland. In the more rugged places among the canyons, you may see signs of mountain lion (*Felis concolor*). These wary and wily animals usually will not show themselves to humans, but their large tracks can be followed in snow, mud, or sandy creek bottoms. Smaller mammals also abound, and the Colorado Division of Wildlife has installed many "wildlife guzzlers" around the grassland where fauna will naturally congregate. The guzzlers collect and protect water for use by small mammals and birds.

The Comanche National Grassland has about 275 different species of birds that live in or migrate through the region. These include the game species scaled quail (*Callipepla squamata*) and ring-neck pheasant (*Phasianus colchicus*). Raptors are numerous and include the prairie falcon (*Falco mexicanus*) and resident golden eagles (*Aquila chrysaetos*). Bald eagles (*Haliaeetus leucocephalus*) can be seen along water courses, especially the Arkansas River north of the grassland, as they migrate through the area.

The most celebrated bird of the region is the lesser prairie chicken (*Tympanuchus palliodicinctus*). A threatened species in Colorado, the lesser prairie chicken is making a comeback as a result of conservation efforts here and elsewhere in the state. One of the world's best viewing areas for the unforgettable courtship rite of the lesser prairie chicken is in the Comanche National Grassland. There is a viewing blind built by the Forest Service and the Division of Wildlife where the male's ritual can be observed. The lek, or dancing ground, is usually on a rise or slight hilltop. The observation blind overlooks a large lek and is located about 12 miles east-southeast of Campo; exact directions are provided on a brochure available at Forest Service offices. Because the dance of the male lesser prairie chicken and the observation blind are so popular, you need to make reservations for using the blind. From early March through the end of May is the best time to observe this display of avian affection.

FINAL THOUGHTS

The soil is an apt vehicle to use in describing the complex and intricate relationships of this environment; the grassland ecosystem is dependent upon and a contributor to the soil. Soil also can be used as an analogy for the restoration of the prairie. The U.S. Forest Service has managed the restoration of the Comanche National Grassland to a healthier vegetation cover and has overseen the improvement of its grazing, recreational, and historical resources. The soil is also being rebuilt; new soil is slowly made from parent material and incorporates new organic matter from decaying plants. The process is slow, and the cycles of nutrient reuse, rain and drought, good year and bad, can only be thought of in terms of centuries. Without intervention by the Forest Service or some other organization, the prairie soils would soon have reached a point of no return; with it we are gradually producing a viable ecosystem.

This is not to imply that we will ever reestablish a truly natural grassland ecosystem. The natural prairie's demise started with the overuse of fire centuries ago but was finalized by the plow and the overgrazing of the last century or so. We will never regain the old ecosystem; it is gone forever. But we have shown here in the Comanche National Grassland that we can live within constraints imposed by natural laws.

One other thing needs to be restated: nature is adaptable and prolific and astounding in almost all environments. The dry, windy, inhospitable plains still host a myriad of flora and fauna that are seemingly out of place. Huge herds of buffalo lived and roamed for centuries in balance with this fragile environment. A little spring rain can turn a brown and desolate expanse into a lush, green pasture. Deep canyons and soft, rolling prairies coexist in an area where the horizon looks infinitely far away. The high plains in general and the Comanche National Grassland in particular are places of diversity, beauty, fecundity, and surprise.

ADDITIONAL READINGS

Caughey, B., and D. Winstanley, 1989. *The Colorado Guide — Landscapes, Cityscapes, Escapes,* Fulcrum, Inc., Golden, Colo.

Costello, D. F., 1969. *The Prairie World,* University of Minnesota Press, Minneapolis, Minn.

Curry-Lindahl, K., 1981. *Wildlife of the Prairies and Plains,* Harry N. Abrams, Inc., Publishers, New York, N.Y.

Friedman, P. D., 1988. *Valley of the Lost Souls — A History of the Piñon Canyon Region of Southeastern Colorado,* Colorado Historical Society, Denver, Colo.

Kent, H. C., and K. W. Porter, eds., 1980. *Colorado Geology,* Rocky Mountain Association of Geologists, Denver, Colo.

Laurion, T. R., 1988. "Underdog," *Natural History* 97 (9), pp. 66–70.

Lockley, M. G., 1984. "Dinosaur Tracking," *Science Teacher* 51 (1), pp. 18–24.

Lockley, M. G., K. J. Houck, and N. K. Prince, 1986. "North America's Largest Dinosaur Trackway Site: Implications for Morrison Formation Paleoecology," *Geological Society of America Bulletin* 97, pp. 1163–1176.

Pearl, R. M., 1969. *Exploring Rocks, Minerals, Fossils in Colorado,* Swallow Press, Chicago, Ill.

Prince, N. K., 1983. "Late Jurassic Dinosaur Tracks from SE Colorado," *Colorado University at Denver Geology Department Magazine* 2, pp. 15–19.

Scott, G. R., 1968. *Geologic and Structure Contour Map of the La Junta Quadrangle, Colorado and Kansas,* U.S. Geological Survey Miscellaneous Geological Investigations Map I-560.

U.S. Forest Service, 1969. *Colorado National Grassland (Map),* U.S. Department of Agriculture, Denver, Colo.

Wright, H. A., and A. W. Bailey, 1982. *Fire Ecology — United States and Canada,* John Wiley & Sons, New York, N.Y.

8

TAMARACK RANCH

An old saw says that the Platte River of Colorado and Nebraska is "a mile wide and an inch deep — too thin to plow and too thick to drink." As with most such sayings, there is some hyperbole and some truth involved. The Tamarack Ranch State Wildlife Area near Crook in the far northeastern corner of Colorado is an area that typifies the truth in the saying. Here the South Platte River is broken into numerous channels and branches that spread out over a width of up to a half-mile. The stream here carries so much sediment and debris that it looks more like a collection of wet, slow-moving sandbars than one of Colorado's major rivers.

But there is much more to this river and its valley than clever sayings. If you were to view this place from the vantage point of an airplane, the river and its environment would more resemble a ribbon of life than a river of sand. Even from Interstate 76 just to the south of the ranch, the river looks like a verdant and life-sustaining linear oasis. In this kind of lowland riparian ecosystem more fauna flourish than anywhere else in the state. It is a place where western species of plant and animal interfinger with eastern species slowly migrating westward along the bottomlands of the riverine environment. Life here has variety, fecundity, beauty, and intensity. At certain times of the year the cacophony of bird sounds is so intense that you can barely hear someone near you speak. This life depends on the river and the life-giving water it supplies. To understand this environment, you must first understand the uniqueness and complexity of the river itself. The Platte is exceptional, but only in that it is an extreme example of what can happen to water, geology, climate, and landforms under certain conditions.

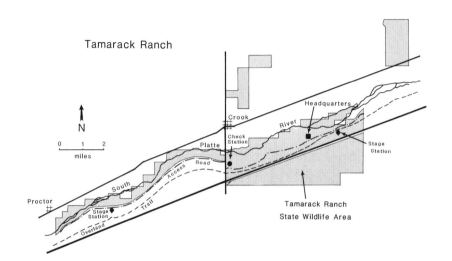

Tamarack Ranch

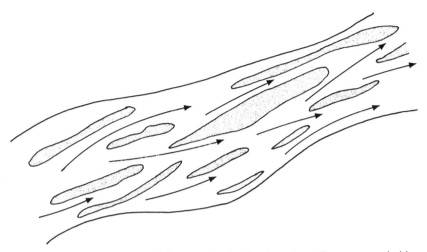

Figure 8.1. Braided streams exhibiting multiple islands and sandbars surrounded by flowing water and complex channels.

THE RIVER

Geomorphologists — earth scientists who study the shapes and processes of landforms — call rivers like the South Platte "braided" rivers. From above, such streams give the appearance of braids of hair intertwining randomly (Figure 8.1). Rivers take on this form from a unique combination of factors not seen in most places.

Many people from other parts of the country, upon seeing the South Platte for the first time, are amazed at the strangely flattened river valley. They are used to streams and rivers with a single channel carrying relatively steady flows throughout the year. Major rivers in the East such as the Ohio, the Hudson, the Tennessee, and the Mississippi are all single-channel rivers with considerable flows all year long. There are recurring floods and intermittent droughts, but by and large the streams run copiously year round.

The Platte and other such streams in the West have very different controls than these more "normal" rivers. The story of the South Platte here at Tamarack Ranch, and for most of its length, is complex and intricate but also intriguing and revealing. The river valley here is underlain by Cretaceous period sedimentary rocks such as the Pierre shale (see Chapter 6, "Garden of the Gods"), but you seldom see any rock because the entire area is covered by extensive sandhills developed during and since the last glacial advances in the mountains to the west. Glaciers added large amounts of sand and other mineral debris to the rivers that flowed from the mountains during the ice melt. These rivers spread and deposited the sand over large regions of eastern Colorado. Subsequent winds reworked the sand and created large dunal areas. The Tamarack Ranch area is located on some of these old dune formations that have since been stabilized by vegetation. These relic sands are the source of much of the sedimentary load now carried by the South Platte River.

The wide, braided nature of the South Platte depends upon these old sediment sources and on the present-day characteristics of the river and its drainage basin. Most of the water in the river comes from the mountains of central Colorado. Spring snowmelt concentrates the water flow so that the river has large discharges during late spring and early summer. The large amounts of water combined with the steep slopes of the mountains make for high-energy flow conditions capable of eroding and carrying large quantities of material, especially sand. As long as the river maintains this high-energy character, the sediments continue to be carried by the water. When slope gradients decline and flows wane, the water can no longer hold the large load of mineral detritus, and deposition of this material occurs all along the valley. Year after year these deposits are added to the valley channel.

From late summer into autumn and winter, the flows of the river steadily diminish to the point of being almost nonexistent. Some experts even believe that before humans altered the river flow regime, the discharge of the South Platte ceased altogether during several months of the year. The reduced flow of water must still negotiate the buildup of debris left by the river over the eons. Since it does not have the force to maintain a main channel, the water flows in an almost deranged pattern, creating the braided pattern of the river.

The elements necessary to the formation of a braided stream are extreme seasonality of water discharge, irregular flows, and high sediment content. The South Platte River at Tamarack Ranch certainly meets these requirements. Ephemeral sandbars and semipermanent sand islands develop here as the river goes through its annual cycles (Figure 8.2). However, the channel patterns of any given moment can be changed in an instant with a single large flood.

Figure 8.2. Sandbars and shallow water, trademarks of this stretch of the South Platte.

THE FLOODS

The water from large snowmelts in the mountains can cause very high flow rates in the river during May and June. When these large snowmelts combine with severe thunderstorms over the plains, devastating floods can result. Flow rates of the South Platte just upstream of Tamarack Ranch have been recorded for the past 57 years. The flow at this location has averaged about 500 cubic feet per second (cfs) (500 cubic feet of water passes a given point on the river each second). Floods occur often on the South Platte and usually range from approximately 1,000 cfs up to 20,000 cfs. These almost yearly floods rework the sediments of the channel, form new sandbars, and even rearrange the islands in the channel. Later in the chapter we also will see how these floods profoundly affect the vegetation of the valley.

One flood in the past 57 years stands out as a reminder of the remarkable power of nature. On June 6, 1965, the entire South Platte River valley from the base of the mountains near Denver to the Nebraska state line was inundated by a monumental flow of water. More than 123,000 cfs moved past the Tamarack Ranch area. This is more than six times the maximum flow recorded for any other year during the period of record. Denver was devastated by the flood — destruction and death were the results. Flooding occurred along the entire valley where channels were redesigned by the sheer force of the water. The magnitude of this flow can be appreciated when you realize that the average low flow during the late summer is 18.5 cfs and the lowest flow recorded during these 57 years is 1.3 cfs. The only constant in this river system is inconsistency, and this inconsistency is what cannot be tolerated by people wanting to exploit the water resources of the South Platte.

THE IRRIGATION

The extensive human use of water from the South Platte River basin began as early as 1838, when Antoine Janis began taking water from the Cache la Poudre River for irrigation of crops. This was the beginning of a massive alteration of the natural river system of the South Platte.

The South Platte River drains a large area of Colorado, at least 24,270 square miles. The river is almost 450 miles long and traverses a complex of landscapes with varying climates and vegetation regimes. The climate here at Tamarack Ranch is cold in winter, very hot in summer, and averages only 16 inches of precipitation per year — not enough to maintain any kind of permanent flow in the river. Although inconsistent flows in the river are the norm, they were even more extreme before human influences produced large alterations in the system. After the spring runoff there was often not enough water added to the river to keep it flowing; many summer days saw no water in the river at all. In fact, there was so little water available that vegetation was sparse along certain sections of the river. Grazing buffalo and prairie fires kept treed vegetation from encroaching into the bottomland, and there was not enough moisture to support the verdant vegetation now seen. In the summer of 1845, John C. Fremont wrote that the river was "merely a succession of sandbars, among which the channel was divided into rivulets a few inches deep" (Fremont 1845, p. 110).

All of this changed with the advent of irrigation in the drainage basin of the South Platte. Because of low summer flows, more water was desired by humans than was available during the summer growing season. Farmers and ranchers along the South Platte River wanted a more permanent and dependable flow of water for crops and stock. The only practical way to accomplish this was to create a system of reservoirs along the South Platte and its tributaries that would capture and save water from the high flow times and release it during low flow periods. Unintentionally, this also led to increases in groundwater due to leaks in dams, reservoirs, and irrigation

Figure 8.3. Bottomland, one of the most diverse and prolific environments in all of Colorado.

canals. More groundwater adds to river flows because springs fed by this increased underground water supply the river throughout the year.

The progressive and aggressive alteration of the South Platte produced two major and unexpected changes that are very evident today. The first obvious change is the dense stands of vegetation growing along the bottomlands of the river (Figure 8.3). This vegetation is in stark contrast to the sandsage community of plants on the hills above and paralleling the river. The prairie cottonwoods, peachleaf willows, green ash, and tamarisk of the river bottom appear lush and verdant in comparison to the sparse and dried grasses and blue-green tints of the sage on the old sand dunes above.

The changes in the vegetational characteristics of the riverine environment in turn changed the character of the river channel. Deep roots of trees and shrubs stabilized sand islands within the river channel. Where the frequent floods once shifted the sands dramatically, they now merely alter the edges of the main sand islands. Only very large floods such as the one that occurred in 1965 can significantly affect the islands. This stabilized land helps promote more plant growth in a continuing cycle.

Two of the best places on the Tamarack Ranch to witness the evidence of these environmental changes are on the main bridge that crosses the river on Highway 55, and near Area 8 south of the highway along the dirt service

Figure 8.4. Shifting sands and shallow channels south of Highway 55.

road where you can walk down to the river. Here you can get a feel for the riverine environment with its massive cottonwoods and the shallow, sandy river flowing slowly at your feet (Figure 8.4).

The Tamarack Ranch State Wildlife Area and the South Platte River together represent an excellent example of the interconnectedness of natural systems. When one thing is changed in a system, there are always accompanying changes that may or may not be anticipated. You cannot do just one thing to a natural system — one thing imperatively leads to others. Consider, for example, the chain of events set off when water is stored behind a dam. This water is released at appropriate times on the human calendar. Some of this water changes underground water regimes and leads to a more consistent river flow regime. These changes alter the vegetation environments by ensuring some water availability in summer months. The vegetation changes alter the geomorphic aspects of the sandbars and islands in the river. All of these changes affect faunal migrations and other human uses such as fishing and hunting. Whether the changes are good, bad, or a combination of each, they do occur. As you hike around the Tamarack Ranch and the other areas discussed in the book, keep these thoughts on change in mind.

THE ECOSYSTEMS

We have talked briefly about the vegetational environment of the Tamarack Ranch State Wildlife Area. Tamarack Ranch is an exceptional place to discuss the juxtaposition of two vastly different vegetation systems and the reasons for their coexistence. The Colorado Division of Wildlife and the Colorado Natural Areas Program have combined efforts to sustain and improve these two ecosystems and have studied both of these areas in terms of vegetation succession and animal habitat. Each ecosystem is unique and intriguing.

THE LOWLAND RIPARIAN ECOSYSTEM

The most obvious characteristic of this ecosystem is the profusion of large, deciduous trees along the river. Plains cottonwoods (*Populus sargentii*) make up the bulk of the treed vegetation in the valley bottom. These cottonwoods were a rare sight in the early 1800s. The combination of drastic seasonal changes in water levels of the river, intense browsing of cottonwoods by buffalo (*Bison bison*), and frequent wildfires kept the South Platte valley relatively clear of these large trees. When the buffalo herds were decimated, the river "tamed," and the fires controlled, the cottonwoods spread rapidly. They were the dominant vegetation by the early 1900s and hit their peak spread in the 1940s and 1950s.

More recently, however, the plains cottonwoods have begun to decline as a species in river bottoms throughout the river systems of the West. They have decreased 9 to 10 percent along the South Platte River and even more in other river systems; the Arkansas River to the south has seen a decline of up to 30 percent. Although the cottonwoods are still the dominant overstory vegetation in most of the riparian regions along the South Platte, the river bottom has become a corridor for biotic invasion from the east. Tamarisk (*Tamarix* spp.) and several species of willow (*Salix* spp.) are replacing many of the cottonwoods that are dying off without regeneration. The tamarisk is especially potent as a successor because it is mildly allopathic or toxic to the cottonwood. It is a case of natural chemical warfare by the tamarisk that reduces the competition from other species and allows the tamarisk to proceed toward a takeover.

Green ash (*Fraxinus pennsylvanica*), however, is an even more aggressive interloper (Figure 8.5). It is suspected by many an ecologist of the riparian regions of the West that this fundamentally eastern species could

Figure 8.5. Green ash, one of the many exotic plants invading the river valley.

readily become the new dominant species along the South Platte in the coming decades. The green ash seems designed specifically for this role. It is tolerant of poor, alkaline soils and shade; is not readily killed nor even much affected by flood damage; and is not highly susceptible to livestock browsing.

The high runoff years along the South Platte River of 1982 to 1983 and 1983 to 1984 stimulated cottonwood regeneration. Apparently the reworking of sediments promotes cottonwood reproduction and growth. But subsequent dry years have caused the newly sprouted cottonwoods to literally dry up and die. The invaders still have an edge and will, most likely, continue in their replacement of the plains cottonwood as the dominant species.

Understory vegetation along the bottomlands is varied and dense. Willows make up a large portion of this growth with the peachleaved willow (*S. amygdaloides*) being the most prominent. There are also the sandbar willow (*S. interior*), coyote willow (*S. exigua*), and small stands of diamond willow (*S. lutea*). You will also find several species of brome (*Bromus* spp.), the Virginia creeper (*Parthenocissus quinquefolia*), poison ivy (*Toxicodendron rydbergii*), wild rose (*Rosa woodsii*), western snowberry (*Symphorocarpus occidentalis*), wax currant (*Ribes aureum*), and mulberry bushes (*Morus* spp.). Other treed vegetation, including more eastern invaders, are the American elm (*Ulmus americana*), the box-elder (*Acer negundo*), and the eastern red cedar (*Juniperus virginiana*) in some of the drier locations.

THE FAUNA

This profusion of vegetation spawns a very large and diverse population of animals. In terms of both diversity and density of animals, riparian areas of Colorado are the most prolific of any ecosystem in the state. Along the riparian regions of the state as a whole, at least 283 species of vertebrates have been identified. Along the South Platte River, 129 bird species, 28 mammals, and 20 amphibian/reptile species have been identified. This is far more than any other environment in the state and is even more dramatic since riparian ecosystems make up only 0.2 percent of the land area of Colorado. Animal residents and migrants alike are drawn to this fecund vegetational oasis in the otherwise dry expanses of eastern Colorado.

The Tamarack Ranch itself is a birders' paradise. Great blue herons (*Ardea herodias*), the endangered sandhill crane (*Grus canadensis*), green herons (*Butorides striatus*), and numerous waterfowl such as the Canada goose (*Branta canadensis*), snow goose (*Chen caerulescens*), northern pintail duck (*Anas acuta*), and the mallard (*A. platyrhynchos*) all frequent the quiet back waters of the wildlife area. There are also wild turkey (*Meleagris gallopavo*) and a wide variety of hawks. The endangered bald eagle (*Haliaeetus leucocephalus*) and golden eagle (*Aquila chrysaetos*) are commonly found here during winter months. Dozens of perching and song birds frequent the area during all seasons of the year.

Faunal invasions have also come from the east, in the form of significant herds of white-tailed deer (*Odocoileus virginianus*), the opossum (*Didelphis virginiana*), and the red-headed woodpecker (*Melanerpes erythrocephalus*). Other mammals of the area include the muskrat (*Ondatra zibethicus*), a few beaver (*Castor canadensis*), striped skunks (*Mephitis mephitis*), raccoons (*Procyon lotor*), and coyotes (*Canis latrans*). If you can go to only one place to see animal life in Colorado, go to the South Platte River valley in general and the Tamarack Ranch State Wildlife Area in particular. The fecundity and vibrancy of this ecosystem are amazing, especially juxtaposed with the plains grassland ecosystem.

THE PLAINS GRASSLAND (SAND SAGEBRUSH)

In the eastern half of the Tamarack Ranch State Wildlife Area, south of the dirt access road, lies a second significant ecosystem. This area of dry sand hills covered with relatively sparse vegetation stands in dramatic contrast to the riparian zone above (Figure 8.6). Here the approximately 16 inches of precipitation each year is the only moisture available. Much of it evaporates, or if it is in the form of snow, sublimates, or runs off down the fairly steep slopes of the hills. There is no supplemental water from mountain snows as we see in the river bottomlands. This area is typical prairie landscape, dominated by grasses, small forbs, and low, woody sage.

In 1978 work began here to improve the habitat potential of the Tamarack Ranch sandhill zone by eliminating cattle grazing. Reseeding of warm-season native grasses began in the early 1980s with moderate success. It was decided that more drastic measures should be taken, and in 1984 prescribed burns were begun. These burns were an experiment since little research had been done previously on the potential of burns to improve rangeland in eastern Colorado. There was some success; this technique did improve blue grama (*Bouteloua gracilis*) and prairie sandreed (*Calamovilfa longifolia*) growth.

Figure 8.6. Sandhills lie in stark contrast to the adjacent bottomland.

These habitat improvement efforts were undertaken to enhance the area for reintroduction of the greater prairie chicken (*Tympanuchus cupido*). In 1984 36 greater prairie chickens were reintroduced to these sandhills. An additional 40 were brought in during 1985, and 23 more were added in 1990. These endangered birds, once numerous in several of Colorado's northeastern counties, had declined rapidly due to loss of native prairie caused by overgrazing and the change of grasslands to croplands during the first half of this century.

This larger cousin of the lesser prairie chicken (*T. pallidicinctus*) discussed in Chapter 7 has very similar characteristics to its smaller relation. The leks, or mating areas, are very similar, and the elaborate dance and posturing of the male during courtship is comparable. The greater prairie chicken is the more threatened species of the two, and its survival, even here at the Tamarack Ranch, is not a certainty. At least one-third of the greater prairie chickens introduced have already been lost through predation.

Ironically, the greater prairie chicken faces competition from another endangered species, the plains sharp-tailed grouse (*T. phasianellus*). This bird is a direct competitor for habitat with the greater prairie chicken and is so closely related that there have been sightings of hybrid birds coming from the mating of the two species. The loss of two leks of the greater prairie chicken by various causes and the establishment of a third by the hybrids is an interesting and puzzling twist to the reintroduction efforts.

The locals call this part of the Tamarack Ranch State Wildlife Area the sand sage area because the vegetation of these sandhills is not restricted to blue grama and prairie sandreed. The dominant, or at least co-dominant, species is the sand sagebrush (*Artemisia filifolia*), also commonly known as silvery wormwood (Figure 8.7). This is a small, woody shrub that gives a bluish-gray tint to the hillsides and vistas. Significant stands of needle-and-thread grass (*Stipa comata*) and sand dropseed (*Sporbolus cryptandrus*) are also found here. As in most grassland areas, several other species of grasses and small forbs can also be seen here.

FINAL THOUGHTS

THE OVERLAND TRAIL

In the 1850s a massive migration of people moved westward through the Great Plains and the mountain regions of the West. Many routes were pioneered for these treks, such as the Santa Fe and Oregon trails. The Overland Trail followed the North Platte and Sweetwater rivers to South Pass in Wyoming. Between 1858 and 1859 a spur of this trail was begun that followed the South Platte River to the Front Range foothills near the present site of Denver. The impetus for the South Platte spur of the Overland Trail was the "Pikes Peak or Bust" gold rush that in reality was a rush to Cherry Creek and eventually to Clear Creek west of Denver, where the Central City gold strikes were made. Part of this trail goes through the Tamarack Ranch State Wildlife Area, paralleling the dirt access road. The Lillian Springs stage station, established in 1859, is marked by a rock monument located just south of Area 18 in the western half of the ranch. Spring Hill stage station, established in 1860, is marked by a similar monument just south of the road near Area 15 of the eastern half of the ranch. Little is left of the trail itself — the sand foundation of any trail here is soon reworked by wind and water, eliminating the impressions of wagon wheels and footsteps.

Figure 8.7. Sand sagebrush dominates the hills above the river bottom.

THE HUNTING SITUATION

The Tamarack Ranch State Wildlife Area includes over 10,600 acres of prime habitat for a myriad of fauna. From the lush bottomlands where waterfowl and small mammals abound to the sand hills where prairie chicken and grouse intermingle, this large area is devoted to animal production and proliferation. The land was purchased by the State of Colorado between 1949 and 1964 for the purpose of providing increased game for hunting. The positive side of this is that the area is a verdant and prolific fauna factory. Without the development of the area by the Colorado Division of Wildlife for hunting, the place would not exist in its present form or with the density and diversity of life that exists here. Another positive is that many nongame species are also encouraged. Songbirds abound, for example, in this place where east meets west and ranges overlap. The Division of Wildlife even plants crops meant solely for feed for the wildlife. Milo, corn, millet, sorghum, barley, oat, and wheat fields are very visible along the access road in the eastern half of the wildlife area.

The negative side is that the area is principally designed for hunting, with various seasons occurring throughout the year. This means that nonhunting naturalists must take care when visiting the ranch. The numbered areas along the dirt access road are waterfowl hunting areas assigned to hunters to keep them spread out. Other hunting, such as deer hunting, takes place in and around the wildlife area where hunters are not confined to the assigned spots. Please, if you are going to visit the Tamarack Ranch State Wildlife Area, check the hunting season schedule at your local Division of Wildlife office.

ADDITIONAL READINGS

Beidleman, R. G., 1978. "The Cottonwood-Willow Riparian Ecosystem as a Vertebrate Habitat, With Particular Reference to Birds." In *Lowland River and Stream Habitat in Colorado: A Symposium,* Colorado Division of Wildlife, Denver, Colo.

Chronic, H., 1980. *Roadside Geology of Colorado,* Mountain Press Publishing Co., Missoula, Mont.

Colorado Division of Wildlife, 1989. *Wildlife in Danger,* Department of Natural Resources, Denver, Colo.

Eschner, T. R., R. F. Hadley, and K. D. Crowley, 1983. *Hydrologic and Morphologic Changes in Channels of the Platte River Basin in Colorado, Wyoming, and Nebraska: A Historical Perspective,* USGS Professional Paper 1277-A, U.S. Government Printing Office, Washington, D.C.

Fremont, John C., 1845. *Report of the Exploring Expedition to the Rocky Mountains,* Gales and Seaton, Washington, D.C.

Griffiths, M., and L. Rubright, 1983. *Colorado,* Westview Press, Boulder, Colo.

Hall, T., and A. Yasky, *Birds of the South Platte Wildlife Area,* Colorado Division of Wildlife, Denver, Colo.

Johnsgard, P. A., 1984. *The Platte: Channels in Time,* University of Nebraska Press, Lincoln, Nebr.

Lindauer, I. E., 1983. "A Comparison of the Plant Communities of the South Platte and Arkansas River Drainages in Eastern Colorado," *Southwest Naturalist* 28, pp. 249–259.

McGreager, R. L., 1986. *Flora of the Great Plains,* University of Kansas Press, Lawrence, Kans.

Monahan, D., 1985. *Destination, Denver City: The South Platte Trail,* Swallow Press, Athens, Ohio.

Propst, N. B., 1979. *Forgotten People: A History of the South Platte Trail,* Pruett Publishing Co., Boulder, Colo.

Reisner, M., 1986. *Cadillac Desert — The American West and Its Disappearing Water,* Penguin Books, New York, N.Y.

Scott, T. G., and C. H. Wasser, 1980. *Checklist of North American Plants for Wildlife Biologists,* The Wildlife Society, Washington, D.C.

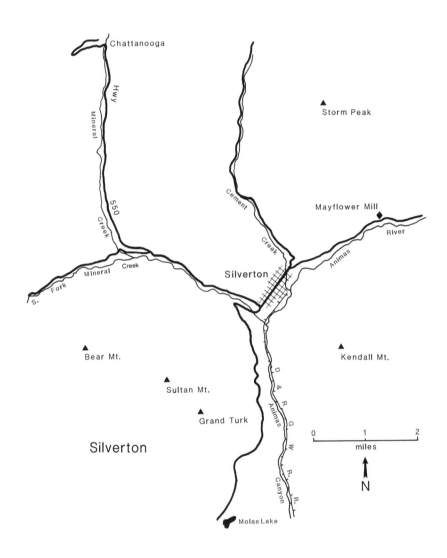

Chattanooga

Hwy

Mineral

550

Creek

S. Fork

Mineral   Creek

Storm Peak

Cement

Creek

Mayflower Mill

River

Animas

Silverton

Bear Mt.

Kendall Mt.

Sultan Mt.

Grand Turk

Silverton

D & R G W R. R.

Animas

Canyon

0   1   2

miles

N

Molas Lake

9

SILVERTON

The San Juan Mountains of southwestern Colorado have often been referred to as the "Alps of America" because of their steep sides and glacially scoured, U-shaped valleys (Figure 9.1). The San Juans rival any mountains in the world for scenic grandeur, but the title is somewhat inappropriate for a number of reasons. The Alps have been settled for millennia, the San Juans for barely a hundred years; the Alps are densely populated, the San Juans thinly peopled (entire counties in the San Juans have fewer than 1,000 people); the Alps contain verdant meadows and productive farmlands, San Juan County no farmland whatever; mining is not a large part of the economy in the Alps, but it has been and continues to be central to the economy of the San Juans, with tourism growing fast only in the last decade or so. The San Juan Mountains of Colorado are unlike the Alps or any other mountain range. This is what makes them a special place to visit and experience.

If any single place can represent the sum of the San Juan Mountain region, it is surely the area in and around the town of Silverton where you can get an almost complete perspective of the region over time. The geologic timescale is characterized here by Precambrian metamorphic rocks, sedimentary layers of the Paleozoic and Mesozoic, massive Tertiary volcanic eruptions, and extensive Pleistocene glaciation. Human time is characterized by Indian dominion, land-usurping treaties, prospecting and mining exploitation, engineering marvels, and a real Old West aura.

The San Juans are a spectacular mountain system where fourteen peaks rise higher than 14,000 feet. The summers are short and cool, the winters

Figure 9.1. Steep valley walls and alpine character typical of the Mineral Creek valley landscape.

long and severe. Because the San Juans are the first major mountain range east of the plateau region of Utah and Arizona, moist winds from the Pacific easily reach them. This situation produces copious snowfalls in winter and infrequent, but heavy, thunderstorms in summer. As much as 43 feet of snow falls in the Silverton area during a winter. The harsh climate, high mountains, and mineral wealth of the region combine to make this a lucrative but Spartan mining district.

THE GEOLOGY

Although the San Juan Mountains are by far the largest agglomeration of volcanic mountains in Colorado, they are more than just a mass of volcanic peaks. They are a geologically complex system of terrains that include Precambrian crystalline intrusive and metamorphic rock, Paleozoic to Cenozoic sediments of all types, innumerable and extensive fault and fracture zones, karst topography, and geologic phenomena of almost any other description. This geologic complexity adds to the mystique of the range and produces infinitely variable landscapes that catch the visitor's eye. In the Silverton area alone, you can see Precambrian metamorphics, Devonian period limestones, Permian sandstones, and a myriad of Tertiary volcanics.

The southeast corner of the Silverton Quadrangle contains a large collection of Precambrian metamorphic gneisses and schists. Many of these old rocks are dissected by much newer volcanic intrusions of rhyolite, porphyry, andesite, and latite. A large proportion of these intrusions have accompanying mineralization, evidenced by the numerous mines in this section of the quadrangle. The Precambrian rocks may also be covered by large masses of Tertiary volcanic tuffs, flows, and breccias.

The southwest corner of the quadrangle, to the west of the Animas River valley and south of Silverton, contains several examples of sedimentary rock. Here we find the red beds of the Permian Cutler and Rico formations. Sultan Mountain and Grand Turk both consist of these sedimentary rocks overlain by large deposits of tertiary volcanics. We also can see a scene that is relatively rare in the Colorado mountains — a karst landscape. The area in and around Molas Park is underlain by the Leadville (Ouray) limestone, which has the property of dissolving into complex patterns. Here it has created a series of large "potholes" that are filled with water and form the many ponds and lakes atop the Molas Pass divide.

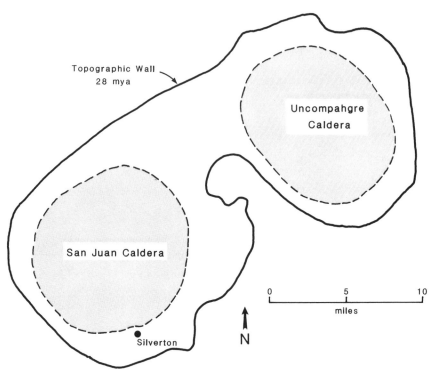

Figure 9.2. Map showing the position of the San Juan and Uncompahgre calderas 28 million years ago.

The most notable geology of the Silverton region, however, lies in the northern part of the quadrangle. This is the far northwestern extent of the most dramatic volcanism of the Tertiary period that occurred in what is now Colorado. A series of nested calderas make up the core of the volcanic activity here. Calderas were formed when large masses of volcanic material were ejected from deep within the Earth and overlying rock was weakened to the point of massive collapse. The calderas in the Silverton region were tens of miles in diameter and immense compared to recent volcanic activity around the world. Their formation began about 28 million years ago (mya), when widespread ejection of molten material and ash created the collapsed landforms of the San Juan and Uncompahgre calderas (Figure 9.2), irregular circles of fractured and faulted crust at the surface. Huge amounts of tuff-producing ash and lava spread over the surrounding land and filled the large depressions of the calderas themselves. About 27.5 mya renewed volcanic activity caused the collapse of the Silverton caldera (Figure 9.3).

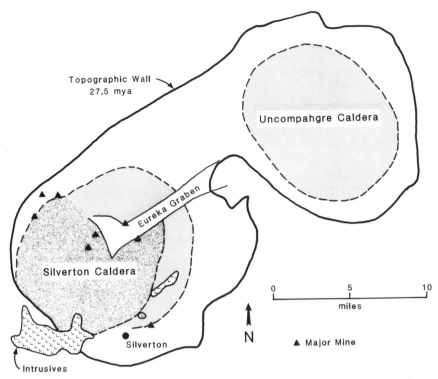

Figure 9.3. Diagram indicating the superposition of the Silverton caldera coincident with the location of the older San Juan caldera.

The town of Silverton lies at the far southwestern edge of this caldera; the western side of the caldera runs in close proximity to Mineral Creek valley toward the north. Although the center of the caldera was a large depression, the magnitude of the ejected material was such that the basin created by the collapse was filled with volcanic debris. This created the topography we see today: the center sections of the caldera are now high mountains to the north and east of Silverton and the fractured edges of the caldera are now valleys.

The violence of this volcanic activity resulted directly from the chemical makeup of the magma. More acidic, less dense rock of continental areas is very viscous; basic, more dense rock of ocean areas flows much more easily. The viscous nature of the rock here allowed great pressures to build before the eruption took place. When this pent-up energy was finally released, the pressures caused very rapid and unbridled expulsions of magma and the subsequent collapse of the caldera.

Volcanic activity of this magnitude was occurring throughout the San Juan Mountains at this same time and continued sporadically for several million years. As discussed in Chapter 12, "Slumgullion Slide," the Lake City caldera developed about 22.5 mya. By 22 mya the most extensive volcanic eruptions had ceased.

This series of episodes left a legacy to the Silverton region. First, the San Juans are characterized by massive amounts of volcanic rock. This is, by far, the largest center of volcanic activity in Colorado and one of the largest in the entire United States. Second, the sedimentary and Precambrian crystalline rocks that once dominated the geology of the region are deeply buried beneath the volcanic debris. Some of these sediments are visible below volcanic rocks around the edges of the volcanic field, such as at Sultan Mountain and Grand Turk. In most other areas of the San Juans, the volume of volcanic rock is so massive that the sedimentary and crystalline rocks once prevalent are entirely buried and invisible at the surface. Third, the caldera edges, where innumerable fractures and faults occurred, were conduits for fluids carrying minerals in solution. These conduits became the ore veins searched for and mined over the past 150 years. Gold, silver, lead, copper, zinc, and other metals have been found along the fringes of these old calderas (Figure 9.3).

THE MINING INDUSTRY

Early efforts to exploit the mineral riches of the San Juan region were slowed by the fact that the Confederated Ute Reservation in southwestern Colorado extended as far east as the 107th west meridian. This meant that most of the region in the San Juans west of Creede, including the Silverton area, was not legally open for prospecting and mine development. The treaty did not keep miners and prospectors out, but it did cause numerous conflicts and curtailed serious development of the mineral wealth in the San Juan Mountains. In 1873 the Utes were "convinced" to sign a treaty ceding this area to the U.S. government and, therefore, to the territory of Colorado. Weminuche Tribe members of the Utes, the ones divested of the land, were not even invited to the treaty negotiations. Nonetheless, the Brunot Treaty of 1873 opened the floodgates to legal mine development, and the history of the San Juans, in general, and Silverton, in particular, took a significant turn.

As early as 1860, Charles Baker prospected the area where Silverton now sits; however, it was not until 1870 that significant deposits of mineral ore were discovered near Silverton. Development was slow until the signing of the Brunot Treaty; following that event mining boomed. Gold and silver were the main attractions. There were rich finds, but access to markets and supply routes proved difficult. In 1882 the Denver and Rio Grande Railroad finished its tracks to Silverton from Durango along the Animas Canyon to the south. The railroad was a boon to the mining industry and population growth of the region. In late November 1884, Otto Mears completed the "Million Dollar Highway" from Ouray to Silverton. This engineering marvel doubled access to Silverton from the outside world and provided needed redundancy to the often snow-bound train service.

Silver, not gold, became the mainstay of mining in Silverton until the 1893 Silver Panic, when many mines and mills shut down. By this time Silverton was an established community and able to weather the crisis. From 1895 until about 1908, the town grew and regained its former prosperity. Gold had become the main mineral; however, after 1908 even gold mining declined slowly but steadily until 1991, when the last large mine (the Sunnyside) closed down. There are still tailings recovery operations and small-scale mining taking place, but the future of mining and the City of Silverton are in considerable doubt. Scattered throughout the area are reminders of better economic days such as the old headframe just above Chattanooga (Figure 9.4) and the now-silent tramway of the Mayflower Mill (also called Shenandoah-Dives) (Figure 9.5) just east of Silverton. The mining industry in Silverton is comatose; the legacy of mining in the community will live for a long time to come.

THE GLACIAL STORY

The San Juan Mountains are the quintessential glacial terrain in Colorado. The "Great Ice Age" that created this landscape is really a very complex series of glacial advances and retreats that occurred throughout the world over the past 2 million years or so. Glaciers occur in high latitude and high altitude locations for two reasons: at such locations the temperature decreases (by 5 to 9 degrees F) and snowfall increases. Basically, more snow falls in winter than melts in summer. This unbalanced condition allows for great masses of snow and ice to build up over centuries to thicknesses of hundreds to thousands of feet. Ice is produced from the copious snows

Figure 9.4. Old headframe above Chattanooga, a poignant reminder of the "glory" days of mining in the area.

Figure 9.5. Overhead tramway by the Mayflower Mill, an impressive remnant from a past era.

by the weight of new snow compressing and changing the buried snow crystals into ice crystals.

Two terms are used to name this 2-million-year glacial period. The "Pleistocene" is the geologic period of time from the beginnings of the glacial advances until about 10,000 years ago. "Holocene" is the term for the time from 10,000 years ago to the present. Some scientists prefer to use the term "Quaternary," which encompasses all 2 million years, including the last 10,000. This book uses the term Pleistocene.

According to the classic theory of glaciation in North America, there were four major periods of glacial advance with "interglacials," or warmer times, between them. These glacial periods are called, from youngest to oldest, the Wisconsin, Illinoisan, Kansan, and Nebraskan. These names refer specifically to the vast continental glaciers that covered large areas of the northern United States. Alpine or mountain glaciers of the United States occurred in general accord with the continental ice sheets. However, recent evidence indicates that there may have been up to seven extensive glaciations just in the last 700,000 years with as many as 21 identifiable ice advances in the past 2.1 million years.

THE EVIDENCE IN THE SAN JUANS

Evidence for three substantial ice advances exists in the Silverton area. There may have been others, but the ice from subsequent advances obliterated any clues. The oldest advance in the San Juans is called the Cerro glaciation, which is believed to have occurred in the early Pleistocene. Most of the debris left by this glacial episode is gone, but a few remnants still exist far beyond the mountain fronts to the north and south of the San Juans. Another glaciation, the Durango, is thought to have occurred from 300,000 years ago to about 200,000 years ago. Very little evidence is left of this period either, except in valleys beyond the limits of the more recent glacial episode.

The most recent glacial period here in the San Juans is simply called the Late Wisconsin. It probably corresponds to the Pinedale and Bull Lake advances in other areas of the Southern Rocky Mountains. It lasted from 30,000 years ago to the final melting of the last ice about 10,000 years ago. Almost all of the glacial landforms of the San Juans are the final result of this event. This was a massive ice inundation of the entire mountain range, and evidence for it is remarkably preserved throughout the region. The Silverton area is an excellent place to see the enduring evidence of glacial erosion and deposition.

THE LAST GLACIAL PRESENCE

Glaciation near Silverton can be represented well by the description of a single glacier, the Animas Glacier. This huge agglomeration of ice followed the valley of the current Animas River from its head in the valleys just to the east and northeast of Silverton to the present location of the City of Durango. The Animas Glacier, 50 miles long and up to 2,000 feet thick, covered all of the mountains except the very highest peaks (Figure 9.6) and collected ice from 75 separate catchment basins. The main tongue came down the Animas Valley to Silverton, where branches of ice contributed to the flow from Mineral Creek, the South Fork of Mineral Creek, and Cement Creek valleys. One can only imagine the sight of these deep valleys filled with ice, moving slowly but surely. Only the landscape remnants remain to help us conjure up the images of this frozen world. Luckily for our imaginations glaciers leave undeniable, tell-tale landforms for us to see.

THE GLACIAL LANDSCAPE

Alpine glaciers created dozens of unique and descriptive landforms; this book will discuss a few of the most distinctive and easily identifiable. The most widespread and largest of these landforms are the glacial valleys themselves. When a stream or river is the sole creator of a valley in steep mountain terrain, the cross-section of the valley is V-shaped with relatively straight walls and angular slopes. Glaciers, because of their mass, carve and erode the bottom of the valley and steepen the sides (Figure 9.7), producing a U-shaped cross-section. If you see this profile, you are almost certainly in a glacial landscape.

The second most distinctive feature of alpine glaciers is the cirque. This French word is used to describe the bowl-shaped depression high up on the mountain at the head of the valley where the glacier began. The weight of accumulating snow and ice carves out this depression. Often, after the ice melts, the bottom of the cirque contains a small lake as a remnant of glacial erosion. This lake is called a tarn. The cirques on Bear Mountain, Kendall Mountain, Storm Peak, and others in the Silverton area contain tarns.

Where several cirques surround a peak and lead to multiple valleys, the peak itself is steepened and termed a horn. The Matterhorn of the Swiss

Figure 9.6. Top of Sultan Mountain, one of the few peaks in the region not completely covered by ice during the Pleistocene.

Figure 9.7. Mineral Creek valley, the quintessential U-shaped glacial valley.

Alps is the archetypical horn in glacial terrain. Sultan Mountain and Grand Turk are very good examples of horns visible from Silverton. A rugged, saw-toothed ridge that separates two cirque basins is called an arete. Aretes exist to the east and west of the Bear Mountain cirque and are visible from Highway 550 along Mineral Creek valley. All of the features mentioned thus far are erosional landforms; glaciers also leave behind deposits, which are evident throughout the San Juan Mountains.

Glacial deposits are more difficult to recognize than erosional features. It is possible, however, to distinguish the kind of debris that makes up most glacial deposits. This material is called till and is a mixture of all sizes of mineral matter laid down by melting ice. When till is found in a curved ridge at the lower end of a glacial valley, it is called a terminal or end moraine. If it lies like a veneer on the basin floor, it is called ground moraine. When it occurs along the valley sides, it is a lateral moraine. Examples of these landforms can be found in the Silverton area, but because of reworking by streams and vegetation growth, they are not easily distinguished.

One distinctive depositional feature that can be seen is a rock glacier in the Bear Mountain cirque visible from Mineral Creek valley (Figure 9.8). The hummocky ground within the cirque is composed of rock and a substantial amount of ice in the spaces between the stones. The ice deforms slowly and promotes sluggish downslope movement as gravity pulls on the landform. Snow falls in winter, melts in the spring, and trickles down into the rock glacier only to refreeze and continue the creep downhill.

THE AVALANCHE THREAT

Although the glaciers are long past, snow still exerts a great influence on the natural environment of the Silverton area. Snow accumulation and distribution, for example, significantly affect the patterns of vegetation growth. And the sudden and massive movement of snow in the form of avalanches dictates winter lifestyles for the hardy, year-round inhabitants of the area. Avalanches disrupt transportation, interfere with mining operations, and loom over everyday life during the winter. Avalanches are common here not because so much more snow falls than in other mountainous regions of the state, but rather because environmental conditions are conducive to avalanche production from the snow that does fall. Intense solar radiation and cold air temperatures combine to form weak areas within the snowpack. Additional weak zones are created during the freezing

Figure 9.8. Rock glacier on Bear Mountain, visible from the floor of Mineral Creek valley.

and thawing cycles of spring. When the snow layers become weak and overloaded with new snow, rapid and sudden movement of the pack follows. Topography is also a factor in the number of avalanches or snow slides. Avalanche starting zones usually average 30 to 45 degree slope angles. Many of the steep, upper slopes of the mountains in the San Juans fit precisely into this range. The intense, if intermittent, snowfalls of the region can load these slopes very quickly with large quantities of snow, producing severe avalanche problems.

The almost infinite variety of avalanche types are generally classed in two categories: the loose snow, or "powder avalanche," which usually starts out as a small movement of snow and gains momentum as it moves downslope, and the "slab avalanche," which occurs in well-bonded, cohesive snow packs with a weak zone at the bottom of or within the pack. The width of the fracture in the snow that starts a slab avalanche may be as wide as one-quarter to one-half mile long, producing a huge slide.

It is easy to see the remnants of avalanches in the landscape. Large swaths of treeless avalanche tracks mark the sides of every valley in the area (Figure 9.9). The runout zones spread across the valley floors and sometimes up the opposite valley walls. Avalanche galleries protect automobile traffic in some of the most hazardous areas (Figure 9.10). Most of the main avalanches run year after year, and their tracks are obvious, but some are insidious, only revealing their danger when some unsuspecting skier crosses a slope at the wrong time or place. During the winter care must *always* be taken in the mountains, especially in the San Juans where avalanches are an ever-present winter hazard.

THE VEGETATION

Silverton sits solidly in the subalpine life zone at 9,305 feet above sea level. Where the vegetation has not been totally altered by mining, milling, and avalanches, typical subalpine ecosystems abound. Good examples of mountain riparian ecosystems, characterized by lush grasses and sedges and extensive willow growth, can be seen along Mineral Creek valley and the South Fork of Mineral Creek.

The subalpine spruce/fir forest is well represented on the mountain sides. The San Juan spruce/fir forest is somewhat unique in two respects. First, many blue spruce (*Picea pungens*) grow near the wetter places along the valley floor, as is typical in these forests; but in the San Juans the blue

Figure 9.9. Avalanche scars abound on all the valley walls of the area.

Figure 9.10. Snow shed on Red Mountain Pass portends the severe avalanche threat to Highway 550.

spruce also tends to grow in drier areas on the hillsides above the wet bottomlands. Blue spruce intermixes with the Engelmann spruce (*Picea engelmannii*) and subalpine fir (*Abies lasiocarpa*) all the way through the subalpine to near treeline. In many cases it is very difficult to distinguish between the blue and Engelmann spruce. There has been some discussion over the years about hybridization of these two species, but no genetic studies have been completed to prove or disprove this hypothesis. If it does occur, this may be one area where hybridization exists.

The second special characteristic of the subalpine forest here is the inclusion of corkbark fir (*Abies lasiocarpa* or *Abies lasiocarpa arizonica*) as a species or subspecies in the subalpine forest. These trees look identical to subalpine fir except for the thick, corky bark that encases the trunk. Botanists are not in agreement about whether the corkbark fir is a separate species or just a subspecies/variety of the subalpine fir in Colorado.

FINAL THOUGHTS

The San Juan Mountains are a vivid collage of the mountains of Colorado. Pristine forests and verdant meadows share the land with mining slag heaps and toxic settling ponds; glacially formed landscapes linger while avalanche-created scenes are reworked each year; the old, harsh lifestyle of the miners is slowly being replaced by tourist trains and fashion boutiques. The colors and textures are an odd but fascinating composite that, somehow, goes together.

One thing, however, is becoming clearer through the years. The mining industry that impacted the area so much and for so many years is no longer the major force in the lives of the residents here. With the closing of the Sunnyside Mine, the era of extraction also closed. There will be enduring reminders of this industry, cleaned up and displayed for the transient visitor, but the industry itself is gone. The environment will be better served and the landscape will slowly heal the scars from human exploitation. There is poignancy, however, about the loss of a heritage and the diminishing hope for a future. This is inevitable in the boom and bust cycle of mining in the West. Hopefully 50 years from now, Silverton will still exist as a vibrant community that can be sure of its past and sanguine about its future.

ADDITIONAL READINGS

Armstrong, B. R., 1976. *Century of Struggle Against Snow: A History of Avalanche Hazard in San Juan County, Colorado,* Institute of Arctic and Alpine Research, Occ. Paper 18, Univ. of Colorado, Boulder, Colo.

Atwood, W. W., and K. F. Mather, 1932. *Physiography and Quaternary Geology of the San Juan Mountains, Colorado,* U.S. Geological Survey Professional Paper 166, Washington, D.C.

Benham, J. L., 1981. *Silverton and Neighboring Ghost Towns,* Bear Creek Publishing Co., Ouray, Colo.

Bird, A. G., 1990. *Silverton Then and Now,* Access Publishing, Englewood, Colo.

Chronic, H., 1980. *Roadside Geology of Colorado,* Mountain Press Publishing Co., Missoula, Mont.

Kent, H. C., and K. W. Porter, 1980. *Colorado Geology,* Rocky Mountain Association of Geologists, Denver, Colo.

Larsen, E. S., and W. Cross, 1956. *Geology and Petrology of the San Juan Region, Southwestern Colorado,* U.S. Geological Survey Professional Paper 258, Washington, D.C.

McTighe, J., 1984. *Roadside History of Colorado,* Johnson Books, Boulder, Colo.

Perla, R. I., and M. Martinelli, Jr., 1978. *Avalanche Handbook,* U.S. Department of Agriculture Handbook 489, Washington, D.C.

Shoemaker, J., ed., 1968. *Guidebook of San Juan — San Miguel — La Plata Region, New Mexico and Colorado,* New Mexico Geological Society, Socorro, N.Mex.

Steven, T. A., and P. W. Lipman, 1976. *Calderas of the San Juan Volcanic Field, Southwestern Colorado,* U.S. Geological Survey Professional Paper 958, Washington, D.C.

Varnes, D. J., 1963. *Geology and Ore Deposits of the South Silverton Mining Area, San Juan County, Colorado,* U.S. Geological Survey Professional Paper 378-A, Washington, D.C.

10

PICEANCE CREEK BASIN

This is the land of the purple sage, the land of the Old West complete with wild horses, tumbleweed, and big skies. Isolated and at times stark, this land is a part of Colorado relatively unknown to most visitors and many residents of the state. This chapter is about the Piceance (pronounced: 'pē änts) Creek Basin of northwestern Colorado near the town of Meeker. This basin is defined by the surrounding land features: to the west are the Cathedral Bluffs; to the north is the White River; to the east is the Grand Hogback; and to the south are Roan Creek and the Book Cliffs.

Although most people have never seen this place, Piceance Basin is one of the most written about and studied places in Colorado and the entire West. Hundreds of books, articles, and especially, government documents have been produced covering the geologic, vegetational, cultural, political, and historical aspects of the basin. Why should this remote, seemingly desolate, and harshly beautiful place attract so much attention? The answer lies in just two words: oil shale!

The specific details and geology of the oil shale will be discussed later in the chapter; for now suffice it to say that the oil shale of this region has the *potential* to supply enough hydrocarbons to satisfy the United States's appetite for oil products for decades. The equivalent of an estimated 288 billion barrels of oil is recoverable from the rocks in this region. To put this in perspective, in 1987 the United States used approximately 15.5 million barrels of petroleum per day. At that rate the potential oil in the oil shale regions, of which the Piceance Basin is a main part, would satisfy 50 years of United States oil demand.

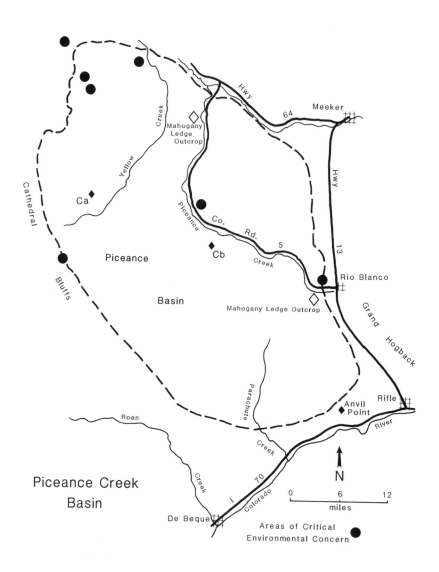

Piceance Creek
Basin

Areas of Critical
Environmental Concern ●

OIL SHALE DEVELOPMENT

The first oil shale development project in the area began in 1917 on Dry Fork near the small town of De Beque, Colorado. The oil recovery facilities here were modeled after a retort process devised in Scotland. This process worked, but as one workman described it later, "We proved you could make oil, but you couldn't make any money at it" (Murray 1974). Almost from this meager beginning, the United States government has been involved in oil shale research and experimentation.

The U.S. Geological Survey, Bureau of Land Management, Bureau of Mines, and Navy have all been involved in oil shale at some level. In 1916 the Navy started exploration of 50,000 acres known as the Naval Oil Shale Reserves Nos. 1 and 3. Along with the Navy, the Bureau of Mines began the Anvil Points oil shale recovery project near Rifle in 1946. Corporations have also bought and leased private oil shale patents since 1921. The two federal oil shale lease tracts located in the Piceance Creek Basin are designated Cb (Occidental Petroleum) and Ca (Amoco). These leases to private companies were part of the "prototype oil shale leasing program" for the states of Wyoming, Utah, and Colorado in 1974. Both of these parcels, like most of the Piceance Basin, are managed by the Bureau of Land Management.

Oil shale development here has waxed and waned over the years with booms and busts occurring at almost regular intervals. Andrew Gulliford has written a poignant history of the human toll these cycles have taken in his book, *Boomtown Blues*. Currently, the Piceance Basin is in the bust mode with no operating oil shale development sites, but the fascination with huge petroleum reserves lying just under the surface still pervades the psyche of this region. The causes for this phenomenon and the consequences of it are the motivation for this chapter.

THE ECOSYSTEMS

If one were to stand on the Cathedral Bluffs and look eastward, the view over the Piceance Creek Basin would seem almost uniform. The steel-blue hues of the sage and the intermittent dark-green punctuations of piñon pine and juniper go on and on (Figure 10.1). This seeming homogeneity disguises a wide variety of vegetational environments. Changes in topography and local variations in the availability of moisture cause abrupt and unexpected changes in vegetation patterns. Precipitation varies here

Figure 10.1. Long vistas of sagebrush country.

from about 11 inches per year in the northwest corner of the basin to almost 25 inches per year in the far southwestern area. The average precipitation at Meeker, northeast of the basin, is 17.5 inches per year. Effective precipitation, however, varies even more than these figures indicate. Slope angles and aspect combine to create small niches of vibrant growing conditions in some spots, while causing desertlike conditions in others. These sudden changes add a certain natural mysticism to the Piceance Basin that may startle the first-time visitor.

This natural variation is increased by the intensity of grazing that has occurred here for more than 100 years. Intensive cattle grazing in the basin began in the 1870s, and sheep grazing followed in the 1890s. Cattle grazed throughout the open ranges of the basin whereas sheep were mostly confined to the southern edge of the area from Thirteen Mile Creek to Rio Blanco. Overgrazing was the rule rather than the exception during this early period. Only after the Taylor Grazing Act of 1934 did the vegetation cover of the land improve. Even now little can be found of the pre-grazing, natural vegetation pattern. The intensive grazing not only caused losses of vegetation cover but increased soil and gully erosion and changed the mix of flora species. Be aware of this history when looking at the ecosystems discussed below.

SAGEBRUSH SHRUBLANDS ECOSYSTEM

Almost anywhere on the rolling uplands of the Piceance Creek Basin you can smell the sweet, pungent aroma of sage. The odor permeates the place even when you may be in another ecosystem. The vast majority of sage here is the big sagebrush (*Artemisia tridentata*), although there are other species of smaller sages present such as prairie sage (*A. ludoviciana*) and pasture sage (*A. frigida*). The big sagebrush, the largest sage bush in Colorado, stands up to 2.5 feet tall. Other plant species commonly found in conjunction with the sage are the Utah serviceberry (*Amelanchier utahensis*) (Figure 10.2), primarily in the higher elevations of the sage zone; the shadscale saltbush (*Atriplex confertifolia*); and, in abandoned agricultural fields, rabbitbrush (*Chrysothamnus* spp.).

The sagebrush ecosystem generally occupies elevations between 5,300 feet and 6,000 feet in the basin. Most of the area has moderate precipitation and is characterized by gently rolling hills with deep, loamy-to-sandy soils cut by innumerable arroyos. The vegetation changes, however, when bottomlands are encountered where high salt concentrations occur. These

Figure 10.2. Utah serviceberry and big sagebrush often grow near each other in northwestern Colorado.

areas are so different that they are given a new ecosystem designation: the semidesert shrubland ecosystem.

SEMIDESERT SHRUBLAND ECOSYSTEM

This ecosystem is distinguished by vegetation that is resistant to highly saline water. Plants here grow in areas where salt concentrations would be toxic to other vegetation. In fact, greasewood (*Sarcobatus vermiculatus*), the principal plant of the ecosystem, increases surface alkalinity by bringing salts up through its vascular system and into the leaves. As leaves fall and decompose, salt is added to the surface layer of the soil. Although there is some big sagebrush here, it occurs only where salt levels are relatively low. Most of the other plants of this area, like the greasewood, are salt tolerant. These include Gardner's saltbush (*A. gardneri*), winter-fat (*Ceratoides lanata*), and the shadscale saltbush.

PIÑON PINE/JUNIPER ECOSYSTEM

As elevations increase to around 7,500 feet and soils become rockier and coarser, the piñon-juniper woodland emerges. Piñon pine (*Pinus edulis*) and Utah juniper (*Juniperus osteosperma*) are the dominant overstory vegetation in this ecosystem (Figure 10.3). The dark-green stands of piñon-juniper woodland rise in vivid contrast to the more muted hues of the sagebrush. Many of the piñon-juniper stands are almost equal mixes of piñon pine and juniper trees; others may be almost 100 percent juniper or piñon pine. There is also a real mix in ages among the different stands. You will see young and expanding piñon-juniper areas whereas others are near senescence. Understory vegetation varies from dense stands of serviceberry, mountain mahogany (*Cercocarpus montanus*), big sagebrush, and several grasses to very sparse areas where the piñon-juniper canopy is almost closed. Fires in certain parts of the Piceance Basin have forced the piñon-juniper woodland to occupy only the rocky ridges and slopes. Where fire has not been much of a factor, the woodland spreads out over large areas.

OTHER REPRESENTED ECOSYSTEMS

Ironically, many of the other ecosystems represented in the Piceance Creek Basin are more readily found in high mountain elevations and far greater moisture conditions. These include the Douglas fir (*Pseudotsuga*

Figure 10.3. Piñon pine–Utah juniper of the uplands surrounding the lower-level sage areas.

menziesii) and quaking aspen (*Populus tremuloides*) ecosystems and nar-rowleaf cottonwood (*P. angustifolia*) stands. All of these vegetational com-munities require considerable moisture and relatively cool temperatures. Elevations in the basin reach 8,800 feet, creating some conditions conducive to these ecosystems. However, most areas of Douglas fir, quaking aspen, and narrowleaf cottonwood occur in deeply cut ravines and small canyons where water collects and shade is available. As you drive along Rio Blanco County Road 5 just west of Rio Blanco, look to the north: every small creek valley (Figure 10.4) contains examples of each of these vegetation types snuggled down below the more exposed ridge-tops that are dominated by big sagebrush.

RIPARIAN ZONES

There are many wide stream bottoms in the Piceance Basin, such as the one that follows Piceance Creek from the southeastern part of the basin to the far north-northwestern edge at the White River. These valley bottoms were once covered by cattail (*Typha domingensis*) wetlands, grasses, and sedges. Now, however, they are dominated by irrigated meadows and the mournful bleating of sheep. Irrigation of almost all of these natural riparian areas for pasture has produced a vegetation zone of rushes and exotic grasses such as Kentucky bluegrass (*Poa pratensis*), conspicuous when contrasted with the surrounding vegetation (Figure 10.5). The grazing sheep and innumerable irrigation ditches dominate an otherwise semiarid, rocky environment. The changes wrought by the development and expansion of irrigation are symbolic of the very great changes made throughout the Piceance Creek Basin by humans. When you travel through the area, remem-ber that few of the vistas you see today are the same as those seen by travelers of the region before 1870.

AREAS OF CRITICAL ENVIRONMENTAL CONCERN

The Bureau of Land Management in conjunction with the Natural Areas Program of the Colorado Department of Natural Resources has designated six areas of the Piceance Creek Basin as Areas of Critical Environmental Concern (ACEC). This designation stresses the importance of these sites and the need for their protection from adverse impacts of development. General locations of these six areas are shown on the map of the Piceance Creek Basin. These six areas combine to contain at least six rare plant species

Figure 10.4. Many hidden ravines surprise the viewer with lush and thriving forests.

Figure 10.5. Many basin valleys are farmed with irrigated water flowing through an intricate system of small canals.

(some rare only in Colorado) and three species endemic to the Green River shale geologic formation. These plants include:

RARE
Piceance twinpod	(*Physaria obcordata*)
Dudley Bluffs bladderpod	(*Lesquerella congesta*)
Piceance bladderpod	(*L. parviflora*)
Uinta gilia	(*Gilia stenothyrsa*)*
Sun-loving meadow rue	(*Thalictrium heliophilum*)
Utah gentian	(*Gentianella tortusa*)*

* = rare in Colorado

ENDEMIC
Dasycl's fescue	(*Festuca dasyclada*)
Yellow milkvetch	(*Astragalus lutosus*)
Barneby's columbine	(*Aquilegia barnebyi*)

The ACEC designation not only serves to protect these plants but also is meant to reserve these sites as outdoor laboratories and classrooms for selected biological research and study.

THE FAUNA

The Piceance Creek Basin cannot match many of the other places in this book for overall density of animals; it can compete, however, in terms of diversity. At least 365 separate species of fauna live in or migrate through the basin. This number includes 78 mammal, 255 bird, 15 fish, 12 reptile, and 5 amphibian species.

Among this gathering of species is the largest migrating mule deer (*Odocoileus hemionus*) herd in North America. Herd numbers have vacillated between 15,500 and 70,000 individuals with the number today around 50,000. During the summer the herd moves to the Roan Plateau to the south and the Flat Tops area to the east. In winter they mostly congregate in the northern-northwestern part of the basin near the confluence of the White River and Piceance Creek. Along the south bank of the White River, the Colorado Division of Wildlife manages a wildlife area to promote deer habitat. This Division of Wildlife area is a focal point for the winter mule deer migration.

There is also a significant herd of Rocky Mountain elk (*Cervus elaphus*), some mountain lion (*Felis concolor*), and a few black bear (*Ursus americanus*). Birds include sage grouse (*Centrocercus urophasianus*) and, blue grouse (*Dendragapus obscurus*), several species of waterfowl, an occasional sandhill crane (*Grus canadensis*), and 22 species of raptor.

One of the more romanticized animals in the basin is the wild horse that roams the sagebrush range. The current wild horse population is somewhere between 250 and 300 head. These animals have characteristics of both wild and domesticated horses because ranchers have been releasing domestic stock into the herd since the early days of ranching. Many of these horses can be seen in the western third of the basin and on the Cathedral Bluffs (Figure 10.6). Today movements of the horses are controlled and limited by the existing fences. Other factors that affect wild horse use of the range include snow depths, exposure to weather, and water sources. In the last few decades the wild horse population has spread beyond the area recognized as wild horse range in 1971, when the Wild and Free-Roaming Horse and Burro Act was passed as a protective measure for the animals. It is difficult to predict what this expansion of range will mean for the wild horses of the basin.

Figure 10.6. Wild horses near oil shale tract Ca.

THE GEOLOGIC STORY

The Piceance Creek Basin lies solidly within the Colorado Plateau geologic province. Here most of the rocks near the surface are relatively new on the geologic time scale; they are mostly sedimentary in character; and, they lie *nearly* horizontal. Unlike places such as the Garden of the Gods where several hundred million years of geologic history can be seen at the surface, the Piceance Basin rocks extend back in time only to the early Cenozoic — some 65 million years ago (mya).

THE GEOLOGIC COLUMN

The oldest rock found at the surface in the Piceance Creek Basin is the Wasatch formation (Figure 10.7). This formation of late Paleocene and early Eocene age is made up of old river bed deposits of mud and sand. The Wasatch formation underlies the Green River formation that was deposited in structural depressions holding the ancient lakes Uinta (in present-day Colorado) and Gosiute (in far northwestern Colorado and southwestern Wyoming). These lakes were extremely saline, much like the Great Salt Lake of today, and the deposits in them were very high in organic matter. Although

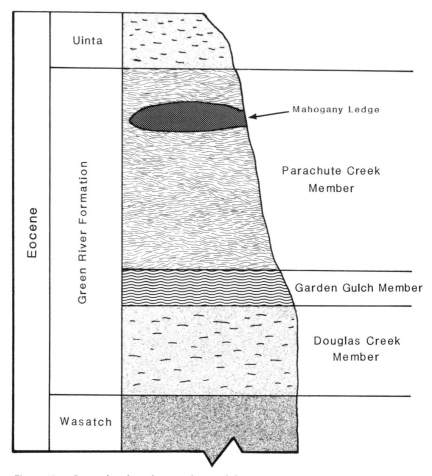

Figure 10.7. Generalized geologic column of the Piceance Creek Basin showing the dominance of the Green River formation and the position of the kerogen-rich Mahogany Ledge.

the Green River formation is considered one formation, it contains a complex of different rock members. In the central section of the Piceance Basin, just west of Piceance Creek, the members include from oldest to youngest: the Douglas Creek member, the Garden Gulch member, and the Parachute Creek member. Lying just above the Green River formation is the Uinta formation, a freshwater lake deposit with sandstones, siltstones, and shale.

THE GEOLOGIC STRUCTURE

Elevations within the Piceance Creek Basin reach 8,800 feet, but these high zones were not caused by the intense, localized stresses of mountain building (orogeny) such as the forces evidenced at Mt. Evans, the Garden of the Gods, or the Crested Butte areas. Here the geologic uplift was more areally constant and wider in scope. This regionwide movement of the Earth's surface is called an epeirogeny. Rocks in places affected by epeirogeny have less-drastic folding and little or no metamorphism. This is not to say that tremendous pressures and energy were not involved in the uplift of the region; it merely means that, as a general rule, the area was uplifted en masse much like a stack of pancakes being lifted as the plate on which they sit is lifted.

There was, nonetheless, some relatively localized warping of the sedimentary rocks of the Piceance Basin. We have seen that the topography of the Piceance Creek Basin resembles a bowl with higher elevations around the outer edge. This is particularly true along the western and southern boundaries of the basin. The "basin" part of the Piceance Creek Basin, however, comes from the fact that it is a geological structural basin. This basin structure is akin to a set of bowls stacked on top of each other where each bowl represents a geological formation. If we were to cut across the bowls (formations) horizontally, we would see that the outer edge of the lowest bowl surrounds the others at this horizontal surface. A cross-section of the Piceance Creek Basin (Figure 10.8) reveals that the Wasatch formation is the lowest bowl, the Green River formation with its various members is the middle bowl, and the Uinta formation is the top bowl.

In geologic jargon the Piceance Creek Basin is bounded by the Rangely-Skull Creek–White River anticline on the north; the Grand Hogback monocline on the east; the Elk and West Elk Mountains and Gunnison uplift on the south and southeast; the Uncompahgre uplift on the southwest; and the Douglas Creek uplift on the west. The center of the sedimentary layers in the basin has been depressed 28,000 feet. Thus the base of the basin (well below the Wasatch formation) is 28,000 feet lower than the same rock formations in surrounding regions.

THE OIL SHALE

Up to this point this book has been somewhat imprecise in its use of the term "oil." The generally accepted name for shale with recoverable

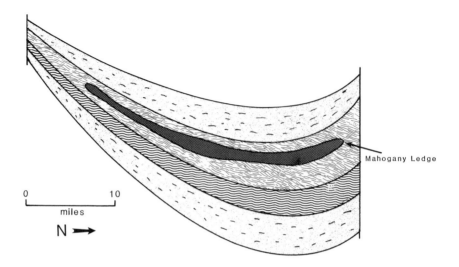

Figure 10.8. Cross-section of the Piceance Creek Basin showing the curved geologic strata stacked like a set of soup bowls.

hydrocarbons is "oil shale"; we are not really dealing with oil itself. The hydrocarbon material held fast in the oil shale is actually a substance called "kerogen." Kerogen is not unique to the oil shales of the Piceance Creek Basin — it is the most common organic material on Earth. It just takes a highly concentrated form in the oil shales of the world.

When petroleum (oil) is naturally produced within the Earth's rocks, a sequence of alteration of organic matter takes place. The sequence begins with plant and some animal matter at the surface of the Earth. This living material dies and begins to decompose. If it stays at the surface it usually totally decomposes and recycles as nutrients for new plants. If it gets covered by some kind of deposit, it may be able to decompose slowly into some form of carbon fuel such as peat, coal, gas, or oil. In general, marine-produced organic matter goes through an anaerobic (nonoxygen) chemical sequence that leads to carbon-rich oil. Terrestrial organisms usually break down to become peat, coal, and natural gas. These processes are complex and the intermediate stages of any of the processes are varied. Kerogen is an intermediate material developed in saline water environments and a precursor to the production of petroleum. What kerogen needs in order to develop into oil is additional heat and/or pressure that "cooks" it until oil is formed.

Figure 10.9. Shadowed area is the Mahogany Zone exposed in the far northwest part of the basin.

Kerogen itself is a very enigmatic chemical substance and takes many different but related forms. The major chemical elements in kerogen are oxygen, hydrogen, and carbon; the forms of kerogen can range from near-coal to near-oil and all conditions between the two. When heated, the kerogen changes mostly into petroleum. Some oil shale rocks contain up to 20 percent kerogen and can yield, upon heating, 100 gallons of oil for every ton of rock processed.

THE GREEN RIVER FORMATION

The oil shale industry of the Piceance Creek Basin has always been interested almost exclusively in the Green River formation. This rock contains an average of 12.4 percent organic carbon in the form of kerogen, which can yield about 28 gallons of oil per ton of rock when processed. As seen in the above geologic column (Figure 10.7), the Green River formation is actually composed of several members; these members were not created equal as far as kerogen levels are concerned. The best member by far in the entire basin for potential oil production is the Parachute Creek member of the Green River formation. Within the Parachute Creek member is a zone of kerogen concentration called the Mahogany bed or Mahogany Zone (Figure 10.9). The Mahogany Zone yields between 35 and 70 gallons of oil per ton of rock processed. Because the Piceance Creek Basin is a structural basin, the Mahogany Zone is buried up to 1,800 feet below the surface in the central part of the basin and is exposed around the edges. You can see the Mahogany Zone in the north along Rio Blanco County Road 5 about four miles south of White River and again in the east along Piceance Creek two to three miles west of Rio Blanco. You will recognize it as a mahogany-colored layer of sedimentary rock lying in thin layers halfway up the canyon walls, where it was exposed through erosion of the canyon by Piceance Creek.

THE OIL SHALE RECOVERY PROCESS

There is no single best method for producing oil from kerogen, but all of the methods have one thing in common: the oil shale must be heated to temperatures high enough to break the chemical bonds within the kerogen in order to produce crude oil. Two general approaches are the *ex situ* and the *in situ* recovery schemes. Even within these two schemes there are a multitude of possible methods of producing oil. Within the Piceance Creek Basin we have an example of each of these general approaches to oil shale recovery: the Occidental Oil Company site, Cb, was an *ex situ* facility (changed to *in situ* in later years) and the Amoco site, Ca, was developed as an *in situ* facility (Figure 10.10). Only the very basics of each kind of process will be discussed.

THE *EX SITU* PROCESS

This process mines the oil shale much like other minerals are mined. The rock is brought to the surface and crushed. At this point it is taken to a retort (a very sophisticated furnace) and "cooked" at about 500 to 550 degrees C (932 to 1,022 degrees F) until the chemical bonds of the kerogen are broken and gaseous oil is recovered and condensed. The oil is then treated like any other crude oil at the refinery.

The advantages to this process are high-efficiency recovery rates of oil from the shale and the ability to control the retort process very precisely. The disadvantages are the high cost of mining and transporting the ore,

Figure 10.10. Tract Ca and the *in situ* process viewed from Cathedral Bluffs.

pollution production at the retort, and especially, the difficulty in disposing of the waste rock that is left after processing.

THE *IN SITU* PROCESS

This method extensively fractures the oil shale to increase the porosity and permeability of the rock. The fractured rock is then heated in place by some method such as injecting high temperature gases into the subsurface zone. Heat disperses into the fractured rock and cooks the kerogen in place to release the crude oil. The oil is then collected and refined.

The advantages of this method are better environmental conditions (little waste rock for disposal), the ability to use the process on lower grades of oil shale, and cost reductions from reduced mining and transportation expenses. The disadvantages are the much lower efficiency in oil recovery, the possible contamination of groundwater, and the difficulty in controlling the retort process because it is really a remote retort at some considerable depth below the surface.

It is painfully obvious to those who live in and near the oil shale areas of Colorado that neither process has shown exceptional promise. Costs for both are still high and the rates of oil recovery per dollar expense cannot, as of yet, compete with normal petroleum production. The economic balance sheet on the side of full-scale oil shale development is lacking. No operational development of oil shale is currently occurring, and no firm plans are in place for the future. There are other factors that need to be accounted for when considering full-scale development of an oil shale industry, not the least of which are environmental issues.

ENVIRONMENTAL PROBLEMS AND CONCERNS

A significant number of the publications concerning the oil shale region of Colorado are studies of the environmental impacts of oil shale development. Any decision to generate oil at a production level must in large part depend upon the environmental consequences this development would have. What follows is far from exhaustive and only meant as food for thought. The only way of knowing what will actually occur to the environment is to go into full production and see what happens; however, the following speculation is based on comprehensive research by a myriad of scientists over the last several decades. Some of the findings are accepted by virtually all parties involved; many are still quite controversial. No easy answers are going to be found, but a thoughtful weighing of the economic, social, cultural, and environmental factors must be ongoing.

WATER

There are two pivotal problems with water and oil shale development. The first is how to deal with large amounts of contaminated and polluted water either at the surface in *ex situ* facilities or underground at *in situ* facilities. The second and in many ways most staggering problem is where to find all the water that is needed for full-scale shale processing. The average yearly flow of water from the White River measured near the Utah border is 337,000 acre feet per year. The estimates for water need by the oil shale industry range from 121,000 to 500,000 acre feet per year! The impacts on natural ecosystems, domestic uses, and agriculture and other industries of using this much water are mind-numbing.

SOLID WASTE

Any industrial process produces solid waste that needs to be stored, processed, or recycled. The oil shale industry is no exception. If *in situ* processes are used, solid waste problems will be large, but manageable. On the other hand, if *ex situ* processes are used, the problems will be literally mountainous in proportion because the waste shale after the oil is removed will have an equal or greater volume than the shale had before it was extracted from the ground. The scale of this debris would be unprecedented, and it remains a challenge to the industry, the state, and the local residents to propose ways of dealing with it.

REVEGETATION

Huge areas would be devegetated during oil shale production, and many places would be covered with shale detritus from the solid waste generated. Revegetation of land in the semiarid West has always been a problem. The fickle nature of the climate often precludes the easy re-establishment of even native plants. The toxic nature of the shale debris would provide even more challenges to be overcome during revegetation attempts. Acid levels, nutritional deficiencies, and low/sporadic precipitation rates all would contribute to the difficulty of recovering both the natural and newly made human landforms.

OTHER PROBLEMS

Air-quality degradation from dust and retort exhaust, the possible carcinogenic nature of kerogen substances, economic boom and bust, the adequacy and number of schools: the list goes on and on. Some of these problems will arise whether or not development occurs. Government agencies, the oil industry, citizens, and scientists from around the world have grappled with these problems for decades. No one has found the ultimate answers to any of them.

FINAL THOUGHTS

The energy appetite of the United States is not going to lessen any time soon. Someday this place that we call the Piceance Creek Basin and the whole of the oil shale regions of Colorado, Wyoming, and Utah may be one large industrial complex. We may solve some of the daunting environmental problems associated with energy development. If and when it happens, no matter how environmentally and socially conscious we are, the face of this place will be changed dramatically and forever.

For now, in the lull of the current oil shale bust, take the time to visit this place of huge skies, constant wind, infinite vistas, and Old West enchantment. The Piceance Creek Basin is special for many reasons, not just oil shale. Bucolic meadows dotted with grazing sheep, wild horses running amid the big sagebrush, and hidden glens with unexpected firs and aspens are all here and part of today's landscape. Don't just visit, however, for these romantic images; come to see what might be lost or gained if and when big oil comes back. Is economic boom more important than environmental continuum? Can the two exist together? Who should decide? Only after visiting and learning about the Piceance Creek Basin will you be able to give thoughtful, intelligent answers to these questions. Finally, it is ironic to stand atop billions of barrels of nonrenewable energy here at Piceance Basin and be awash in two sources of almost infinitely renewable energy: the sun and the wind.

ADDITIONAL READINGS

Chronic, H., 1980. *Roadside Geology of Colorado,* Mountain Press Publishing Co., Missoula, Mont.

Cook, C. W., ed., 1974. *Surface Rehabilitation of Land Disturbance Resulting from Oil Shale Development,* Tech. Rep. Series No. 1:30-66, Colorado State University Environmental Resources Center, Ft. Collins, Colo.

Energy Development Consultants, Inc., 1979. *Oil Shale in Colorado — the 1980s,* Colorado Energy Research Institute, Golden, Colo.

Epis, R., and J. Callender, 1981. *Western Slope Colorado,* New Mexico Geologic Society, Thirty-Second Field Conference, Albuquerque, N.Mex.

Ferchau, H. A., 1973. *An Ecological Analysis of the Vegetation, Piceance Basin, Rio Blanco and Garfield Counties, Colorado,* Thorne Ecological Institute, Boulder, Colo.

Gulliford, A., 1989. *Boomtown Blues,* University Press of Colorado, Niwot, Colo.

McDonald, A., 1974. *Shale Oil: An Environmental Critique,* Center for Science in the Public Interest, Washington, D.C.

Murray, D. K., 1974. *Energy Resources of the Piceance Creek Basin, Colorado,* Rocky Mountain Association of Geologists, Denver, Colo.

Newman, K. R., 1980. "Geology of Oil Shale in Piceance Creek Basin, Colorado." In *Colorado Geology,* ed. H. C. Kent and K. W. Porter, Rocky Mountain Association of Geologists, Denver, Colo.

Petersen, K. K., ed., 1981. *Oil Shale — The Environmental Challenges,* Colorado School of Mines, Golden, Colo.

——, ed., 1982, *Oil Shale — The Environmental Challenges II,* Colorado School of Mines, Golden, Colo.

Russell, P. L., 1980. *History of Western Oil Shale,* Center for Professional Advancement, East Brunswick, N.J.

Savage, H. K., 1967. *The Rock That Burns,* Pruett Press, Boulder, Colo.

Stone, D. S., 1986. *New Interpretations of Northwest Colorado Geology,* Rocky Mountain Association of Geologists, Denver, Colo.

Vandenbusche, D., and D. A. Smith, 1981. *A Land Alone: Colorado's Western Slope,* Pruett Press, Boulder, Colo.

Weber, W. A., and B. C. Johnston, 1979. *Natural History Inventory of Colorado. 1. Vascular Plants, Lichens, and Bryophytes,* 2nd ed., Univ. of Colorado Museum, Boulder, Colo.

Yen, T. F., ed., 1976. *Science and Technology of Oil Shale,* Ann Arbor Science Publishers, Ann Arbor, Mich.

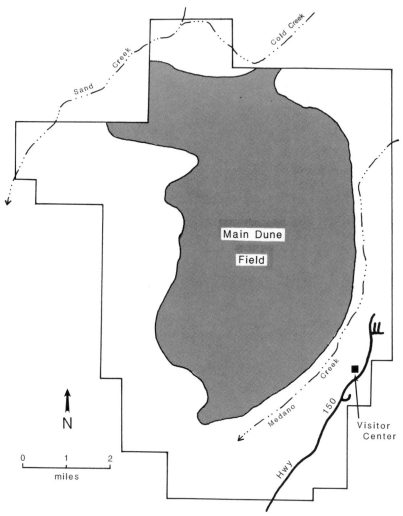

Great Sand Dunes National Monument

11

GREAT SAND DUNES
NATIONAL MONUMENT

"I suspect that people make special pilgrimages here to feel insignificant." Thus Stephen May, in *Pilgrimage,* describes the impact of the Great Sand Dunes National Monument. You feel insignificant because being here takes you out of the context of the normal world. The place is inexplicable to those who happen upon it, and it takes considerable knowledge and effort to understand the phenomena that created the dunes. The enigma that is the sand dunes is a place of contrasts and contradictions, of variety and complexity, of serenity and hostility fused into a single location. These colossal dunes, the largest by far in North America, are a surprise to those seeing them for the first time. From afar the dunes seem like a tan mirage on the horizon; up close they loom large and move like some crystalline chameleon that changes colors depending on the time of day and the atmospheric conditions.

The contrasts and contradictions include the fact that at 8,200 feet above sea level, in an area surrounded by snow-covered mountains that rise to over 14,000 feet, there exists a sea of sand. The air is most often dry, interrupted only by the occasional torrential rain from a thunderstorm or snow from an intense blizzard. Total annual precipitation in the monument is low whereas just a couple of miles to the east, the mountains receive as much moisture as the Midwest.

Variety and complexity include the juxtaposition of three life zones and several ecosystems. There are endemic species of insects and ever-changing environmental conditions. The geology of the monument and the surrounding area is a compilation of many forces and processes including mountain building (orogeny), tectonic fracturing (rifting), volcanic activity, and interminable weathering, erosion, and deposition by wind, water, and ice. Even the sand is a collection of many gradations of sand-size particles of various mineral types, each giving its contributions to the color and shape of the dunes.

It is a serene place when the sky is blue and crystal clear and the wind is calm, but it can become violent and inhospitable when storms converge or when the summer sun beats down on the sand. In many ways its hostility resembles that of the alpine life zone where strong, desiccating winds, intense solar radiation, and too much moisture or severe drought are ever-present possibilities.

The feeling of insignificance described by Stephen May changes to awe and appreciation as you learn more about the how and why of the dunes. Their story is complex and continuing, and it begins with the story of the San Luis Valley.

THE VALLEY

The San Luis Valley is the largest and southernmost of four intermontane basins in the Southern Rocky Mountains of Colorado. North Park, Middle Park, and South Park, along with the San Luis Valley, are all structural basins, created through the faulting and movement of large areas of the earth's bedrock. The basins, although all at relatively high elevations, dropped or were lowered relative to the surrounding mountains.

The basin that is the San Luis Valley is a part of the much larger Rio Grande rift system, which extends approximately 500 miles from central Colorado into Mexico. A rift zone, or system, occurs where the earth's crust is being stretched and pulled apart by the forces created as tectonic plates separate. When this happens certain parts of the affected area are thrust to higher elevations while others, like the San Luis Valley, are dropped down in relative elevation. The development of the San Luis Valley trough began about 27 million years ago (mya) during the early Miocene and has continued into the Holocene. Not all of the basin was dropped at the same rate or to the same depth. The western edge of the valley was downthrown much less than the eastern side and is outlined by the San Juan Mountains. The San

Figure 11.1. The mountains seem to have captured the moving sand of the dunes.

Juans are primarily a volcanic mountain system relatively new in geologic terms; they have developed mostly during the Tertiary period. The eastern side of the valley is made up of a steep scarp along the Sangre de Cristo Mountains. On this eastern edge, the bedrock may be as much as 30,000 feet below the surface. The entire northern end of the San Luis Valley (called the Alamosa Basin) is filled with alluvial material derived from the two flanking mountain systems (Figure 11.1).

Understanding the northern half of the valley is the key to understanding the history of the sand dunes. The major river draining the eastern half of the San Juan Mountains is the Rio Grande. The river exits the mountain front near the city of Del Norte. The Rio Grande carries heavy loads of mineral debris eroded from the high, volcanic mountains. It has been doing so for millions of years, but the most significant amounts of debris have only been available since the intense glaciation of the San Juans from about 2 million to around 12,000 years ago. The glaciers eroded and deposited vast amounts of debris that were then available to the river systems to carry out of the highlands. During the last 10,000 to 15,000 years, much of the material carried by the Rio Grande has been deposited in the Alamosa Basin. Although the course of the river in the San Juans has remained confined by steep valley walls and has therefore been relatively constant, the course of the river across the valley floor has changed considerably. Initially, the river flowed almost due east across the basin to just west of what is now San Luis Lake. The river has slowly moved its bed southwestward, leaving large deposits of loose alluvial debris in its wake. These vast deposits, along with lesser deposits derived from streams like Saguache Creek, have collected here and provide a ready source of sand, silt, and clay for further movement by wind and water.

Much of this area where the Rio Grande once flowed is now a closed basin where there is no external drainage of the surface water. This is much like a half-filled bathtub where water cannot escape on the surface so it either evaporates or sinks into the Earth (the drain) to become part of a vast underground water reservoir. Therefore, it is up to the wind to erode and transport the sediments left by the old Rio Grande and the other smaller creeks still flowing into the basin. This is the source for the sand that makes up the giant dunes toward the northeast. But there are some other players in the scenario that need to be addressed before we know the whole story.

Notice on the map of the monument the change in direction of the Sangre de Cristo Mountains from north-northwest–south-southeast trending to almost due south trending near Medano Creek. This sharp break in the alignment of the steep and high escarpment of the mountains helps to funnel the almost constant southwest wind into this pocket. Moreover, Medano Pass, located just east of the dunes, is at a lower elevation than the mountains to the north or south. Wind will take the easiest route, which here means up and over the mountains at Medano Pass.

The predominant wind across the San Luis Valley is from the southwest blowing toward the northeast. In late spring the wind is generally almost steady at 40 to 50 miles per hour. There are also times of relative calm and times when the wind is much stronger. The sparse vegetation that grows in the San Luis Valley, the one true desert in Colorado where annual precipitation rates average only about 6 to 10 inches per year, cannot hold the loose, dry sediments in place. The forceful winds have free access to these sediments. The combination of all of these factors allows large quantities of sand, silt, and clay particles to blow out of (deflate from) the center of the Alamosa Basin toward the area occupied by the Great Sand Dunes National Monument.

THE DUNES

The dunes are the manifestation of innumerable actions by the individual grains of sediment that move across the valley floor (Figure 11.2). These grains are pushed by an unrelenting wind that not only moves the material but separates it into size and weight classes. The dunes here are *sand* dunes, not clay or silt dunes; just how does the wind manage this selection process?

THE SAND

To understand the processes at work here, a little background discussion on the subject of geomorphology is necessary. Geomorphology is the study of the land surface and how the patterns and shapes of surface features get their form. It is, in essence, the study of the erosion, transport, and deposition of broken rock fragments and debris. Erosion is the process of removing material from its current resting place; this might entail the dislodging of rock debris by glacial ice or the removal of sediment by water or wind. Transport describes how material, once it is picked up, moves downstream, downvalley, or downwind. Deposition addresses the factors involved in determining when and where this mobile material will finally, or at least temporarily, come to rest, maybe to be moved again at some future date or to become new rock in the millennia to come.

The erosion, transport, and deposition of material depends to a very great degree on its size and density. Figure 11.3 is adapted from a Hjulstrom diagram that shows the relationship between wind speed (power) and grain size of material moved. Note that the size of clay and silt particles is just under a tenth of a millimeter and smaller. It takes very little wind speed to keep these sizes of material in transport. As the grain size gets larger or the density increases, it takes ever-faster wind speeds to keep the material moving. Knowing this, it is easy to deduce the reasons for having only sand in these dunes. As the strong and steady southwest wind comes across the relatively barren Alamosa Basin, it picks up sand, silt, and clay. When the wind is funneled into the pocket formed by the change in the directional trend of the Sangre de Cristo Mountains just east of the monument, the wind must ascend up and over this formidable wall of rock. The wind loses much of its energy and carrying power, enough to make it drop most of its load of the larger, heavier sand. The silts and clays, being smaller and lighter, are carried up and over the mountains by the now less powerful wind. The result: *sand* dunes.

Figure 11.2. Medano Creek, the obvious boundary of the dunes on the southeast.

Only a small amount of the sand grains are actually picked up and carried long distances by the wind. This process is called suspension. Most of the sand is moved by a process called saltation. Saltation is the mechanism whereby sand is eroded and moved only short distances before it falls back to earth, usually to bounce and move other grains as it lands. This causes the impacted grains to erode and move a few inches to a few feet, continuing the process ad infinitum. The steady winds and relatively consistent grain size of the sand actually can produce "ripples" where sand is deposited at the crests of the ripples and moved subsequently to the next crest. These small-scale features are usually less than one inch high, and the distance between crests, contingent upon wind speed and grain size, is two to four inches. Look for these as you climb and explore the dunes. Some of the larger and heavier grains never leave the surface but are pushed along by the more active, saltating grains. This process creates a surface creep that helps the total migration of sand downwind.

An intriguing and beautiful aspect of the dunes is their ability to change color depending upon time of day, sun angle, and position of the viewer. Some of this color change results from differences in refraction of the light off the irregular facets of the sand grains themselves, but the primary reason is the multitude of mineral types extant in the sand. At least half of the sand

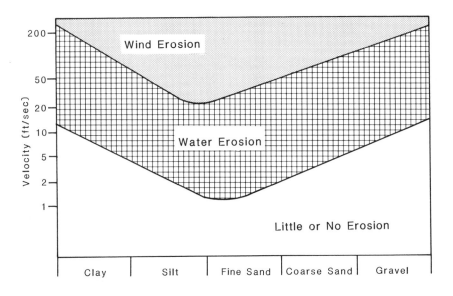

Figure 11.3. Revised Hjulstrom diagram showing the wind and water speeds at which various sizes of sand, silt, and clay are moved.

is made up of both finely and coarsely grained volcanic minerals from the San Juan Mountains. Almost a third of the sand is single and multicrystalline quartz, a component of both volcanic and nonvolcanic rock. There are several trace minerals such as feldspars, pyroxenes, and amphiboles that add color to the dunes. Magnetite, a small percentage of the total, is a distinctive mineral that is visible as black streaks crossing the tans and browns of the dune faces. Magnetite grains are usually smaller than the other mineral grains, but because they are much denser and heavier, they react to the forces of the wind much like the larger, less dense quartz and volcanic minerals; they are eroded, transported, and deposited by wind speeds that erode, transport, and deposit the quartz and volcanic minerals.

THE SHAPES

When visitors first approach the dunes, they are mesmerized by the huge mass of sculpted sand that makes up the bulk of the dunes. The top of this central core of sand stands at least 700 feet above Medano Creek and is made up of a dune type called transverse, or reversing transverse, dunes. This is only one of several dune types that exist in and around the monument

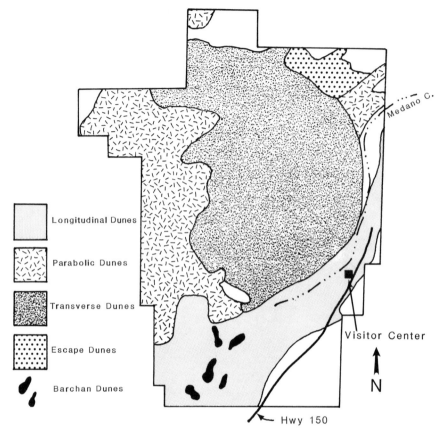

Longitudinal Dunes

Parabolic Dunes

Transverse Dunes

Escape Dunes

Barchan Dunes

Visitor Center

N

Hwy 150

Figure 11.4. Map indicating the position of the various sand dune types within the monument.

(Figure 11.4). The relationship among the dune types is intricate and interesting and deserves understanding.

Figure 11.5 shows the three main variables that affect dune form. This diagram assumes that the wind is steady from a nearly constant direction. This is generally true at the monument with a singular exception to be discussed later. Three factors determine sand dune shape: wind effectiveness (wind speed and consistency), vegetative cover, and sand supply. The following discussion will refer to Figures 11.4 and 11.5 to explain how each dune type forms.

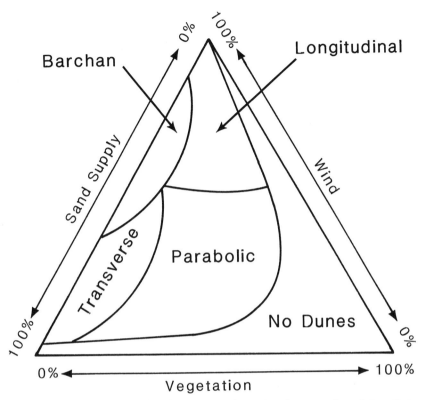

Figure 11.5. Sand supply, wind, and vegetation determine the type of sand dune that develops. Each of these affects what kind of sand dune types are found in the monument, attesting to the complexity of the physical environment of the area.

Parabolic dunes. If you were to drive into the monument from the west along Highway 160, you would cross a nearly flat expanse of ground interrupted by low, elongate, and U-shaped mounds of earth. These features are the first set of parabolic dunes. You will hardly recognize them as dunes, especially compared to the dramatic dunes you see before you in the monument. Parabolic dunes can be considered a transition from no dunes at all to the beginnings of dune features. They develop in areas that have little sand, relatively low wind speeds, and considerable vegetation.

Three subtypes of parabolic dunes exist in the valley. Those near San Luis Lake are the remnants of sand left over after the persistent wind has done its best to erode the sand from the area. These are called the parabolic dunes of deflation — deflation being the term used by geomorphologists to mean the removal of material.

Almost due northeast from the parabolic dunes of deflation you will encounter the fixed parabolic dunes of accumulation. The key words here are "accumulation" and "fixed": accumulation because a small portion of the sand from the deflation area settles here; and fixed because the movement of the sand is so gentle that vegetation has taken hold and stabilizes these dunes. Fixed parabolic dunes of accumulation can be seen just inside the western boundary of the monument.

Immediately downwind is the third type of parabolic dune, which functions as a transition to the main body of sand. These are the active parabolic dunes of accumulation. They are active because the sand is moving at a rate that does not permit a substantial vegetative cover to get established. Remember that all parabolic dunes develop in areas with relatively little sand, moderate winds, and modest vegetation cover.

Longitudinal dunes. Along the southern end of the main dune mass are low-lying, elongate dunes that develop along the Medano Creek valley and toward the northeast. Figure 11.5 shows that longitudinal dunes occur in very windy places with small sand supplies and very little vegetation. Longitudinal dunes are low ridges of sand that generally parallel the wind. These ridges do not build to very high levels and therefore are seen from the road into the monument as a sort of foreground for the larger dunes that loom behind them. Many geomorphologists feel that longitudinal dunes are really exaggerated and broken barchan dunes. This may very well be the case here, since the majority of barchan dunes of the monument are found imbedded among the longitudinal dunes.

Barchan dunes. Barchan dunes have all of the formative characteristics of longitudinal dunes except that they have more sand available. Barchan dunes are often cited as the archetypal dune form. They are crescent-shaped with their horns pointing downwind. Barchan dunes are relatively small and usually isolated from one another, producing distinctive, individual dunes. These beautifully formed features can be seen all along the valley between the main monument road and the large dune mass.

Transverse dunes. Finally, the most dominant and dramatic dune type in the monument is the transverse dune. Transverse dunes make up the great body

Figure 11.6. Large dune mass with mostly transverse dunes.

of sand that so impresses visitors to the Great Sand Dunes National Monument (Figure 11.6). They can become massive, as easily seen in the 700-foot-high sand mass that is visible from miles around. Transverse dunes form in areas where there are very large amounts of sand available, minimal vegetative cover, and relatively low wind speeds. This is the very reason that they are here. The wind loses its energy as it ascends the Sangre de Cristo Mountains and drops its load of sand. You can almost say that this is the final resting place of the sand-size sediments from the valley upwind.

The shapes of the transverse dunes are extremely variable, but the general form is that of piles of sand running perpendicular to the wind. Most often they can be seen as sinuous ridges lying across the path of the prevailing wind. It is difficult to see this general pattern here because of the large number of dunes in a confined area and the infinite, small variations that affect the wind close to the sand surface.

Escape or climbing dunes. A dune type not shown in Figure 11.5 is the escape or climbing dune. These are indistinctly shaped, shifting dunes that appear to be moving even as you watch. Escape dunes can be seen if you drive or walk toward Medano Pass along the eastern and northeastern edge of the monument. These dunes are "escaping" the main sand body and moving upslope into areas previously devoid of large sand deposits. You can almost see this in action; notice the many dead ponderosa pine trees that have been killed recently by this invading sand. These "ghost" trees were killed when they were covered by the sand (Figure 11.7). The trees have since been uncovered and now lie in stark testimony to the transient nature of these ephemeral dunes.

INSIDE THE DUNES

If we were to take a barchan dune and cut it into two equal halves, we would be able to see how the sand is actually deposited. Figure 11.8 shows that the upwind or windward side of the dune is lying at a relatively low angle, somewhere between 10 and 20 degrees. The wind blows the sand up along this moderate incline until it settles on the surface or until it reaches the crest of the dune. Just beyond the crest the wind has little or no effect on the sand because the sand literally falls down the leeward slope under the influence of gravity. The leeward or slip face angle of the dunes will be established at what is referred to as the "angle of repose." The angle of repose is nearly a constant, almost invariably between 31 and 34 degrees for dry sand, and is dependent upon the individual sand grain sizes and shapes. When hiking up a slip face you will swear that the angle is much steeper than this, but if you take a measurement it will be between 31 and 34 degrees.

Figure 11.8 also shows another feature related to the angle of repose. This is the crossbedding that takes place within the dune itself. These beds or layers are created by individual deposits of sand and parallel the angle of repose. Geologists use this information when trying to decipher the depositional environment of certain sandstones. This distinctive crossbedding indicates that the original sand of the rock was part of an ancient sand dune system. We refer to this general concept in geology as uniformitarianism, meaning that the present is the key to the past. The processes that make sand dunes today and the forms that those dunes take are the same processes and forms that operated in the past. This concept is key to understanding rock in general and sedimentary rock in particular.

Figure 11.7. "Ghost trees" stand as reminders of the ever-moving sand.

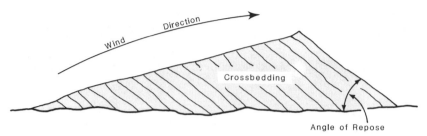

Figure 11.8. Diagram illustrating a typical cross-section of a barchan dune. Notice that the steeper side (slip face) of the dune is away from the direction of the prominent wind.

THE DUNE MIGRATION (OR LACK THEREOF!)

One of the most often-asked questions by visitors to the dunes is, "Are the dunes moving?" The answer to this question is a resounding, "Probably not much." There are the obvious cases of the escape dunes moving over and through previously forested land and killing the trees. There is also the obvious shifting of shapes in the transverse dune areas and, to a lesser extent, in other dune types. But by and large, the consensus is that the dunes do not move or change much. Why? There are at least three known reasons for this long-term stability or equilibrium.

Counter winds. Although the prevailing and dominant wind is steady from the southwest, there are occasions when this wind fails. When major storm systems enter the area just to the east of the Sangre de Cristo Mountains, strong northeast winds can blow over the passes and push the sand back toward the southwest, reshaping the tops of the dunes by reversing the windward/leeward slopes. This creates reversing dunes and helps to build the highest dunes to their impressive elevations. If we were to cut across a reversing dune to expose the cross-section, we would see the crossbedding going in the opposite direction of the normal dune layering. A single storm with these northeast winds has been known to blow the crests of the transverse dunes back toward the southwest by almost 20 feet! The upper layers of sand shift back and forth many times over the years, but there is an overall equilibrium that keeps most of the sand from migrating.

The creeks. There are many creeks that enter the monument, but the most interesting and unique is Medano Creek. This stream enters the monument at the northeast corner and flows along the east and southeast sides of the

Figure 11.9. The shallow water and sand of Medano Creek spreading out for hundreds of feet.

largest dune mass (Figure 11.9). Throughout the late spring, summer, and early autumn of most years it flows past the visitor's center and southwestward until it finally disappears into the ground near the longitudinal dunes in the southwest corner of the monument. During the remainder of the year, its flow is restricted by the cold temperatures that hold water in the mountains as snow and ice. This pattern of flow and ebb varies somewhat over the years but remains relatively constant.

Medano Creek contributes to the stability of the dunes by capturing blowing sand that comes off the dune mass to the west and southwest. The creek then transports much of this sand as bed load back toward the southwest where the prevailing wind can again pick it up and move it back toward the transverse dunes. Medano Creek flowing southwest and wind blowing northeast form a sort of perpetual conveyer belt for moving sand.

The creek is also unique in its own right. It has been studied by geologists and geomorphologists because of the conspicuous buildup of antidunes in its bed and the subsequent bores or stream surges that occur when these antidunes collapse. The antidunes are similar to the wind ripples caused by the saltation of sand grains, but are larger and are produced by the hydraulic character of the water flow. The speed and volume of water in the creek at any one time produce variations in size and movement of the antidunes, but antidunes are produced on the stream bed and appear to move upstream as they are growing. When the dunes are 1 to 2 inches high and several feet long, they act as small dams to pool water behind them. At some point the dunes break, releasing the dammed water, which surges downstream. This bore or surge of water resembles a breaker at the seashore but on a much smaller scale. These antidunes build and break about every 15 to 30 seconds, making bores every 50 to 100 yards. To get to the main transverse dunes, you must cross Medano Creek; stop in midstream and experience this unique fluvial phenomenon.

High water table. The least understood and most controversial contributor to dune stability is the fact that there is water held within the dune mass that stabilizes the sand. This water acts like a weak glue to keep the sand from moving or shifting significantly. All of the San Luis Valley has large, subterranean water reservoirs or aquifers that approach the surface. It is speculated that the top of this water table in the monument actually exists inside the main dune body and holds the sand in place. The water accumulates here through capillary rise in the pores between sand grains. No one, at this point at least, knows just how far below the surface this water is, what the effects of the water are on the sand movement, or what problems might be caused in the dunes if this water were to be removed.

This last concern is of interest because of a proposal being put forth by the Baca Project of the American Water Development Incorporation (AWDI). The proposal by AWDI would take very large amounts of groundwater out of the San Luis Valley for use elsewhere and may lower the total amount of water in the aquifer(s) below the monument. In addition to the problem of dune stability, this proposal might also affect Medano Creek because the creek is a recharge source for the groundwater; a lowering of the water table might cause an overall reduction in the amount of water in the creek. So far this proposal has met with little success in the water courts; no one is certain of what the future of this project or some variant is.

THE CLIMATE

The climate of the San Luis Valley and the Great Sand Dunes National Monument deserves detailed discussion because it is a major part of the enigma that is the sand dunes. This area of Colorado gets the least precipitation and yet has some of the largest groundwater reserves in the state. This desert environment, where the surface temperature of the sand can reach well over 120 degrees F on a summer day, contains the City of Alamosa, which can be the country's coldest spot on a winter night. How and why do these seemingly disparate facts occur?

The dryness of the San Luis Valley is caused by its location with reference to the surrounding landscape. Recall that there are two main directions from which moisture comes to Colorado. There are the Pacific air masses carrying moist air from west to east and the wet air moving in from the Gulf of Mexico to the east-southeast. When the moist winds from either direction encounter mountains and are lifted and cooled, the gaseous water condenses and precipitation is produced. The San Luis Valley is surrounded, except in the very south, by high mountains. The San Juan Mountains capture most of the precipitation from the Pacific, and the Wet Mountains and Sangre de Cristo Mountains receive the water from the Gulf. Little moisture is left for the San Luis Valley. The Great Sand Dunes National Monument averages about 10.04 inches of precipitation per year; the lower and more central areas of the San Luis Valley receive even less. The City of Alamosa gets only about 6.5 inches per year. The internal drainage of the northern part of the valley is evidence that there is not enough water gathered on the surface to enable streams to flow long enough to exit the area.

These same facts explain the huge underground aquifers in the valley. A large percentage of the precipitation captured by the mountains comes in the form of snow. In the spring this frozen water melts slowly, enters fractures, joints, and conduits in the bedrock, and moves leisurely downhill to eventually end up *below* the valley in the large aquifers.

Because the area is so arid and so high, the skies are unusually clear and vibrantly blue. Most clouds over the valley occur as cumulus clouds on summer afternoons when the valley gets most of its rain from thunderstorms. At most other times the lack of clouds causes both the very hot temperatures on the dunes and the very cold ones recorded at night during the winter. At 8,200 feet above sea level, the average elevation of the monument, there is considerably less atmosphere between the sun and the Earth's surface than at sea level. High-intensity solar insolation is received by the ground surface, especially on clear summer days. The mineral makeup of the sand allows it to absorb large quantities of solar energy quickly and re-emit that energy as heat — producing very hot sand in the summer. Clouds, when they do appear, act much like greenhouse glass in that they stop thermal energy from reradiating back to space at night when there is little or no incoming energy. Therefore, if you have clouds at night the temperature remains somewhat higher than without them. However, the valley has mostly clear nights during the winter so there is considerable heat loss and cold temperatures. These cold temperatures are reduced even more by the fact that cold air from the mountains is dense and actually flows downhill into the valley at night. Alamosa can get temperatures that reach -30 degrees F or lower during winter nights. The cold-air drainage is particularly severe during the infrequent calm days and nights that can occur in December through February.

These calm days are the true exception in the San Luis Valley in general and at the Great Sand Dunes National Monument in particular. The predominant wind from the southwest blows across the valley, unobstructed by topographic features or vegetation as it travels the almost flat valley floor. The wind is funneled into the area of the monument by the Sangre de Cristo Mountains and can become very strong for extended periods. The windiest season at the monument is definitely during the spring months of April through June, when the wind speed *averages* almost 45 miles per hour. If you happen to be walking on the dunes during this time, you will experience firsthand the effects of sand blasting. The solitary grains of sand get only 3 to 4 feet above the ground but are carried by these strong winds at very high speed. Your head will be safely above the sand storm (assuming you are 5 feet tall or more) but your torso and legs will be mercilessly abraded by millions of sharp-edged sand grains. It is an experience that you should have but once.

Another experience you probably do not want to encounter more than once is to be caught out on the dunes during one of the summer's violent thunderstorms. Two-thirds of the 10 inches of precipitation the monument receives each year comes from May to September. Almost all of this rainfall comes in the form of thunderstorms that drop large quantities of rain during very short periods of time. The greatest concern for visitors on the dunes, however, is the lightning that accompanies most thunderstorms. The violence and intensity of the lightning can be a most frightening and dangerous occurrence. A testament to the power inherent in lightning strikes on the dunes is the fused sand that is found occasionally where the lightning has instantaneously welded a multitude of sand grains together as it strikes. This "fulgurite" is a vivid reminder that you should get off the dunes if a storm is pending.

THE ECOSYSTEMS

Although the dunes themselves are the most spectacular and well-known feature of the monument, the area has a curious and varied mix of ecosystems that make it special if only for the juxtaposition of at least ten of the ecosystems described in Chapter 1. This does not include the ecosystem of the dunes, which is a special case. The spruce/fir forest, limber/bristlecone pine forest, subalpine/alpine ecotone, and alpine tundra ecosystems are all within view as you look toward the mountains. In the monument itself you will find examples of the semidesert shrub, piñon pine/juniper woodland, mountain riparian, quaking aspen forest, ponderosa pine forest, and Douglas fir forest ecosystems. None of these is extensive because they only surround the main core of the monument, but their presence reflects the complex nature of this intriguing part of the state. Although the specifics of these ecosystems are discussed in other chapters, there are important aspects of them that beg consideration here.

THE PERIPHERY

From the western edge of the monument and on into the center of the San Luis Valley, we find a true desert environment. Here the halophytes, or salt-loving plants, such as four-wing saltbush (*Atriplex canescens*) and greasewood or chico (*Sarcobatus vermiculatus*) abound. The plants must be salt tolerant because of the high evaporation rates and the mineral-rich character of the groundwater in the area.

At the eastern and northeastern edge of the monument, we find a very curious phenomenon. There are two treelines here: one at high elevations where the growing season is too short for tree growth and one at low elevations where there is cold-air drainage and little moisture. Evidence of this cold-air drainage can be found if you look closely at the positions of the ponderosa pine and piñon pine stands. The location of piñon pine is very temperature controlled; the tree will not grow *below* about 8,000 feet in the monument due to the cold air drainage. The ponderosa pine is limited only by moisture availability. Being more cold tolerant, it can survive the colder air below 8,000 feet (Figure 11.10). This phenomenon of piñon pines growing at higher elevations than ponderosa pines is a reversal of the norm; in most cases piñon pine is found in the band of foothill elevations below where the ponderosa pine grows (see Chapter 6, "Garden of the Gods").

Figure 11.10. Northeastern edge of the monument covered with montane life zone ponderosa pine and other species.

The monument contains very typical montane fauna. The most common mammals, birds, and reptiles of the montane are found here, but an intriguing change takes place with two species of amphibians that reside in the monument. The Great Plains toad (*Bufo cognatus*) and the spadefoot toad (*Scaphiopus bombifrons*), both usually found in the plains life zone, occur here, but they have altered their metamorphosis processes. They wait for optimal environmental conditions to occur before beginning metamorphosis and then have an accelerated metamorphosis that takes place in only a fraction of the time required by their lowland kin. This attests to the fact that the monument and the San Luis Valley both have a severe and, at times, unpredictable environment.

ON THE DUNES

This severe environment is taken to even greater lengths on the dunes themselves. Most casual visitors, upon first seeing the shifting surface sands, would assume that nothing much could live on the dunes; they are not altogether wrong. But there are both flora and fauna that make the dunes their home.

Like the tundra high above, the dunes are a severely drought-stricken and windblown area. However, there is a sanctuary of sorts in the hollows and leeward sides of the dunes where some moisture collects and winds are tempered. Here at least three species of perennial plants (two grasses and a legume) are beginning to get established: Indian rice-grass (*Oryzopsis hymenoides*), blowout grass (*Redfieldia flexousa*), and scurfpea (*Psoralea lanceolata*). These plants suffer several debilitating environmental constraints including very high and very low temperature extremes, abrasion by blowing sand, shifting sand around their roots, lack of moisture, and a dearth of nutrients. They survive anyway! As you walk on the dunes, you will encounter these patches of vegetation and will witness firsthand the tenacity of nature. Some time in the far-distant future, these plants and others may cover the dunes and stabilize them against even minor movement. You were there when this process began.

On the fringes of the dunes you also encounter the slow but inexorable encroachment of other plants that will contribute to eventual dune stability. The prairie sunflower (*Helianthus petiolaria*), for example, is an annual plant that is an opportunist. It grows during more benign years and adds stabilizing roots to the sand surface. Thistles (*Cirsium* spp.), wild geraniums (*Geranium fremontis*), primroses (*Oenothera* spp.), and sand begonias (*Rumex venosus*) are also encroaching around the border of the dunes.

The dunes are a special place for fauna as well. There are three endemic insect species that inhabit the sand of the dunes. These include the Great Sand Dunes tiger beetle (*Cicindela theatina*), the giant sand treader camel cricket (*Daihinibaen giganteus*), and the circus beetle (*Eleodes hirtipennis*). The tiger beetle feeds on other insects, and its bite is very unpleasant. The larvae dig vertical tunnels where they lie in wait to capture passing insects. The camel cricket, which has shovel-like features on its hind feet that help it to dig its burrow, is basically nocturnal, so you may never see it. The circus beetle is a dull, black insect that sprays a very malodorous inky fluid to ward off its predators. The only predator that is not put off by this smelly liquid is the northern grasshopper mouse.

Although there are several snake species found in the San Luis Valley, no one has ever seen the one rattlesnake of the area, the western prairie rattlesnake (*Crotalus viridis*), on the dunes. Because they are cold-blooded, the very high and low temperatures of the sand make the dunes extremely inhospitable to them.

FACTS AND MYTHS

If the natural history of the sand dunes is not enough to entice you to visit, the mystical quality of the area will surely do it. This book is not about human history and mythology, but I do want to tantalize you with just a few examples of local lore.

The human history of the region takes us back many millennia, to the Folsom peoples. Evidence exists in the valley of these people who traveled and hunted the area some 10,000 years ago. There is something profound and reassuring about the continuum of human involvement with the natural world here for these many, many years.

On a more mythical and legendary level, you may have a vision of web-footed horses crossing the dunes on bright, moonlit nights. The eerie stories of these fleeting horses may be inspired by the wild horse herds that have roamed the edges of the dunes in years past. There are also legends of mysteriously disappearing sheep flocks and their shepherds. Many flocks and herders passed through the area and were never seen again. These stories probably developed from the flocks that went up and over Medano and Mosca Passes into the Wet Mountain Valley beyond. Then there is the story of the Martinez family who homesteaded near the dunes. One day the Martinez boy was found wandering and dazed. Neighbors found his dead mother and father in their cabin; no explanation of their deaths has ever emerged.

The Great Sand Dunes National Monument is a very special place not only in Colorado but in North America and the world. It is a place where the naturalist can find unique and enchanting qualities. Endemic species, singular geology, and forbidding environments beg to be discovered. But the dunes can also be enjoyed for the sole delight of playing in America's largest sandbox. Children of all ages can come and enjoy this treasure and rest assured that the signs of their presence will be erased by the wind soon after their departure. Your footprints on the dunes are ephemeral, but your memories and experiences here will last a long time.

ADDITIONAL READINGS

Burford, A. E., 1961. "Petrology of the Great Sand Dunes, Colorado," *Proceedings of the West Virginia Academy of Science* 33, pp. 87–89.

Chronic, J., 1960. "Geology of South-Central Colorado." In *Guide to the Geology of Colorado,* ed. R. J. Weimer and J. D. Haun, Geologic Society of America, Denver, Colo.

Fleck, R. F., 1971. "The World of the Sand Dunes," *Colorado Outdoors* 20 (5), pp. 31–36.

Hansen, H., 1970. *Colorado: A Guide to the Highest State,* Hastings House, New York, N.Y.

Harris, D. V., 1980. *Geologic Story of the National Parks and Monuments,* John Wiley & Sons, New York, N.Y.

James, H. L., ed., 1971. *Guidebook of the San Luis Basin, Colorado,* New Mexico Geological Society, Santa Fe, N.Mex.

Johnson, R. B., 1967. *The Great Sand Dunes of Southern Colorado,* U.S. Geological Survey Professional Paper 575-C, pp. C177–C183.

May, S., 1987. *Pilgrimage,* Swallow Press, Athens, Ohio.

Merk, G. P., 1960. "Great Sand Dunes of Colorado." In *Guide to the Geology of Colorado,* ed. R. J. Weimer and J. D. Haun, Rocky Mountain Association of Geologists, Denver, Colo.

Tilden, F., 1986. *The National Parks,* Alfred A. Knopf, New York, N.Y.

Trimble, S. A., 1981. *Great Sand Dunes — The Shape of the Wind,* Southwest Parks and Monuments Association, Globe, Ariz.

Upson, J. E., 1939. "Physiographic Subdivisions of the San Luis Valley, Southern Colorado," *Journal of Geology* 47 (7), pp. 721–736.

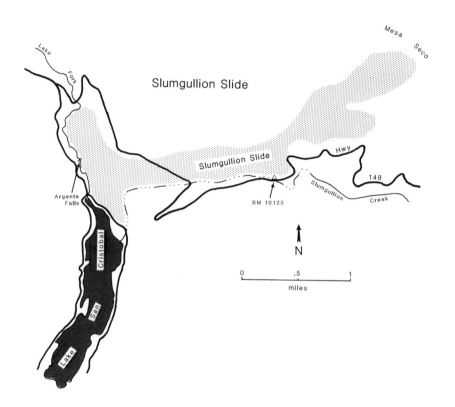

12

SLUMGULLION SLIDE

This chapter is unique for this book — it is about a solitary geological event that created a singular landscape. Four miles south of Lake City in the San Juan Mountains is Lake San Cristobal (Figure 12.1). Lake San Cristobal is much like other reservoirs in Colorado that are produced by dams that hold back the flowing waters. This dam, however, was not built by the U.S. Army Corps of Engineers or the Bureau of Reclamation; this dam was created by a gigantic earthflow that blocked the Lake Fork of the Gunnison River (Figure 12.2). The name given this earthflow is the "Slumgullion Slide."

Visitors here can witness firsthand the power and the interconnectedness of nature. They can see the result of Earth processes culminating in the collapse and movement of a mountainside; they can see the effects upon the vegetation regimes of the past and present; they can see the products of chemical changes in rock and mineral that create eerily lying ground; and in their mind's eye they can see the inevitable continuation of these phenomena into the future. This strange and wonderful landscape is disconcerting because of the abnormal landforms produced, the awesome power unleashed by nature, and the unusual effects on the vegetation and the ecosystems. This is why the Slumgullion Slide is such a singular place — it is a showcase for the raw power of nature and the multitude of landforms that natural processes can produce. The Slumgullion Slide is a living testament to the complexity, vitality, and creativity of the natural environment.

What extraordinary processes and forces produced this phenomenon we call the Slumgullion Slide? The answer to this question is the central focus

Figure 12.1. Lake San Cristobal, the product of the massive flow of the Slumgullion Slide.

Figure 12.2. The light-colored earth at left center is the dam for Lake San Cristobal.

of this chapter. The chapter will also look at the resulting characteristics of the environment.

MASS MOVEMENT OF EARTH MATERIAL

Whenever there is a slope consisting of any type of Earth material, the force of gravity incessantly pulls upon it. Only the coherence and strength of the rock and soil that make up the hill or mountainside prevent the slope from moving toward the valley below. If the pull of gravity exceeds the strength, the slope fails, and the rock and soil move downhill. The generic term for this process is "mass wasting" or "mass movement." The manner in which this movement takes place primarily depends on the type of material making up the slope and the amount of water mixed in with the earth constituent.

Mass movement slopes may take many forms, as seen in Figure 12.3. The particular form that occurs depends upon the rock/soil mixture, the speed of movement, and the amount of moisture incorporated in the earth mass. The Slumgullion Slide is defined as an earthflow; it contained considerable water and moved very rapidly (at least the first major flow). The mass of

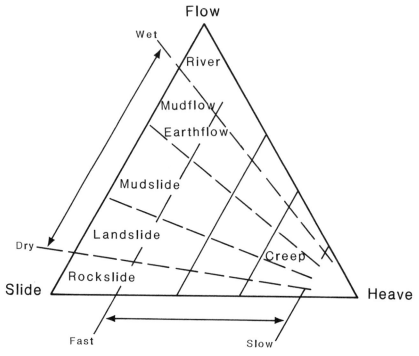

Figure 12.3. Diagram showing how moisture and the speed of movement determine the kind of mass wasting that will take place. The Slumgullion Slide is really an earth- and mudflow.

rock and soil that make up the Slumgullion Slide flowed much like a heavily mud- and rock-laden river. To get a feel for how this might have looked at the moment of failure, imagine millions of tons of wet concrete being released instantaneously and flowing downhill. What could have caused the movement of material on this scale? The answer is complex and not yet fully understood, but earth scientists have pieced together the major elements involved.

THE SLUMGULLION SLIDE

The story of the slide began about 28 million years ago (mya). At that time the area that we now know as the San Juan Mountains was beginning a period of intense volcanic activity (see Chapter 9, "Silverton"). A cataclysmic series of volcanic eruptions occurred, of a size to make the 1980 Mount

St. Helens eruption look minuscule. These eruptions created the Uncompahgre caldera, a large depression produced when the top of the volcanic center collapsed upon itself (Figure 12.4). Because so much molten rock (magma) was evacuated from the chamber below the Earth's surface, the summit area no longer had the underlying rock to support it. In a violent and rapid moment, the top collapsed and generated a depression with innumerable faults, fractures, and broken (brecciated) rock.

Tremendous masses of ash, lava, and other volcanic debris were ejected during this episode. For the next several million years, volcanic activity continued in the region, including the development of the Silverton caldera (27.5 mya) and the Lake City caldera (22.5 mya) (Figure 12.5). More volcanic debris was produced during these eruptions, and layer upon layer of volcanic rock was formed over much of the San Juan Mountains. These volcanic rock types include rhyolite, andesite, and many varieties of welded and unwelded tuff. Tuff is formed when volcanic-ash flows consolidate to eventually form rock; welded tuff is created when the ash is hot enough at the time of deposition to "weld" itself together.

The upper reaches of the Slumgullion Slide sit just above the highly fractured zone of rock along the eastern flank of the Uncompahgre caldera. There are numerous other faults that crisscross this zone, and there may be a substantial fault that runs directly under the slide itself. These fractures and fissures allowed gases and fluids to travel from great depths to the surface. The gases and fluids have chemically altered the rock and caused tremendous weathering and erosion of the high rock walls. At the very head of the slide along Mesa Seco is a large basin nearly four-fifths of a mile wide. The basin is surrounded by volcanic rock cliffs that average nearly 500 feet high. These cliffs are the ready source of weathered rock and mineral debris that, over innumerable millennia, have fallen into the basin. The continued weathering of this debris once it fell from the walls produced a clay mineral called "montmorillonite." The crystalline pattern of montmorillonite is such that it takes water directly into the crystal structure of the clay, causing the mineral to expand and swell. When the clay particle dries, the water leaves the crystal, and the clay shrinks back to its former size. This swell-and-shrink capacity of montmorillonite is very destructive to other rock and soil because tremendous pressures can be exerted by the swelling particles. The montmorillonite agitated and lubricated the massive buildup of fallen debris.

The debris finally and catastrophically collapsed and flowed down the mountainside about A.D. 1270 (Figure 12.6). Scientists are confident of this date because of radiocarbon dating of dead trees that were killed by the

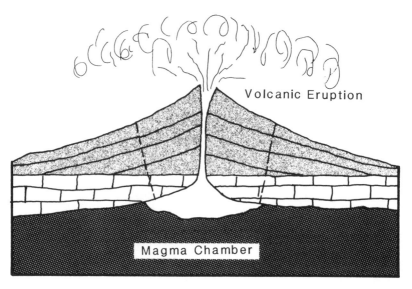

Volcanic Eruption

Magma Chamber

Stage 1

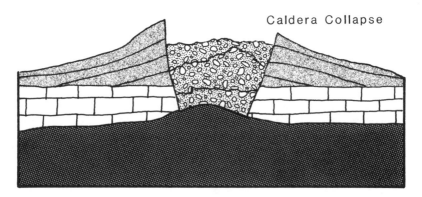

Caldera Collapse

Stage 2

12.4. Schematic showing the process of creating a caldera. Massive amounts of magma are removed from the chamber. This weakens the rock and causes the upper part of the mountain to collapse.

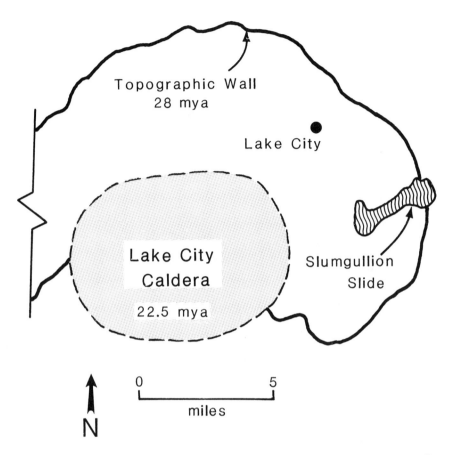

Topographic Wall
28 mya

Lake City

Lake City
Caldera

22.5 mya

Slumgullion
Slide

0   5
miles

N

Figure 12.5. The location of the Slumgullion Slide at the edge of the large caldera wall aided the development of the slide as we see today.

flooding of Lake San Cristobal. The dimensions of the flow are staggering — it is almost 4.5 miles long, 500 to 2,000 feet wide, and contains an estimated 8.5 billion cubic feet of earth.

The toe or end of this flow formed the dam that created Lake San Cristobal. As the flow hit the valley bottom, it spread both north and south along the Lake Fork valley. Eventually, the lake found an outlet on the western side of the toe; it now flows over Argenta Falls and on to the main branch of the Gunnison River and Blue Mesa Reservoir. The lake formed is just over 2 miles long and 2,060 feet at its widest, with a maximum depth of about 90 feet.

Figure 12.6. The slide from the opposite valley wall.

Rock and soil debris continued to collect in the basin, and about 350 years ago another flow began. This flow was much slower but more persistent than the first — in fact, it is still moving. The second flow starts at the top of the original slide and reaches down the slope some 2.5 miles.

THE SECOND FLOW

The second flow is moving incessantly if inconsistently. The speed of the flow varies from year to year and from place to place. Rates of movement have been measured for decades. The general conclusions are that the middle of the flow moves faster, the edges slower; the upper areas move swiftly, the toe barely creeps along. The speeds vary from about 2 feet per year to almost 20 feet per year. Two distinguished researchers of the slide, Dwight Crandell and David Varnes, both with the U.S. Geological Survey, have even observed slowly moving waves in the mass of rock and soil. The whole effect is a jumbled and chaotic landscape (Figure 12.7).

For those who wish to explore this surrealistic terrain firsthand, a good place to reach the upper slide is near the 10,123-foot bench mark (see the Lake San Cristobal Quadrangle, U.S. Geological Survey, 7.5-minute map series) where Slumgullion Creek crosses Highway 149 between Lake City and Slumgullion Pass. Be careful if you do venture onto the earthflow; precipitation can make much of the ground a quagmire because of the high clay content. You will know when you reach the currently moving part of the flow, because the vegetation here is strikingly different from that on the older flow and even more different from that on the surrounding nonflow areas.

THE VEGETATION

The elevation of the slide ranges from 8,840 feet at the base of the dam/toe to approximately 11,600 feet at the top of the earthflow near the summit of Mesa Seco. Thus the region of the slide spans the montane and subalpine life zones and approaches the alpine. Ecosystems on the undisturbed mountainsides and valleys are typical of those found elsewhere in central Colorado. The montane is dominated by ponderosa pine (*Pinus ponderosa*) and Douglas fir (*Pseudotsuga menziesii*) ecosystems whereas

Figure 12.7. Jumble of trees and other vegetation on the slide surface.

Figure 12.8. Very little vegetation survives on the active part of the slide.

the subalpine contains the spruce/fir ecosystem of Engelmann (*Picea engelmannii*) and blue (*P. pungens*) spruce and subalpine fir (*Abies lasiocarpa*) and many examples of mountain riparian and mountain meadow ecosystems.

The relatively stable lower and older slide areas also reflect these typical ecosystems. Only a smattering of bent and dislodged trees indicates that this area is still not totally motionless. The vegetation on the newer slide, however, reflects the awesome power unleashed here by nature.

THE VEGETATION OF THE ACTIVE SLIDE

If an ecosystem is defined as the composite of all organisms and physical factors that occur in one place, then the active earthflow zone of the Slumgullion Slide could be described as having its own ecosystem — the "slide" ecosystem. This designation would hardly be accepted formally by ecologists, but it does give an idea of just how unique the vegetation environment is here.

Although this part of the slide underwent its most drastic movement 350 years ago, there are, as yet, few mature trees (Figure 12.8). It resembles a "zone of death" where new, young trees and shrubs begin life but never make it to maturity. Not only is there little older vegetation, there is little vegetation at all! Where other places discussed in this book may have several full-fledged ecosystems in close juxtaposition, here there is only a handful of species in total. Constant moving and shearing of the root zones of most plants cause weakness and death over a span of a few years. If movement is rapid, plant destruction may be immediate. Many of the smaller forbs have adapted to the motion and the high clay content of the soils. They have developed a "rubbery" root modification such that their root systems resemble "rubber bands"; this elasticity absorbs some of the lesser motion. These roots also spread very dramatically in the lateral direction, with almost no vertical growth downward into the soil.

Only three species of trees make up the arboreous vegetation. Alder (*Alnus tenuifolia*) is found only at the slowly moving toe of the active slide. Engelmann spruce and quaking aspen (*Populus tremuloides*), the only other tree species, are widely spread across the flow in seemingly random patterns. Evidence of the movement of the flow is easily seen in the chaotic character of the tree trunks (Figure 12.9). Trees normally attempt to grow vertically, in direct opposition to gravity. If a tree is bent as a result of being pushed at its base through slope movement, subsequent growth will be vertical from that point in time. When the tree is bent anew it will again attempt to grow vertically. The result can be grotesquely twisted trunks. Because the roots are under tremendous stress, most trees will eventually be killed by the constant motion, leaving only the younger trees in the slide ecosystem. This age structure of the vegetation is a striking characteristic of the Slumgullion Slide.

Grasses are almost nonexistent in this zone. Small quantities of Junegrass (*Koeleria macrantha*) can be found, and several flourishing areas of sedge (*Carex* spp.) spread across the undulating ground, but very few other species of grass are present. Sedges are more opportunistic than grasses; once established they reproduce more vigorously especially in the wetter areas on the flow. Rushes (*Juncus* spp.) are also relatively abundant because of their affinity for saturated ground and their ability to reproduce from underground shoots. Other plants that make up the sparse vegetation on the flow include milkvetch (*Astragalus* spp.), kinnikinnick (*Arctostaphylos uva-ursi*), dandelion (*Taraxacum officinale*), and lambstongue groundsel (*Senecio integerrimus*). Few of these are found as mature plants because the age structure of even the forb vegetation on the slide favors only the young.

Figure 12.9. A forest of crooked trees created by the movement of the Earth.

Figure 12.10. Small ponds of water support masses of aquatic vegetation and eerie ecosystems.

On more stable sections of the flow, you will find older plants of many species. You will even find several species of grass, including Arizona fescue *(Festuca arizonica)*, mountain muhly *(Muhlenbergia montana)*, and blue-grass *(Poa* spp.).

OTHER SURFACE FEATURES

Scattered throughout the active slide area are numerous small ponds and pools of water (Figure 12.10). The sedges and rushes mentioned above thrive in and around these moist areas. Ponds are also filled with colorful mosses at various levels within the clear water. Interestingly, many of these ponds appear to lack any input or output flows — no streams enter or exit the pools.

Whereas most of these pools are remnants of intermittent streams that were diverted, leaving the ponds isolated, some of the ponds are the result of perched water tables that reach the surface in the minor depressions occupied by open water. A perched water table is created when groundwater sits atop an impervious surface of some sort that prevents the water from percolating farther into the ground. The most likely material for the impervious surface here is clay — recall that a large component of the flow is the clay, montmorillonite. When packed and wet the montmorillonite produces a very impermeable surface. Its exceptional qualities in this regard allow it to be used to line the bottoms of toxic waste sites to prevent the leaching of hazardous materials into groundwater sources. These isolated ponds lend to the strangeness of the landscape on the slide; verdant mosses hovering in the water and deep green sedges and rushes ringing the pools lie incongruously among the bare and jumbled ground of the otherwise moon-like surface.

On the surface of the Slumgullion Slide are many examples of geomorphic processes occurring on much smaller scales. The surface is marked by innumerable intermittent streams that erode and rework the loose soil and rock. Wind scours the surface of the flow and sculpts fine features into the landscape. One of the most interesting of these processes involves the presence of smaller and very fluid mudflows that occur on top of the main mass of the large flow. These smaller mudflows are typical of those where there is an abundance of loose, fine-grained rock and soil, relatively steep slopes, sparse vegetation, and large but intermittent flows of water. Large quantities of water come from quick snowmelts in spring or severe thunderstorms in spring and summer. The landforms resulting from these mudflows are the small, steep-sided ravines with substantial natural levees paralleling the sides of the small valleys. These levees look incongruous because they seem like human-made features that required large earth-moving equipment. They are natural, however, and a part of the enigmatic and strange earth forms we experience at the Slumgullion Slide.

FINAL THOUGHTS

One definition of the word "slumgullion" is "a stew of meat, vegetables, potatoes, etc." A meal made up of this stew would seem to have something for every taste, especially when the "etc." can mean almost any other ingredient available. The Slumgullion Slide is like a stew of this kind; it has something for every taste. The botanist can ponder the sparsity of flora species and the awkward lean of the young trees. The geomorphologist can study the perched water tables and the mudflow levees. The geologist can study the origin of the slide and the mineral potential of the hidden fault zones of the area. The soil scientist can analyze the modification of the minerals to clay particles and determine the value of the ground for future vegetation growth. The list could go on and on. Whatever your interest in the natural world, there is something for you at the Slumgullion Slide. This unique landform is strange and wonderful, and it is easily accessible to most people. This is a naturalist's opportunity you should not miss.

ADDITIONAL READINGS

Carson, M. A., and M. J. Kirkby, 1972. *Hillslope Form and Process,* Cambridge University Press, Cambridge, Mass.

Chronic, H., 1980. *Roadside Geology of Colorado,* Mountain Press Publishing Company, Missoula, Mont.

Kuntz, D. W., H. J. Armstrong, and F. J. Athearn, 1989. *Faults, Fossils, and Canyons: Significant Geologic Features on Public Lands in Colorado,* U.S. Bureau of Land Management, Denver, Colo.

Lipman, P. W., 1976. *Geologic Map of the Lake City Caldera Area, Western San Juan Mountains, Southwestern Colorado,* U.S. Geological Survey, Map I-962, Denver, Colo.

Mohlenbrock, R. H., 1989. "Slumgullion Slide, Colorado," *Natural History* 98 (4), pp. 34–37.

13

COLORADO NATIONAL MONUMENT

On a sunny, warm, calm day, a person sitting almost anywhere in the Colorado National Monument and viewing the multicolored rocks and subdued vegetation of the land has a nearly overwhelming sense of tranquility. It seems as though this landscape has been here forever, that nothing much changes now, nor has it changed even in the far-distant past. This peaceful facade masks the turbulent geologic history of this region we call the Uncompahgre Plateau. The 32 square miles of the Colorado National Monument are but a small part of the Uncompahgre Plateau, which in turn is but a small segment of the 130,000-square-mile Colorado Plateau geologic province of Colorado, Utah, New Mexico, and Arizona (Figure 13.1). The Colorado Plateau is the home of some of the world's most beautiful, awe-inspiring, and famous natural landmarks such as the Grand Canyon, Arches, Canyonlands, Zion, Bryce Canyon, and Monument Valley.

Colorado National Monument sits at the very northeastern edge of the Colorado Plateau and is, therefore, a perfect place to witness the geologic development of the province with reference to the lands surrounding it. Here you can see the relationship between the high mountain orogenies of the Rockies and the broad, regional uplifts of the plateau epeirogenies. An epeirogeny is an uplift, on a grand scale, of vast land areas without much folding, faulting, or tilting. You see the flat yet elevated plateaus, mesas, and buttes of the monument in relation to the Grand Valley below that belongs to the Colorado (Grand) River and to people who base their lives on the

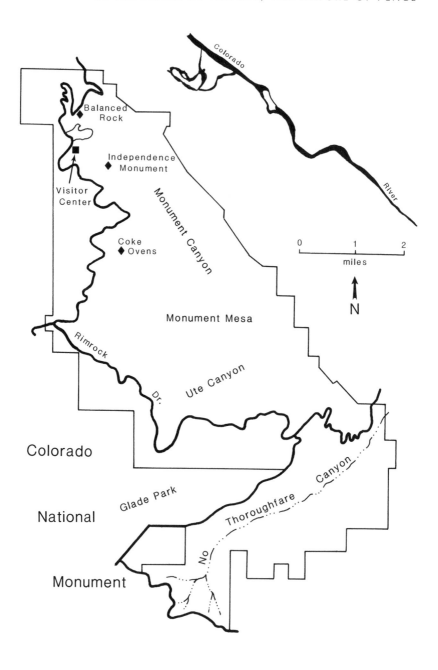

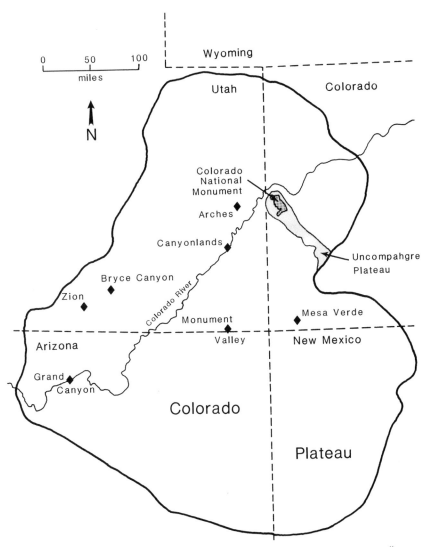

Figure 13.1. Colorado National Monument and the Uncompahgre Plateau, a small part of the Colorado Plateau that makes up a large segment of four states.

productive orchards of the bottomland. The town lying just north of the monument is appropriately named "Fruita" in honor of the economic mainstay here.

The principal story of the Colorado National Monument, however, lies in its rock and canyon landscapes, its distinctive flora and fauna, its long human record, and its place in the chronicle of the land between the Rockies and the Great Basin. The foundation for the landscape lies firmly in the geologic history of the Uncompahgre and Colorado plateaus.

THE GEOLOGIC TALE

The germane history of the Uncompahgre Plateau and the Colorado National Monument began about 300 million years ago (mya), at the same time as the orogenic uplift of the "Ancestral Rockies" (see Chapter 6, "Garden of the Gods"). East of here high mountains were formed from the relatively localized, violent, and uneven uplift of sections of the Earth's crust. At the site of the Uncompahgre Plateau, the 1.6-billion-year-old gneisses and schists of the Precambrian were elevated high above the surrounding lands. The difference between the mountains and plateaus was that the plateau land rose more uniformly — much like lifting up a layer cake while it is still on the platter. The increased altitude of the land created an erosional environment in which almost all rocks atop the Precambrians were eroded away and the land again approached sea level. What remains of these Precambrian rocks is seen today in the canyons of the region (Figure 13.2).

THE SEDIMENTARY ROCK LAYERS

From about 300 mya we begin to get a series of sedimentary layers laid down almost horizontally. Many variations of sediments deposited in many kinds of environments are stacked one upon the other. The first layer is the Chinle formation: a dark red siltstone and shale lying directly atop the Precambrian metamorphic rocks. This contact is called the "Great Unconformity" because of the long (1.3-billion-year) break in the geologic time sequence between the two formations.

On top of the Chinle lies the most dramatic rock of the monument. The Wingate sandstone is a tan to light red rock that forms the very high cliffs so dominant along Rimrock Drive. These sandstone cliffs form so vertically

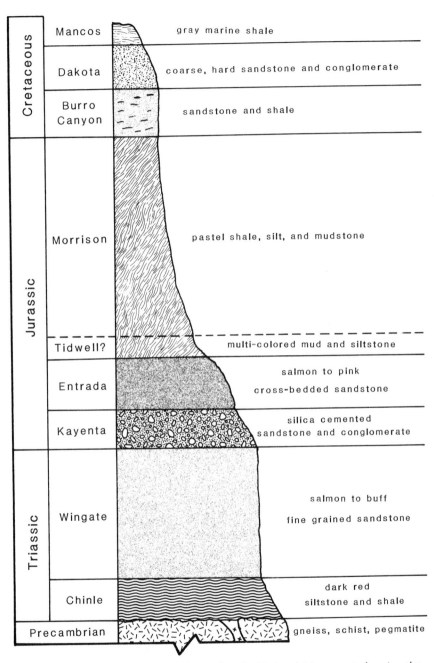

Figure 13.2. Geologic column of the Colorado National Monument showing the temporal relationship among the various rock types of the region. The Wingate sandstone near the bottom of the column is the main cliff-forming rock of the monument.

because of the way that the Wingate sandstone fractures. Most major pieces of the rock break off in large vertical slabs (Figure 13.3).

The Wingate formation is not a very resistant rock and would weather and erode very quickly if not for the protection of the rock lying just above it. The Kayenta formation is a hard, red sandstone and conglomerate cemented by silica, one of the most resistant minerals. Much of the monument — including Rimrock Drive, the monument headquarters, and the campground — sits on the Kayenta.

Some of the most beautiful rock seen in the monument, especially in the northwestern half, is just above the Kayenta and is called the Entrada sandstone. This light salmon-red ancient sand dune deposit weathers to very muted and rounded forms. All over the West it is referred to as "slick rock" because of its propensity to be slippery as sand dislodges underfoot. The Entrada is also famous for the natural arches formed of it throughout the Colorado Plateau and in particular in Utah's Arches National Park, less than 50 miles to the west.

Most of the higher lands of the monument lie in the southeastern half. The rocks here are layered above the Entrada and include the Summerville formation — now thought to be the lower Tidwell member of the Morrison formation just above. The shales, mudstones, and siltstones of the Morrison and the thin beds of the Burro Canyon formation are all capped by hard, resistant Dakota sandstone. This Morrison is found throughout the state and is famous for its dinosaur fossils. No fossils have yet been found in the monument, but given enough time and erosion, some future hiker in the monument might stumble upon some. For now the only sign of dinosaurs in the Colorado National Monument are tracks of tetradons found along the Chinle/Wingate contact. These are much older creatures (about 200 million years old) than those found elsewhere in the Morrison.

THE MONOCLINE

A dominant feature of the monument and the Uncompahgre Plateau can be seen with amazing clarity if you enter through the Fruita side. This is the rock-warping, monoclinal fold you traverse as you ascend into the monument. A monocline is the bending of horizontal rock layers as they are uplifted on one side but not the other (Figure 13.4). Renewed uplift of the Uncompahgre Plateau about 8 mya created the heights we see today in the main part of the monument. The monocline as seen near "balanced rock" (Figure 13.5) is one piece of evidence for this great uplift. The vertical extent

Figure 13.3. Fractures and cracks that keep the face of the Wingate sandstone vertical.

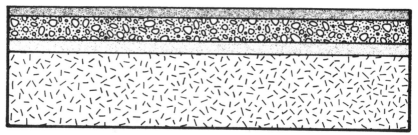

Horizontal Sediments Lying on
Precambrian Basement Rock

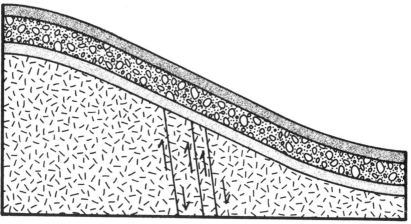

Monoclinal Fold in Sediments with
Faults in the Basement Rock

Figure 13.4. Schematic showing the bending of the monocline and creation of the upland that is now a major part of the monument. You can see this monocline easily as you enter the northern entrance and drive the curving road into the monument.

Figure 13.5. Balanced rock and the warping of the monocline in the northwest part of the monument.

of the Earth's movement is manifest if you look across the valley to the north and see the Book Cliffs. These cliffs are composed mainly of Mancos shale capped by a resistant sandstone and lie 1,500 feet above the valley floor. In the geologic column the Mancos is above the rocks in the monument. As you stand on the Kayenta formation you are at eye level with Mancos shale that should be thousands of feet above you. This is the vertical displacement that occurred here to create the monocline and the Uncompahgre Plateau.

THE EROSION

The rocks of the Uncompahgre Plateau and the Colorado National Monument have not been immune to the landform processes of weathering and erosion. In fact, without erosion, the creative force of the monument, we would not be very impressed with this landscape. It is the weathering and erosion of millions of years that created the stark contrasts of plateau and canyon. And it is the differential erosion of the assorted rock types that gives us the varied nature of the landscape.

The most famous landform in the Colorado National Monument is Independence Monument (Figure 13.6). This 450-feet-high monolith is but a temporary rock bastion defying the relentless gnawing of erosion. Independence Monument has outlasted much of the other rock only because of the tough caprock (the Kayenta) that sits atop it. The thick layer of Wingate sandstone that makes up most of the monolith is a relatively weak rock that is removed rapidly in geologic timescales. If the Kayenta did not protect Independence Monument, the result would be similar to the Coke Ovens formation seen along the canyon walls of Monument Canyon (Figure 13.7). The Coke Ovens have lost their protective Kayenta caprock and are being summarily destroyed by wind, rain, and ice. These elements are constant and dogged. The entire Uncompahgre Plateau will eventually become a series of disconnected mesas, then buttes, then monuments, then pinnacles, then sky. Without renewed uplift in the future, the entire plateau will some-day, eons hence, be leveled. This is the eventual fate of the Colorado Plateau and the Rockies themselves. It will take millions upon millions of years, but it will happen.

Figure 13.6. Independence Monument, a lone bulwark against the relentless forces of erosion.

Figure 13.7. The Coke Ovens have lost their protective cap of the Kayenta formation and will soon be gone.

THE LIFE OF THE MONUMENT

The flora and fauna of the Colorado National Monument must survive on only 10 to 12 inches of precipitation each year. This near-desert amount of rainfall is accompanied by intense sunshine and dramatic temperature fluctuations between night and day and winter and summer. In addition to these weather extremes, soils upon which the vegetation depends are alkaline, rocky, and far from fertile.

Plants here must adapt or die. Desert and semi-desert flora abound in water-conserving tricks that allow a surprising variety and density of vegetation cover to exist here. Some plants have leaves that are small and waxy, keeping the loss of water through transpiration to a minimum. Piñon pine (*Pinus edulis*) and Utah juniper (*Juniperus osteo sperma*) exhibit this water-saving trait. Plants such as Mormon tea (*Ephedra viridis*) go so far as to eliminate leaves altogether. This strange looking shrub resembles a small stand of green sticks two to three feet high. Other plants use small hairs on their leaves to reduce water loss; the cactus takes this practice to an extreme, with leaves that have become sharp spines. Everywhere you look you can find wondrous and ingenious adaptations that enable plants to live and flourish in this dry environment.

THE CANYON BOTTOMS

The life zone classification scheme used throughout the rest of the book does not work particularly well for the vegetation of the monument. There is an elevation differentiation for vegetation communities, but it is more akin to that in other parts of the Colorado Plateau and the desert southwest than to the elevation differentiation of the mountains and plains of Colorado.

The lowest, driest, and harshest environment of the monument is the canyon bottoms where vegetation must struggle with low precipitation rates and the very poor soils developed on the Precambrian rocks. These areas are dominated by grasses and low-stature, salt-resistant shrubs such as rubber rabbitbrush (*Chrysothamnus nauseosus*), several sage species (*Artemisia spp.*), and numerous saltbush species (*Atriplex spp.*) (Figure 13.8). The stark nature of these canyon floors is softened by the multicolors of blossoms in spring and summer. The Stansbury cliff rose (*Cowania mexicana*), Fendler bush (*Fendlera rupicola*), and cactus flowers abound and brighten this otherwise bleak landscape.

Figure 13.8. Desertlike vegetation in the bottoms of one of the monument canyons.

In dramatic contrast to most of the forbidding canyon bottoms are the riparian ribbons that wind wherever water accumulates and intermittently flows. These places are quite evident, with their canyon (*Populus fremontii*) and narrowleaf cottonwoods (*P. angustifolia*), willows (*Salix spp.*), and human-introduced tamarisk or salt-cedar (*Tamarix ramosissima*).

If you hike along these bottomlands you are likely to notice the multitude of reptiles and amphibians. In one two-hour hike along the bottom of No Thoroughfare Canyon, I saw red-spotted toads (*Bufo punctatus*), canyon treefrogs (*Hyla arenicolor*), western whiptails (*Cnemidophorus velox*), desert striped whipsnakes (*Masticophis taeniatus*), the yellow-headed collared lizard (*Crotaphytus collaris*), and the eastern fence lizard (*Sceloporus undulatus*). This trail, like others in the canyons, is alive with scurrying, desert-defying fauna.

The largest animal of the Colorado National Monument lived most of its life in these deep canyons but was removed several years ago. The American bison or buffalo (*Bison bison*) was introduced to the monument by John Otto in 1926. This species thrived — at times so much so that it had to be thinned. Many sections of the delicate, desertlike ecosystems of these lower elevations were destroyed or seriously damaged by the bison. Occasionally, monument rangers sighted bison on the Kayenta bench far above the canyon floor; no one has ever been able to determine how the bison got up the cliffs. In 1983 the 43 to 45 animals that still lived here were finally removed. The National Park Service decided that these large, voracious herbivores did not belong in this fragile environment.

THE CANYON WALLS

To many people the seemingly bare rocks of the cliffs several hundred feet high are a sterile and forbidding landform. This impression is not without some merit; gravity, water, ice, and wind remove soil and rock fragments that might otherwise provide soil for plants. The beautiful and vibrant colors of the cliffs are those of fresh rock because the detritus of the weathered rock are constantly being removed.

In spite of the meager prospect for life to exist and thrive on these crags, it does survive here. Tenacious piñon pines and Utah junipers hold fast to the smallest cracks and crevasses in the rock faces. At times the roots of these trees follow fissures tens of yards down through the rock in search of water and nutrients. Cliff rose, Fendler bush, mountain mahogany (*Cercocarpus montanus*), and Utah serviceberry (*Amelanchier utahensis*) all cleave to the precarious ledges and joints along the more northern walls of the canyons.

The cliffs are a comfortable home to several bird species as well. The aerial displays of the white-throated swift (*Aeronautes saxatalis*) and several swallow types including the cliff swallow (*Hirundo pyrrhonota*) can be seen in spring and summer. The majesty of the golden eagle (*Aquila chrysaetos*) graces the monument in all seasons. Prairie falcons (*Falco mexicanus*) exhibit their wonderful flying skill and diving speed in search of a meal. The monument is even home to at least one pair of the endangered peregrine falcon (*F. peregrinus*). These birds seek the high vantage points of the cliffs to propel them into their 100-mile-per-hour dives.

Fewer mammals inhabit or visit the steep slopes of the monument cliffs. One exception is the desert bighorn sheep (*Ovis canadensis*), first reintroduced in 1979. No hard evidence exists that these ungulates lived here before, but the prevailing assumption is that they were once native to the area. About 15 animals were transplanted to the monument and to the area just west of the monument, and several more were brought in over the next few years. There are now about 150 sheep that frequent the area near Kodels Canyon in the far northern part of the monument property.

THE RIMROCK

To the majority of visitors, the most familiar biotic area of the monument is the rimrock or Kayenta bench area on top of the Kayenta formation. Extensive piñon-juniper woodland marks this mesa-top vegetation zone. Below 6,000 feet the Utah juniper is the dominant species of the piñon-juniper woodland. These gnarled and aristocratic trees (Figure 13.9) are able to withstand lower precipitation levels than the piñon pines. Above 6,000 feet the pine slowly becomes dominant. It takes several human generations of time for these trees to become mature in the dry and windy climate of the Uncompahgre Plateau (Figure 13.10). The understory vegetation in the woodland is sparse, with considerable bare ground between plants. The shrubs that exist here, much like those on the canyon floors, are very closely related to Great Basin species far to the west in the Nevada deserts and mountains. There are Mormon tea, single-leaf alder (*Fraxinus anomala*), Russian olive (*Elaeagnus angustifolia*), several sage species, and greasewood (*Sarcobatus vermiculatus*).

Most of the more well-known mammals of the Colorado National Monument live and travel on the bench. The mountain lion (*Felis concolor*)

Figure 13.9. Utah junipers dominate the lower piñon-juniper woodland of the monument.

Figure 13.10. Piñon pine becomes increasingly dominant as the elevation increases.

thrives on the large herds of mule deer (*Odocoileus hemionus*). Coyotes (*Canis latrans*), foxes (*Vulpes macrotis* and *Urocyon cinereoargenteus*), and bobcats (*F. rufus*) keep the jackrabbit (*Lepus spp.*) and rodent populations at bay. The sparse vegetation supports a surprising variety and density of fauna throughout the rimrock area and in the higher grounds to the west and south.

In the more isolated uplands along the southwest edge of the monument, you will even find small stands of ponderosa pine (*P. ponderosa*), Douglas fir (*Pseudotsuga menziesii*), scrub oak (*Quercus gambelii*), and scattered aspen groves (*Populus tremuloides*). These areas get slightly more precipitation than the rest of the monument. Most visitors never venture into these more inaccessible enclaves of varied and unexpected ecosystems.

HUMAN HABITATION

The most famous occupant of the land that we now know as the Colorado National Monument was John Otto. His persevering, tenacious, and often eccentric one-man campaign to turn his beloved canyons and mesas into a protected area succeeded. He was the singular force behind the creation of the Colorado National Monument on May 24, 1911. Otto served as the first custodian of the monument until 1927. He eventually left the country he cherished and never returned.

A more intriguing and certainly longer occupation was that by the Native Americans. Paleo-Indians lived and lingered here at least 8,000 years ago and maybe even earlier. Clovis or Folsom projectile points have been found in Glade Park just to the southwest of the monument. These quartzite points probably were made from local deposits of the mineral that are found on Black Ridge. This archaic culture survived until approximately A.D. 400 when a new culture, the Fremont people, started to emerge.

The Fremont were closely related to the Anasazi who lived south of here at Mesa Verde and in what is now New Mexico and Arizona. Agriculture was the basis of livelihood for these people, who developed irrigation projects to help in raising crops of beans, squash, and corn. The Fremont, who may or may not have been a separate group from the Anasazi, disappeared at about the same moment that the Anasazi left the canyons of Mesa Verde — about A.D. 1,300.

The Utes replaced and may have overlapped with the Fremont culture. When the Utes acquired horses from the Spanish, they became the dominant tribe in what is now eastern Utah and the western two-thirds of Colorado. They thrived for centuries, but not long after the 1879 "Meeker Massacre" they were driven from the region. By 1881 they were relegated to reservations in Utah and southwestern Colorado.

The fertile valleys to the north and east of the monument were settled by whites who created a thriving agricultural economy based primarily on fruits and vegetables. Few of these settlers ventured into the canyons of the monument area except for some ranchers who grazed cattle on the tops of the mesas. John Otto, virtually alone, lived in and promoted the lands of this most beautiful corner of the Uncompahgre Plateau.

FINAL THOUGHTS

Colorado National Monument serves Colorado as the door to the landscapes of the southwest. The monument, with its flora and fauna, its red rock and sheer cliffs, its grand vistas and intimate corners, is the beginning of the Colorado Plateau country and the strange and intense canyon lands that so densely populate it. The protracted story of millions upon millions of acres of land is summarized here where we can read it on a human scale. Once you have seen and fathomed this corner of mesas and buttes, go discover the other spectacular and grand sites across the southwestern horizon. The Colorado National Monument is merely the titillating hors d'oeuvre for the main course.

Discussion of the Colorado National Monument was saved for this chapter because it summarizes so well many of the canons of nature discussed at length throughout the previous chapters. Here we see the ebb and flow of life as it battles for moisture; the recycling of mineral matter — once a sand dune, now the Entrada formation; the intermittent, yet relentless, work of erosion that sculpts and destroys the land. We also see the colossal forces of the Earth's crust, where horizontal sediments are lifted en masse thousands of feet above the surrounding terrain. We can experience the gentler side of nature as well — the soft breezes, colorful sunsets, and solitude of a mesa top. This place is unquestionably a monument to Colorado and the natural landscapes of the state.

ADDITIONAL READINGS

Baars, D. L., 1983. *The Colorado Plateau,* University of New Mexico Press, Albuquerque, N.Mex.

Chronic, H., 1980. *Roadside Geology of Colorado,* Mountain Press Publishing Co., Missoula, Mont.

Chronic, J., and H. Chronic, 1972. *Prairie, Peak and Plateau,* Colorado Geological Survey Bulletin 32, Denver, Colo.

Elmore, F. H., 1976. *Shrubs and Trees of the Southwest Uplands,* Southwest Parks and Monuments Association, Globe, Ariz.

Harris, D. V., 1980. *The Geologic Story of the National Parks and Monuments,* John Wiley & Sons, New York, N.Y.

Houk, R., 1987. *A Guide to the Rimrock Drive — Colorado National Monument,* Colorado National Monument Association, Fruita, Colo.

Kania, A. J., 1984. *John Otto of Colorado National Monument,* Roberts Rinehart, Inc. Publishers, Boulder, Colo.

Lohman, S. W., 1981. *The Geologic Story of Colorado National Monument,* U.S. Geological Survey Bulletin 1508, Washington, D.C.

Zarn, M., 1979. *Ecological Characteristics of Piñon-Juniper Woodlands on the Colorado Plateau,* U.S. Bureau of Land Management Technical Note 310, Washington, D.C.

14

EPILOGUE

If you visit even a few of the places described in this book, you will surely come away with the impression that Colorado is a place of daring beauty and dazzling complexity. You may also get the distinct and accurate impression that what has tantalized you in this book is only a small sampling of sights chosen from an almost limitless number of landscapes. To tantalize you was an express purpose of this book.

If one word could summarize the special, striking identity of Colorado, the word might simply be "up." The elevation, altitude, height, stature, and uplift of Colorado all mean one thing — up. The lowest point on the plains of Colorado is higher than most of the Appalachian Mountain chain. The highest mountain east of the Mississippi River is at about the same elevation as the western edge of the Garden of the Gods in Colorado Springs. And the word "up" here means "mountains."

Colorado is a paraphrase for the past and current generations of mountains that formed here. Even the eastern plains are defined by mountains. The detritus of ancient uplands to the west, they are literally built on the fabric of former mountains and can be thought of as the wearing-down of the heights. This "up" and "down" of mountains defines other parts of the state as well. The plateaus and canyons of the southwest are of and by mountains. The sediments of the horizontal rock beds of canyon country are remains of older uplands, lifted anew and now dissected by waters that begin flowing in the mountains. You simply cannot get away from the elevation of the state — it surrounds and inundates the place.

The up-ness and down-ness of Colorado is inevitably altered and sculpted through the passage of time. Time, then, could also be a word used to explain Colorado: time in all its dimensions from eons to years to seasons to minutes. The eons are measured in terms of millennia of millennia and are punctuated by mountain uplift after mountain uplift. These geologic time-scales are basically unfathomable by us but are, nonetheless, very real. Time is as much a part of the rock as the crystal matrix of minerals of which the rock is composed. Through the ages time has altered and transformed life here in all of its forms. Animals have become extinct or evolved into new forms; plants have migrated from place to place depending upon climate and other environmental factors; and people have come and gone following their own destinies.

Time also comes in scales other than the unimaginable — the scales of decades, years, and months. To enjoy Colorado fully, for example, is to enjoy the rhythm of the seasons. The to and fro of Canada geese as they travel their migration routes, the near hibernation of the black bear, the incongruity of the snow buttercup blooming amid the snow fields of the alpine are all part and parcel of what natural Colorado is. The most engaging aspect of the seasons, however, may be the annual creation of Colorado organic gold — the aspen color show of autumn. As Aldo Leopold wrote in *A Sand County Almanac* (Oxford University Press, 1949), "Other months were constituted mainly as a fitting interlude between Octobers."

Time comes in days and hours and minutes too. These shorter spans of time can often be the most dramatic of all. Who cannot fail to be impressed with the speed and intensity of a summer thunderstorm that builds, inundates, and dissipates in just a few minutes, leaving the land soaked and the sky sparkling? Or with the deadly instant of a snow avalanche booming down a mountainside with uncontrolled energy? Other more benign instants of time are seen in the brief minutes of alpenglow on a summer's evening in the mountains, or in the flashing rumps of escaping pronghorn as they move over a rise on the prairie.

Elevation and time have combined to produce a multitude of places with innumerable landscapes. Hopefully, this book has, at the least, high-lighted the place that nature holds here and given residents and visitors alike a better idea of the nature of the many places we collectively call Colorado.

Maps Available

COLORADO NATIONAL MONUMENT

U.S. Geological Survey
7.5-Minute Series
Colorado National Monument, Colorado

Colorado National Monument Association
Colorado National Monument

COMANCHE NATIONAL GRASSLAND

U.S. Geological Survey
7.5-Minute Series
Several dozen included in the following coordinates:
north half 37º 37' 30" N to 38º N
103º 22' 30" W to 104º 7' 30" W
south half 37 N to 37 30 N
102º 15' W to 103º 37' 30" W

County Series
Baca Co. 1, 2, 3, and 4
Las Animas Co. 2, 3, and 7
Otero Co. 2

U.S. Forest Service
Comanche National Grasslands

CRESTED BUTTE

U.S. Geological Survey
7.5-Minute Series
Crested Butte
Gothic
Mt. Axtell
Oh-Be-Joyful

County Series
Gunnison Co. 2 and 3

U. S. Forest Service
Gunnison Basin Area

FLORISSANT FOSSIL BEDS NATIONAL MONUMENT

U.S. Geological Survey
7.5-Minute Series
Divide
Lake George

County Series
Teller Co.

U.S. Forest Service
Pike National Forest

GARDEN OF THE GODS

U.S. Geological Survey
7.5-Minute Series
Cascade
Manitou Springs

County Series
El Paso Co. 1

GREAT SAND DUNES NATIONAL MONUMENT

U.S. Geological Survey
7.5-Minute Series
Liberty
Medano Pass
Mosca Pass
Sand Camp
Zapata Ranch

County Series
Alamosa Co.
Saguache Co. 4

Great Sand Dunes National Monument Quadrangle

U.S. Forest Service
Rio Grande National Forest

MT. EVANS

U.S. Geological Survey
7.5-Minute Series
Georgetown
Harris Park
Idaho Springs
Mt. Evans

County Series
Clear Creek Co.
Park Co. 2

U.S. Forest Service
Arapaho National Forest

PICEANCE CREEK BASIN

U.S. Geological Survey
7.5-Minute Series
Several maps included in the following coordinates:
39º 37' 30" N to 40º 7' 30" N
107º 52' 30" W to 108º 30' W

County Series
Garfield Co. 3
Rio Blanco Co. 2 and 6

U.S. Bureau of Land Management
Piceance Creek Basin Oil Shale Status Map (February 1981)

SILVERTON

U.S. Geological Survey
7.5-Minute Series
Silverton

County Series
San Juan

U.S. Forest Service
San Juan National Forest

SLUMGULLION SLIDE

U.S. Geological Survey
7.5-Minute Series
Cannibal Plateau
Lake City
Lake San Cristobal
Slumgullion Pass

County Series
Hinsdale Co. 1

U.S. Forest Service
Gunnison Basin Area

STEAMBOAT LAKE

    U.S. Geological Survey
        7.5-Minute Series
          Hahns Peak, Colorado

    U.S. Forest Service
        Routt National Forest, Colorado

TAMARACK RANCH

    U.S. Geological Survey
        7.5-Minute Series
          Crook
          Proctor
          Tamarack Ranch

        County Series
          Logan Co. 2

INDEX